The D*of*E Expedition Guide

This *Expedition Guide* provides advice and guidance for Duke of Edinburgh's Award (D*of*E) Leaders running D*of*E expeditions.

The Duke of Edinburgh's Award is a voluntary, non-competitive programme of activities for anyone aged 14-24. Doing their DofE gives young people the opportunity to experience new activities or develop existing skills. There are three progressive levels of programmes which when successfully completed lead to a Bronze, Silver or Gold Award. Young people create their own DofE programme by choosing a volunteering, physical and skills activity, going on an expedition and, for their Gold only, taking part in a residential activity.

The Duke of Edinburgh's Award is a national youth charity that operates throughout the UK. Founded by HRH The Duke of Edinburgh in 1956, DofE programmes are now delivered under licence by more than 600 partners who offer it through DofE groups in youth clubs, voluntary organisations, schools, colleges, young offender institutions, housing associations and businesses.

Currently over 275,000 young people are doing their DofE in the UK, and over 80,000 achieve a Bronze, Silver or Gold Award each year. They are supported by over 45,000 Leaders.

Our mission

To inspire, guide and support young people in their self-development and recognise their achievements.

Foreword

Every participant in the DofE has to take part in some form
of expedition. This has provided the opportunity for many young
people to find their way through unfamiliar country and to fulfil
their spirit of adventure and discovery. It has encouraged over
seven million participants across the world to overcome challenges
and to discover their own hidden strengths and talents.

This Expedition Guide sets out to explain the risks and challenges
in undertaking expeditions on both land and water. It is intended
to help all involved in expedition delivery, to prepare and plan
demanding expeditions, which young people can then undertake
with confidence.

Safety is the absolute priority in all expedition work. The
advice in this guide is the product of over 55 years' experience, and
careful observance should help to maintain the very satisfactory
record of safety in DofE expeditions.

The knowledge and skills acquired from a study of this guide
will do much to ensure that each expedition is a pleasure and an
enlightening experience and it might, perhaps, even encourage a
desire to continue similar forms of adventurous activity in later life.

Introduction
By Ray Mears

DofE expeditions provide a unique reason and opportunity to explore some of the truly amazing places to be discovered around the British Isles or even abroad.

Without a doubt, the skills that young people learn in preparation for their expedition such as first aid, preparing and cooking their own food, finding shelter from the elements and navigating their way across wild country are powerful life skills that they and others will benefit from for the rest of their lives.

But that is only a small part of the DofE experience, it is on the expedition itself when you are responsible for your own welfare or the lives of fellow team members that you will confront your own personality and come to really know yourself.

It will also provide young people with the opportunity to value the contributions of others and discover the power of camaraderie. These experiences are life-changing and they will discover strengths they never knew they had to overcome challenges and adversity while developing a willingness to step into the unknown.

This is the true spirit of adventure that keeps all adventurers coming back for more. Dare to dream, fight to make your dreams come true.

Ray Mears
Survival and wilderness expert

About this guide

This entirely new DofE Expedition Guide sets out the requirements and processes of the Expedition section and also its aspirations and desired outcomes.

This guide is designed to support DofE Leaders and Supervisors to deliver safe, challenging and positive expedition experiences for young people at Bronze, Silver and Gold levels. It is also designed to help DofE Expedition Assessors.

This guide covers all aspects of DofE expeditions, from the aim to the presentation and sign off. It includes advice and guidance on what is required and how to get the best from each stage of the section, using any of the different modes of travel.

This guide emphasises the core idea of progression. It covers everything from an enjoyable local Bronze expedition designed to spark an interest and curiosity in the outdoors and adventure, to a more challenging Silver expedition which develops and hones expedition skills, to the wild country Gold level expedition which is a comprehensive challenge of a young person's mental and physical abilities.

The Expedition section has been a core part of DofE programmes since its beginnings in 1956. The essence and desired outcomes of the section remain much the same now as they were when captured by Lord Hunt in the first *Expedition Guide* published in 1965.

The recipe for enjoyment is a simple one. There must be an element of physical challenge about the venture; it must also make demands on your knowledge and your skill. There must be an element of risk; this is as necessary to adventure as the flavour of salt in cookery. Spice is added by the inclusion of a human equation; new companions with whom to adjust yourself; old comrades with whom to renew memories of former journeys.

The proportions of the ingredients may vary according to **the nature of the** enterprise; some of them are a matter of personal choice. But the essential condition for enjoying this dish of adventure, is that it should be well and truly prepared before it is eaten. In fact, getting ready to go is at least half of the pleasure. It will probably ensure you succeed in what you set out to do.

John Hunt KG
Expedition Guide (first edition), January 1965

Chapter 5
Types of expeditions

What *The Handbook for DofE Leaders* says...

From cycling in the Galloway Hills, walking in the Brecon Beacons or canoeing down the Thames, to sailing in the Mediterranean, horse riding in Chile or walking in the Atlas Mountains, participants choose where and how they want to undertake their expedition.

Chapter 5.1
Planning D*of*E expeditions

What *The Handbook for DofE Leaders* says...

The team must plan and organise the expedition.

This chapter outlines the processes and requirements of planning a DofE expedition. As around 96% of DofE expeditions are completed on foot, the chapter is written with this mode of travel in mind.

Expeditions using an alternative mode of travel, supporting young people who have additional needs or are taking place outside of the UK, should use this chapter and then refer to the other specific chapters.

The most economical and accessible form of completing a DofE expedition is on foot; it is immensely satisfying for participants as they are fully reliant on themselves. Licensed Organisations often have stocks of equipment and many qualified Supervisors ready to support DofE participants using this mode of travel.

The Expedition section process

The flowchart opposite gives an overview of the steps involved for a young person to complete their Expedition section.

This is a more detailed chart to that shown on page 8 and each step is explained in more detail later on in this guide.

One of the first DofE expeditions. Participants are pictured on 1 February 1957 at Woodrow High House Residential Centre, Buckinghamshire. Woodrow High House is part of London Youth.

Each chapter of this guide is designed to be comprehensive, so people with 20 days or 20 years of DofE experience can dip in and out to find all the information and advice they need. All the DofE terms are defined in the Glossary.

This guide is set out in the chronological order of an Expedition section programme and based around expeditions on foot. Information about other modes of travel in their specific chapters can then be overlaid onto this general expedition advice.

The DofE encourages participants of all levels to consider an alternative mode of travel, on land or water, in the UK or around the world. The DofE hopes participants and Supervisors will embrace and enjoy the spirit of adventure and discovery that this DofE section is all about.

This guide sets out DofE expedition policy and should be read in conjunction with *The Handbook for DofE Leaders* and used alongside the DofE's training resource EX[2].

There are also many essential training and advice documents on the DofE website: **www.DofE.org/expedition**. The DofE programme is achievable by all and so this guide now has a substantially increased section on supporting participants who have additional needs, including guidance on flexibilities to the 20 conditions.

To enrich the advice of this guide, and recognise the input and expertise of the DofE network which enables the DofE to exist; there are 125 hints and tips from people running the DofE throughout the UK. There are also comments from adventurers, DofE supporters and DofE groups to inspire participants and staff alike.

Training, supervising and assessing DofE expeditions is an enormously rewarding undertaking and the DofE hopes this guide will help inspire ever more successful and positive expeditions.

Alex Davies
National Programme & Quality Manager,
DofE Head Office, Windsor.

Contents

Chapter 1
Expedition section aims, principles and benefits

What *The Handbook for DofE Leaders* says...

Expedition section aim: To inspire young people to develop initiative and a spirit of adventure and discovery, by planning, training for and completing an adventurous self-sufficient journey, as part of a team.

From cycling in the Galloway Hills, walking in the Brecon Beacons or canoeing down the Thames, to sailing in the Mediterranean, horse riding in Chile or walking in the Atlas Mountains, participants choose where and how they want to undertake their expedition.

First and foremost, the Expedition section is about developing teamwork. In this way it is very different from the fitness challenges of the Physical section, the technical learning of the Skills section and the support for others in the Volunteering section.

However, the Expedition section draws on all these abilities and, coupled with the location and concentrated time of the challenge, it often becomes the most memorable section and proudest achievement of a young person's DofE experience.

Whilst the Expedition section needs to challenge young people both mentally and physically, it must also be achievable and aim to be enjoyable.

The Expedition section is an adventurous journey of discovery, both in terms of the outdoor environment and personal and team development. It is one of the few opportunities young people get to really separate and isolate themselves from their daily lives and modern mass media and communications.

Teams have to truly rely on themselves. Often the Expedition section creates friendships and bonds which last many years.

Principles

- Participation in shared experiences in the outdoor environment can develop initiative, teamwork, communication, leadership, problem solving and organisational skills.
- Experiencing and overcoming challenges together develops emotional strength and empathy for others.
- Working with a team of peers in the outdoors, experiencing isolation and solitude develops self-reliance and self-confidence.

Benefits

DofE Leaders, Supervisors, expedition support staff, volunteers and Assessors need to support and facilitate an opportunity where, through participation in an expedition, young people:

- Gain an appreciation of, and respect for, the outdoor environment.
- Learn the value of sharing responsibility for success, through leadership, teamwork, self-reliance and co-operation.
- Learn the importance of attention to detail and organisational ability.
- Develop and demonstrate enterprise and imagination.
- Become more self-reliant.
- Become more able to overcome both expected and unexpected challenges.
- Recognise the needs and strengths of themselves and others.
- Improve decision-making skills and the ability to accept consequences.

- Gain the skills to reflect on personal performance.
- Learn to manage risk.
- Learn through experience.
- Develop perseverance and determination.

The proven impact of the Expedition section

The DofE, supported by Pears Foundation, worked with The University of Northampton to produce a comprehensive and systematic research project into the impact and effects of DofE programmes in developing young people.

The positive findings will be of little surprise to experienced DofE Leaders, Supervisors and Assessors. Of course, everyone involved in the DofE Expedition section is always working to make these kinds of benefits even better.

We sorely need something like the DofE to get us out of our chairs and in touch with the real world, even if the real world is trickling down the back of your neck and your tent has blown away. It is important.

It means that you know how to engage with the world and deal with other people. You can't learn that from a computer.

It's about dealing with disappointment, things going wrong and pushing on despite all obstacles. I know it sounds old fashioned, but it isn't.

Young people meet more difficulties, opportunities and challenges than they would have done around the turn of the 20th century.

The DofE can be considered a fundamental part of the 'Make a Human Being' kit.

Sir Terry Pratchett OBE

Sir Terry Pratchett is a novelist best known for the Discworld series. He has written over 50 bestselling books with worldwide sales in excess of 70 million. A DofE supporter, he is also passionate about orangutan conservation, travelling to Indonesian Borneo to support work there.

The impact research concluded the following...

Expedition section principle:
Participation in shared experiences in the outdoor environment can develop initiative, teamwork, communication, leadership, problem solving and organisational skills:

- 93% of participants and 93% of Leaders feel that doing their DofE developed teamwork skills.
- 79% of participants stated they had learned how to work as a team leader and developed greater leadership ability.
- 84% of young people and 95% of Leaders noted improved decision-making skills.
- 78% of young people said doing their DofE had taught them to make decisions for themselves.
- 75% of young people and 92% of Leaders say organisational skills were developed.

Expedition section principle:
Experiencing and overcoming challenges together develops emotional strength and empathy for others:

- 83% stated that taking part in a DofE programme taught them how to work with different types of people.

- 80% of young people and 93% of Leaders said the DofE gave participants the ability to reflect on learning and develop an understanding of their strengths and weaknesses.

Expedition section principle:
Working with a team of peers in the outdoors, experiencing isolation and solitude develops self-reliance and self-confidence:

- 85% of young people believed the DofE had improved their confidence.
- 71% of young people identified that the DofE had improved their self-belief.
- 79% of young people and 94% of Leaders believe participants develop independence.
- 81% of participants and 92% of Leaders feel that their DofE makes young people more adventurous.

Concluding review

The Expedition section is often cited by young people as both the best and the worst part of their DofE experience.

Some reasons for it being their worst experience relate to the physical and mental difficulties encountered which, when overcome, led to it being their best experience.

Doing their DofE gives young people practical skills and new experiences. It also gives them a spirit of adventure; the desire to seek out and engage with new and different activities.

Building self-esteem and friendships were considered by participants to be some of the main benefits of doing a DofE programme. Young people were asked if they had changed the way they felt about themselves by taking part in a DofE programme. The overwhelming answer to this was 'yes' and most felt that this change was in gaining or building confidence.

Having fun was an important aspect for young people taking part in programmes, and this, combined with support from Leaders and their friendships, keeps them engaged with a DofE programme.

Chapter 2

D*of*E expeditions –
requirements and conditions

What *The Handbook for DofE Leaders* says...

The Expedition section involves planning, training for and completing an unaccompanied, self-sufficient expedition with an agreed aim.

All participants must have appropriate training, do at least one practice expedition in the UK, complete a qualifying expedition (the one that is assessed) and deliver a presentation in order to complete the section.

Expeditions must be completed by the participants' own physical efforts with minimal external intervention and without motorised assistance.

The *DofE Handbook for Leaders* sets out the rules and conditions of the Expedition section.

This *Expedition Guide* sets out, in specific chapters, further information and clarification about this section and its delivery. This particular chapter summarises the key information about the section which is then developed further in future chapters.

The five steps to completing the Expedition section

This flowchart gives a simple overview of the steps involved for a young person to complete their Expedition section. Each step is explained in more detail on the following pages.

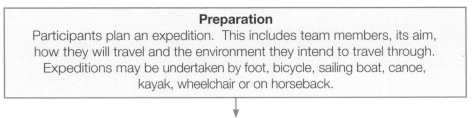

Preparation
Participants plan an expedition. This includes team members, its aim, how they will travel and the environment they intend to travel through. Expeditions may be undertaken by foot, bicycle, sailing boat, canoe, kayak, wheelchair or on horseback.

Training
Participants undergo training in expedition skills and their chosen mode of travel.

Practice expedition
Participants must undertake sufficient practice expeditions to enable them to travel safely and complete their qualifying expedition.

Qualifying expedition, debrief and presentation
Once prepared, participants undertake their expedition, which will be observed by their Expedition Assessor. On completion they will be debriefed by their Assessor and then prepare and give a presentation, in any medium, of their expedition which covers their aims, experiences and outcomes.

Assessment
The Expedition Assessor should provide their report for eDofE following the qualifying expedition and reports should also be provided by a person who saw their presentation.

Recording the Expedition section on *eDofE*

As the Expedition section is a team activity, both Leaders and participants are able to record training, practice journeys, qualifying expeditions and presentation details, as well as other evidence into *eDofE*.

Leaders are able to do this for the whole team at the same time and the Leader entries do not need further approval. All participants must still enter their own personal aim and goals for their qualifying expedition before the section.

Timescales for qualifying expeditions

Level	Duration	Minimum hours of planned activity each day
Bronze	2 days and 1 night	At least 6 hours during the daytime (at least 3 of which must be spent journeying)
Silver	3 days and 2 nights	At least 7 hours during the daytime (at least 3½ of which must be spent journeying)
Gold	4 days and 3 nights	At least 8 hours during the daytime (at least 4 of which must be spent journeying)

- Time associated with overnight accommodation and catering is additional to the minimum daytime hours of planned activity.
- Reasonable time for lunch and other appropriate breaks can be included within the hours of planned activity.
- 30 minutes should be considered a reasonable amount of time for DofE groups to plan for their lunch stop.

Recommended environments

General requirements	
Land environment (walking, cycling and horse riding)	All expeditions should avoid villages and populated areas unless that is impossible. Long distance footpaths should not be used, particularly by Silver and Gold teams, except in small sections to link up other paths or areas outside of the UK where they are the only routes available. Teams should not aim for more than 500m of height gain or descent on any one day although cycling expeditions may climb more.
Canoeing and rowing	Local access agreements must be checked in advance for all expeditions.
Sailing	Practice and qualifying expeditions should take place in different areas. Where this is not practical, different routes over the same area can be used.

Bronze*	
Land environment (walking, cycling and horse riding)	Normal rural countryside which can be familiar and local to the participants.
Canoeing and rowing	Canals, rivers or other inland waterways and lakes.
Sailing	Inland waters or sheltered estuaries well within the participants' competencies.

Silver*	
Land environment (walking, cycling and horse riding)	Normal rural, open countryside or forest, which is unfamiliar to the participants. The environment should be more demanding for participants than at Bronze level. Where possible the expedition should all be in, or at least include, areas of open country or forest.
Canoeing and rowing	Canals, rivers or other inland waterways and lakes in rural areas.
Sailing	Inland waters, estuaries or sheltered coastal waters.

The DofE Expedition Guide

Gold	
Land environment (walking, cycling and horse riding)	Wild country** (remote from habitation) which is unfamiliar to participants. The environment should be more demanding for participants than at Silver level. Remote estuaries, marshes, fens and coastal areas may provide an appropriate environment for an expedition with the emphasis on exploring rather than journeying.
Canoeing and rowing	Rivers or other inland waterways and lakes in rural areas, sheltered coastal waters or estuaries.
Sailing	Inland waters, estuaries or sheltered coastal waters. Yachts may be used in open sea areas.

Bronze and Silver teams who plan expeditions in surroundings more demanding than those recommended must be trained and equipped to enable them to meet any potential hazards. The DofE Expedition Training Framework for the appropriate environment should be used. Teams should consider how they will continue to progress their expedition challenge at subsequent levels.

*** Wild country is defined as an area remote from habitation. DofE expeditions should be through, rather than over, wild country – it's all about solitude not altitude.*

The expectation at Gold level is that all expeditions take place in wild country.

More information about recommended environments can be found in the appropriate mode of travel chapter.

For a map of UK wild country areas see **www.DofE.org/go/expeditionareas**

Each expedition area has an Assessor Network Co-ordinator and a group of experienced Network Assessors able to assess teams and provide local expedition information.

Contact details of Expedition Network Co-ordinators are available from **www.DofE.org/go/expeditionareas**

The 20 conditions of the Expedition section

	DofE qualifying expedition conditions	Further explanation and interpretation of conditions
1	All expeditions must be by the participants' own physical effort, without motorised or outside assistance.	Motorised wheelchairs may be used where appropriate to the needs of the participant.
2	All expeditions must be unaccompanied and self-sufficient.	a) The team must be unaccompanied, unguided and supervision must be carried out remotely. b) As part of effective remote supervision, teams may be more closely supervised for parts of the expedition where specific hazardous areas are unavoidable. This supervision should be kept to an absolute minimum. c) If a team does not possess the necessary physical, first aid and expedition skills required for an area, then they should not be in that area.
3	All expeditions must be supervised by an adult who is able to accept responsibility for the safety of the team.	
4	The expedition must have an aim.	
5	All participants must be properly equipped.	
6	Participants must have completed the required training and practice expeditions.	The qualifying expedition must not be over the same route or in the immediate vicinity of routes used in practice expeditions.
7	At least one practice expedition must be undertaken at each level of the programme, in the same mode of travel in a similar environment to the qualifying expedition.	For overseas assessed expeditions, at least one UK practice must have taken place in an appropriate environment.
8	The team must plan and organise the expedition.	Multiple teams should not travel in convoy but have individual routes from campsite to campsite. Where this is absolutely unavoidable at least 30 minutes must separate each team using the same route and they must operate as discrete teams.
9	Assessment must be by an approved Accredited Assessor.	
10	There must be between four and seven in a team (eight for modes of travel which have tandem).	Unless in the event of an emergency, the team must always keep together.

11	All participants must be within the qualifying age of the programme level.	This is regardless of whether they are under assessment or not.
12	Participants must be at the same level of assessment.	Participants should have a similar ability or level of experience and must make a full contribution to the team.
13	The team must not include those who have completed the same or higher level expedition.	Participants should have a similar ability or level of experience and must make a full contribution to the team.
14	Accommodation should be by camping.	See page 42 for further details.
15	The expedition must be of the correct duration.	a) The expedition must be of the minimum number of days and nights and must include appropriate acclimatisation/final preparation time. b) An acclimatisation day during an expedition due to extreme altitude may be included as long as the minimum hours of activity and journeying are still completed. c) An additional acclimatisation/rest day may be included during an expedition but this will not count toward the expedition days.
16	The expedition should normally take place between the end of March and the end of October.	The expedition must take place at an appropriate time of year for the expedition's location and aim and the enjoyment of the participants.
17	The expedition should take place in the recommended environment.	The expedition should take place in an appropriate and challenging environment. At Silver and Gold levels this must be unfamiliar to the participants. Overseas expeditions should take place in an area appropriate to the level of the expedition.
18	The expedition must meet the minimum hours of planned activity.	a) Six hours at Bronze, seven hours at Silver and eight hours at Gold. At least half of these daily hours must be spent travelling. b) Time associated with overnight accommodation and catering is additional to the minimum daytime hours of planned activity. c) Reasonable time for lunch and other appropriate breaks can be included within the hours of planned activity.
19	A substantial meal should be cooked and eaten by participants each day.	This is optional on the final day.
20	A presentation must be prepared and delivered after the expedition.	The presentation or report, which may be in any format the participants or teams choose, must be related to the expedition's aim.

Variations to the 20 conditions

Where participants have individual needs that mean one or more of the 20 conditions cannot be met, they may apply for a variation to enable them to complete their DofE expedition.

Variation application forms and guidance on how to apply are available on the eDofE Resource Zone and at **www.DofE.org/expedition** or from Licensed Organisations. Variation forms must be approved at the appropriate level. Always get advice from the Licensed Organisation before submitting a variation form.

Variations should be requested at the earliest opportunity, particularly for overseas expeditions, and be submitted in sufficient time to reach the relevant office at least 12 weeks prior to the date of departure. Written approval of these variations should be included in the appropriate notification process to help the Assessor.

Advice and guidance for working with and including young people who have additional needs in DofE expeditions can be found in Chapter 12, on the eDofE Resource Zone and at **www.DofE.org/go/additionalneeds**

Multiple teams

Some large DofE centres may have several expedition teams being assessed in the same area, at the same time. The DofE strongly discourages multiple teams using the same expedition route as teams should plan their own journey.

Multiple teams must always operate independently, discreetly and must not follow each other.

Where the use of the same route is absolutely unavoidable, usually due to the expedition environment, for example canoe expeditions, rather than the availability of Supervisors, then teams must be separated by at least 30 minutes journeying time. Recommended good practice is that Centres use multiple start points (see page 42)

Other modes of travel and multiple modes of travel

Please refer to Chapters 13 and 6.9 for more information.

Expeditions outside the United Kingdom

Expeditions outside the UK provide varied challenges which can inspire and broaden young people's experiences. All Expedition section conditions apply equally to expeditions taking place outside the UK. Please refer to Chapter 5.2 for more information.

Something else...

The Expedition section aims to inspire young people to develop initiative and a spirit of adventure and discovery. The DofE encourages and will always consider innovative and creative expedition proposals from participants even if they do not meet all of the 20 conditions. These will be one-off expeditions in the UK or overseas and can only be used by participants over the age of 16 for any DofE level. Please refer to Chapter 14 for more information.

Preparing for a wild country expedition

Wild country expeditions are exciting and rewarding but it's essential that the team is fully prepared for the environment and know how to use their equipment. A map of DofE wild country areas can be found at **www.DofE.org/go/expeditionareas**

Teams intending to travel through wild country areas must ensure that the appropriate Assessor Network Co-ordinator has been notified. Route notifications must include alternative, low level (lower risk) routes that can be used in the event of adverse weather.

Teams who would like to use a Network Assessor will need to book and pay for these services in advance of the expedition. Information about the process for expedition notifications and the booking of Assessors can be found at **www.DofE.org/expedition** or through the Licensed Organisation.

For expeditions in wild country, participants should always arrive the day before the start of their qualifying expedition. This way the entire team and the Supervisor can meet the Assessor and make an early start. At Gold, the team must set aside an acclimatisation day before the expedition in order to get used to the environment.

Supervisors can use this time to check local access and complete any additional practical risk assessments. This also provides the team with an opportunity to undertake research for their aim and to experience the local environment.

To enhance the experience, the base campsite should not be used by the teams as an expedition campsite.

Chapter 3

Delivering D*of*E expeditions, and staff roles

What *The Handbook for DofE Leaders* says...

Every centre and group must be authorised by a Licensed Organisation (LO). To get a licence, LOs must satisfy the DofE that they understand the full implications of running DofE programmes.

They must:
- Be able to safeguard young people.
- Maintain the DofE's aims and standards.
- Have relevant policies and procedures in place.
- Have an administrative framework to function correctly and ensure continuity.

Management

Each Licensed Organisation (LO) and centre will decide how best to manage the Expedition section for their participants. It is usual for one person to have an overall view of the Expedition section, including the training programme, supporting adults and all the participants' progress throughout the training process.

Most centres have a team of adults who share different aspects of the section, using their skills and experience to deliver the DofE to as many young people as possible.

The DofE discourages individuals from taking on the whole of the sectional delivery themselves. As this is enormously time consuming, it usually limits the number of young people who can participate.

LOs and Approved Activity Providers (AAPs) must ensure that all staff have appropriate qualifications, experience and competence to the level that they deem appropriate, for the safe and effective delivery of the DofE Expedition section. For more information about AAPs, please see page 22.

This will allow them to deliver the Expedition Training Framework in an engaging and enjoyable way, ensuring that participants complete it to the appropriate level and in their chosen mode of travel. Please refer to Chapter 6 on training.

Safety

LOs are responsible for the safety and well-being of participants. They also approve their Supervisor's and Assessor's experience and/or qualifications and set the training that is required. The DofE Leader must ensure that all LO requirements are fulfilled, including appropriate public liability insurance.

Whilst the DofE does not insist on specific qualifications, it is strongly recommended that suitable national qualifications for the chosen modes of travel are obtained.

The DofE Leader, or the chosen expedition provider, is responsible for the suitability of expeditions, safety aspects, the adequacy of the training and the emergency procedures. They should ensure that any AAP used is reputable, risks have been assessed and that Supervisors and Assessors are suitably competent, meeting the LO's requirements.

Vehicles and trailers must be properly serviced, maintained and comply with EU regulations.

It is essential that appropriate risk assessments, preventative actions, emergency procedures and reviews are completed for all expeditions to ensure the safety of the young people involved.

The impact of the expedition on the local environment

The DofE Leader and Supervisor both have a key role in ensuring that the impact of the Expedition section is a positive and sustainable one, for both the participants and the local communities, where the expedition takes place.

Everyone participating in the DofE should follow the DofE Environmental Impact Policy (Chapter 6.6) and behaviour expectations (Chapter 6.10).

Parents, guardians and carers:

It is essential that parents, guardians and carers be told what a DofE Expedition entails. They need to understand what their young person will be doing and the steps taken to ensure their safety, welfare and enjoyment. This is particularly important for adults acting 'in loco parentis'.

Make sure clear expectations are set, for example, parents must understand that they will not hear from their child while they are undertaking their expedition.

Where necessary, parental consent forms should be obtained in line with the LO/AAP policy and processes.

Parents, guardians and carers have a responsibility to keep DofE Leaders and Supervisors informed of any illness, treatment or condition which may have an impact on a participant's participation in a particular activity. Direct communication with the DofE Leader is recommended.

Note that some open expeditions are privately arranged and do not involve the LOs or necessarily meet their requirements. Refer to Chapter 5.4, for more information.

Expedition roles

Within the Expedition section there is a considerable amount of interaction between the participants and the adults who are supporting them.

Within each centre and each LO/AAP these descriptions may change slightly but these are the main roles to be considered.

Role	Description
DofE Leader	The adult responsible for a DofE group. They lead, guide and encourage young people, agree their programme choices and sign off sectional activities in eDofE. The DofE Leader: • Arranges for the expedition team to be trained in all of the required areas. • Supports the team with their expedition planning. They may deliver some or all of the expedition training or delegate training to an appropriate person (an '**instructor**'), to ensure all participants are adequately trained. Full details about the role of the DofE Leader are set out in *The Handbook for DofE Leaders.*
DofE Expedition Supervisor	A person who is responsible to the LO/AAP for the safety and welfare of young people whilst they are carrying out their DofE expedition. The Supervisor may also be the DofE Leader. The role of the DofE Expedition Supervisor is set out in Chapter 8. It is the Supervisor who signs off the participant as ready to undertake their qualifying expedition. It is up to the LO or AAP to decide how many young people, spilt into expedition teams, a Supervisor is responsible for. Where there are multiple teams, there are often multiple Supervisors, each with designated young people/teams they are responsible for.
Expedition support staff	On most DofE expeditions there are expedition support staff who are approved by the LO or AAP. These often include people with outdoor education training or experience and, if appropriate, experience in the relevant mode of travel. These individuals might be LO or AAP staff or volunteers. This may include an instructor who delivers the Expedition Training Framework to DofE participants. Expedition support staff can help their Supervisor, who is the lead adult responsible for designated young people/teams, to deliver an expedition safely, using remote supervision. At all times the LO or AAP ratio of Supervisors to teams must be followed.
DofE Co-ordinator	The person who sets up and manages the DofE in a centre, supporting Leaders and overseeing groups. The DofE Co-ordinator will: • Ensure that all adults working with young people have been appropriately checked and approved. • Ensure that all necessary expedition paperwork has been appropriately submitted. The DofE Co-ordinator may also be a DofE Leader or a Supervisor.
DofE Expedition Assessor	The accredited adult, linked to an LO, who checks on the expedition team's progress and agrees the young people's completion of the Expedition section against the 20 conditions, providing an Assessor's Report as evidence in eDofE. For more information see Chapter 10.

Organisations within the Expedition section

DofE Leaders, Supervisors, Co-ordinators, expedition support staff and Assessors may all interact with the following organisations:

Role	Organisation
Assessor Network and Network Assessors	Assessor Networks provide support to teams planning and undertaking expeditions in areas deemed by the DofE to be wild country. The Assessor Networks will: • Check all notifications to an expedition area in wild country and where requested appoint a Network Assessor. • Offer local information to expedition teams. • Issue a unique reference number for the expedition. • Maintain good relations with local landowners, campsites and residents. Assessor Networks comprise: • An **Assessor Network Co-ordinator** who co-ordinates all expeditions in their area. • A number of accredited volunteer **Network Assessors** who may be asked to assess an expedition. A full list of the DofE's expedition areas can be found on the DofE website at **www.DofE.org/expeditions**.

Role	Organisation
Licensed Organisation	An organisation licensed to manage the delivery of DofE programmes and authorise Awards. The Licensed Organisation will: • Provide policies on safeguarding, health and safety, emergencies and the supervision of expeditions. • Provide public liability insurance for participants and Supervisors whilst on expeditions. • Approve Supervisors.
The Charity	The DofE Charity defines and manages overall DofE policy and central administration. The DofE Charity: • Defines the programme and requirements for the Expedition section. • Provides national resources to support the Expedition section.
Approved Activity Providers (AAPs)	The Duke of Edinburgh's Award licenses external organisations that provide opportunities for the Expedition and Residential sections. These opportunities have been proven to meet our conditions and so can count towards the achievement of an Award. We call these partners Approved Activity Providers (AAPs). They can be commercial organisations or charities and are usually able to provide a section in its entirety, including accredited assessment and providing Assessor reports on eDofE. DofE Leaders can confidently recommend AAPs to their participants. Commercial organisations wishing to deliver the Expedition section on behalf of a Licensed Organisation must be an AAP. The AAP licence is a quality standard on an organisation's activity, meeting the programme and sectional requirements of the DofE. Please note that the AAP licence does not guarantee the suitability of an AAP in terms of health and safety or its financial stability. LOs using AAPs will have their own process for checking the suitability of AAP programmes in terms of health and safety requirements for their young people and they have the final say on the appropriateness of a course in this respect. AAPs who deliver the Expedition section must still meet all of the requirements of the LO, with regards to notifications and qualifications. Any organisation or individual who is not a part of the LO and who wishes to deliver the Expedition section as the Supervisor is required by the DofE to be an AAP. A list of current AAPs is set out at **www.DofE.org/aap** together with details of how organisations can apply for this status.

The DofE Expedition Guide

Chapter 4
Expedition aims

What *The Handbook for DofE Leaders* says...

The expedition must have an aim.

The expedition's aim should relate to the interests and abilities of those taking part and the area they will be travelling through.

This is the key to any expedition's success.

Before any planning, the first thing an expedition team needs to do is decide on their expedition aim. Without it, the team cannot plan an effective and challenging expedition with a clear outcome. From thinking about the aim come all the other decisions like location and mode of travel.

The aim may change, for example following a practice expedition, but it must be agreed with the DofE Leader and Supervisor before the qualifying expedition. It may be altered again if circumstances change. It can be helpful to have a backup investigation plan.

The aim sets the destination/ environment, the mode of travel and the project theme on the qualifying expedition. It will also provide a guide as to the amount of time a team will spend journeying or exploring.

For example: 'Completing a Silver expedition using the cycle system in the Netherlands, to undertake an investigation project on the provision and quality of cycle paths compared to the UK'.

Supporting participants to choose their aim

Participants should think about their interests and abilities and then develop an aim which enhances these within their expedition.

The DofE produces a range of resources about expedition aims; to help inspire participants and support Leaders to facilitate participants to make a decision that suits them.

More information is available from **www.DofE.org/expedition** and in the *Programmes Pack* (available from **www.DofEshop.org**)

It is the role of the supporting staff to help participants to think clearly and logically about their ideas for destinations, mode of travel and project themes. It is important that Supervisors do not force participants to choose locations or a mode of travel because they know them well. Teams should be encouraged, particularly at Gold level, to push themselves and broaden their horizons. Supervisors should be as inspired as the participants.

However, it can be a balancing act for Supervisors to support and empower participants' ideas against the real practicalities, time and cost of those ideas, and the resources available to the DofE centre. The reality for some groups is that 'yes, you can go anywhere in the world, but the minibus is going to Snowdonia'.

Through a process of logical reasoning considering time, money, staff availability and their project, the team should conclude entirely for themselves that Snowdonia is the place that best suits their chosen aim.

If the DofE centre and staff feel they cannot facilitate an aim the team wants to undertake, then there are many open expeditions and Approved Activity Providers who may be able to help. Participants can fundraise to help cover the costs; this adds another level to their development and commitment.

> **TOP TIP...**
> Participants - don't be led astray! Remember it is your expedition, so don't allow your Leaders or Assessors to dictate what you should do for your aim. It's better to use their knowledge as part of your research!
>
> Aled Davies,
> Mid Wales DofE Assessor
> Network Co-ordinator

Some examples of aims could include:
- A piece of work related to the environment they're travelling through, for example, examining footpath erosion, soil samples or studying the local wildlife.

- Monitoring and evidencing the impact of a physically demanding expedition on the body by walking all day and measuring calorie intake, blood pressure and pulse compared to normal.
- Using canoes to explore and research historical buildings on a lake system.
- Examining group dynamics and teamwork, by applying theories like Belbin or Tuckman to a study while on expedition, then producing a detailed statistical research presentation.

> **TOP TIP...**
> Choose an aim carefully that the team will enjoy researching and focusing their presentation on. They could try it out on their practice expedition too.
>
> Tony Cluxton, DofE Manager,
> Birmingham City Council

Get expert advice

As the aim takes shape, participants should talk to someone who has relevant expedition experience and knowledge. This helps participants avoid poor decisions and get the most out of their efforts and their Expedition section experience.

This person's help may be about the mode of travel, the destination area, local culture, flora and fauna or interesting ways to investigate the chosen project. Participants can get information from DofE Assessor Network Co-ordinators or National Park/ Countryside Rangers (UK only).

Getting the right balance and expeditions with a project focus

All expeditions are focused on their aim and it is up to the participants to decide how much time they will give to exploring and investigating their qualifying expedition project. The expedition needs to stretch the participants physically and mentally. There should be an honest balance between the time genuinely spent exploring and investigating the aim and the time spent journeying.

Teams should be prepared to explain to their Assessor what investigations they intend to do to fill the stated time spent on the aim and how it is appropriate to them.

Participants should start by assuming that they will journey for all the required hours and then deduct how much time they will need for rests, lunch and project investigations, based on their aim.

Remember that the minimum hours of activity requires at least half the time to be spent journeying and it may be that teams need to complete more than the minimum required hours to meet the needs of their aim.

As part of good planning and the notification process, when completing their route cards participants need to clearly show what time will be spent on investigating their aim and what it is they will be doing.

While all expeditions are focused on their aim, some teams will put much

more time into their expedition project, these are referred to as 'project focused expeditions'. Teams undertaking expeditions with a project focus will usually identify a knowledgeable and experienced person to support them with their aim. This person may act as a second (non-accredited) Assessor focusing on the aim and receiving the presentation after the expedition. (See page 197.)

As the exploring and project element of the expedition is enlarged, so must be the corresponding amount of research before and after the expedition, the investigation during the expedition and scale of the presentation. Some teams may want to focus on their project so as to reduce the physical demands of their expedition. The expedition must still remain a challenge and an adventure, meeting all of the 20 conditions and Expedition section outcomes.

Local culture and environment

Gaining an understanding of the local culture of an area is vital to any trip,

TOP TIP...
Give time and care in the selection of achievable aims. Decide the aim at the beginning of planning; not as an after-thought.

Jane Morse,
DofE Supervisor,
ATC Devon and Somerset

particularly outside the UK. However, the isolation aspect and required environments of the section means that investigating local culture cannot be an expedition aim.

Any local research, for example visiting a museum, town or village; must be undertaken in the acclimatisation period or after the expedition. This also applies to busy tourist locations, including historic sites and trails.

Think about the presentation

The aim and presentation are closely linked, so participants should think about what kind of presentation they might create at this early stage of the expedition process. Their initial ideas for the presentation may change and develop over the course of their Expedition section, but it is important participants have this end point in their minds.

Cycling around the world

I first got hooked into adventures through reading books of the great adventurers and explorers. I was also lucky to have teachers who took me out into the wild – the Lake District and the Highlands of Scotland. I was struck by their beauty, a sense of achievement, and a realisation that I was capable of more than I thought.

It wasn't until I started planning my round-the-world bike expedition that I realised how important it was to create a goal and a focus point to aim for. The trip was self-funded, I went alone – although complete strangers became my team mates. My aim of cycling round the world and raising money for a good cause kept me going through the toughest of times.

Whilst the physical element can be the most challenging of any expedition, developing an aim or project can be the most beneficial element as it gives you direction and the greatest sense of achievement when you complete it.

I think the key to any successful expedition is to remember that the hard times will pass and you will feel very proud of yourself if you persevere. It's a far greater feeling than the very brief relief of giving up.

Alastair Humphreys

Alastair completed an extraordinary adventure of cycling around the world by bike, visiting 60 countries in five continents over four years. Alastair cycled a total of 46,000 miles, all whilst on a tiny budget and raising money for charity.

Filming expeditions

with Russ Malkin

Russ Malkin is a British television producer and director who has years of experience filming expeditions. He has put together numerous motorcycle adventures with Charley Boorman and Ewan McGregor; made a record- breaking film; founded production company Big Earth which focuses on adventure travel programme making; all the while capturing every moment of his adventures on film.

For me, the object of having an adventure is to really feel alive.

To have that sense of excitement and unpredictability that not only provides a thrilling experience and that takes you out of your comfort zone but that also leaves an amazing memory afterwards.

The planning of an adventure is a very exciting process, staring at maps and picking routes but fundamentally it is very important to record your adventure.

TOP TIPS...

Remember, remember, remember to continue to film even when things are going wrong. If necessary, brief one member to film whatever happens as this drama will undoubtedly become the most important part of your show - so long as no one is in physical danger!

Russ Malkin

I would suggest that you do two things:
- Keep a written diary.
- Keep a video record of your experience so that you can look back on your trip years in the future and relive the moment.

Equipment

First, it is important not to be put off by the thought of making a documentary similar to those made on television. It is now very easy to film your expedition and post the results online. It's a great way to engage your audience!

I would suggest that you buy a camera that takes good quality photographs and high quality video. You can also download apps that allow you to edit this video to a point where you can make well produced mini documentaries perfect for YouTube etc.

You can buy more expensive video cameras for under £1,000 from high street stores that will give you more quality and control over the image but you will then have to purchase editing software to match. There is always the option of renting or buying professional cameras but this is much more costly.

Editing

If you are editing short video clips for the internet make sure that they are punchy and entertaining but keep the editing to a minimum as if you cut too often it could become confusing. Avoid using commercial music as this can cost a lot of money to get clearance.

Here are some more useful tips:

- For documentaries sound is often more important than pictures so ensure good audio.
- Record a video diary at the end of each day expressing your emotions and feelings about what you did that day.
- Shoot establishing shots of where you are (a wide shot of the location, local people, town signs etc).
- Keep your shots as steady as possible as shaking images become very difficult to watch.
- Even on small, short video clips, tell a story that is entertaining.

Master class

For those that have a bit more time and knowledge about filming, bear in mind the following:

1. Perhaps have a great opening sequence that could be a series of highlights for the coming shows. Fast cut, high tempo and entertaining, possibly ending on the title of your programme.

2. Use a voiceover if needed, but try and remember when filming to have your on-screen talent set up what the programme/activity is about.

3. Keep up the momentum, avoid long drawn out sections and keep the edit focussed.

4. Use the video diary mentioned earlier for the source of your voiceover as it will have a lot more emotion than voiceover recorded in the studio. Start the video diary from day one.

5. Use great music, there are a number of websites online where you can use library music for free and remember this music really helps create the mood behind the piece.

6. Try and use maps/graphics to show where you are in the world and a more detailed map to show your route as it progresses (you can download maps, add the route with dotted lines and place names).

7. Remember to have a resolution at the end of the story or section where people express how they felt (joy, pain, fear, sadness etc.).

Team: Participants form a team of between four and seven - eight for modes of travel which have tandem.

↓

Aim and mode of travel: The team will agree their expedition aim and from that their mode of travel. At this stage participants will often decide on likely expedition environments to help direct their training and practice expeditions.

↓

Training: Participants will complete the appropriate level of the Expedition Training Framework, mode of travel training and any other training required by the Supervisor (representing the Licensed Organisation or AAP) to be signed off as competent to successfully and safely undertake their expedition. Participants will also begin physical and fitness training for their practice and qualifying expeditions.

↓

Paperwork: Before undertaking expeditions, participants will need to complete the necessary notification paper work required by their Licensed Organisation, AAP and the DofE. Participants considering undertaking expeditions outside of the UK or who would like a variation should have these in hand at this stage.

↓

Practice expeditions: Participants must undertake sufficient practice expeditions to enable them to travel safely and complete their qualifying expedition. Practice expeditions will be followed by reflection and additional training to fully prepare participants for their qualifying expedition.

↓

Planning and preparation: The team will ensure they have everything in place for their qualifying expedition including notification paperwork, approvals, access, project investigation techniques and presentation.

↓

Supervisor's pre-expedition check: The Expedition Supervisor will conduct a check on all the equipment that the team will need and use during their expedition, ensuring it is fit for purpose.

↓

First contact and Assessor's pre-expedition check: The Accredited Assessor will discuss the proposed route with the team, provide any local information that may be helpful and once agreed, approve the route. The Assessor will meet the team in the expedition area either the day before or on the morning of the expedition. The Assessor will ask the team to confirm their training, chat through their expedition and agree their contract. The supporting adults and DofE team(s) will all review and agree expedition policies, the supervision plan and emergency procedures.

↓

Qualifying expedition: Once fully prepared the team will undertake their expedition, which will be remotely supervised and observed by their DofE Accredited Assessor. The Supervisor and Assessor will meet the team from time to time, keeping intrusion to a minimum, ensuring the team's safety and that the DofE's 20 conditions are being met.

↓

Debrief: At the end of the expedition the Assessor will conduct an oral debrief with the team. This is an opportunity to congratulate the team and help them to review their expedition.

↓

Presentation: At some point after the expedition, all participants will deliver a presentation, in any medium, of their expedition which covers their aims, experiences and outcomes.

↓

Assessment: The Accredited Assessor should provide their report for eDofE following the qualifying expedition and reports should also be provided by a person who saw their presentation.

DofE expedition requirements

The requirements for expeditions on foot are the same for all other DofE expeditions. See Chapter 2. Teams must always adhere to the DofE's behaviour expectations (Chapter 6.10), follow the DofE environmental impact policy (Chapter 6.6) and uphold the good reputation of the DofE.

Recommended environments

All teams must follow the recommended environment guidelines set out on page 10 and ensure they have appropriate access permissions. Some additional considerations are set out below.

Bronze

At Bronze level, one of the outcomes of the section is to inspire young people to gain an interest and appreciation of the outdoors near to them. A Bronze level expedition is all about young people enjoying the outdoors and wanting to go on to Silver level.

Bronze teams should complete their practice and qualifying expeditions close to home. Teams should not usually need to travel more than 30 miles away, often starting and/or finishing at their DofE centre, if in rural areas.

Routes still need to embrace the spirit of isolation but Bronze expeditions often aim to take in some of the famous local landmarks, to spark an interest in the team.

Silver

Silver expeditions take place in normal rural, open countryside or forest, which is unfamiliar to the participants. The environment should be more demanding for participants than at Bronze level. Where possible the expedition should be in, or at least include areas of open country or forest.

As part of the progressive nature of the DofE, teams who have completed their Bronze Award should progress to more challenging environments. Silver expeditions are an opportunity to develop and hone expedition skills and the environment should be thought of as an intermediate stage between normal rural environment (Bronze level) and wild country (Gold level), placing more demands on the participants.

Some Silver teams may go to wild country areas if they are local or it is the best place to meet their aim.

Appropriate training and the Gold level Expedition Training Framework will need to be completed, including a practice in wild country before the qualifying expedition. However, Silver teams doing this must consider how they will increase the challenge of the environment at Gold level.

Gold

The expectation of all Gold teams is that they are in wild country. These are areas that are remote from habitation and unfamiliar to the participants. A list of these areas in the UK can be found at **www.DofE.org/go/expeditionareas**.

The chosen wild country must also represent a step up and place more demands on participants who have completed their Silver expedition.

The choice of area should be based on the aim, but considerations of travel costs, staff availability and equipment transportation all need to be addressed.

Gold teams not undertaking their qualifying expedition in wild country must get approval for this in advance from their Licensed Organisation and their DofE Regional/Country Office, following appropriate notification processes.

Remote estuaries, marshes, fens and coastal areas may provide an appropriate environment for an expedition, with the emphasis on exploring rather than journeying, but must still be remote from habitation.

Guidance on wild country can be found on page 15.

Expedition route planning

It is important for participants to pace themselves and plan balanced days of journeying for their expedition.

Both hot and cold weather can cause problems to teams on long days and the impact of a late finish will disrupt good camping and delay planned early starts for the following morning.

Avoid roads and villages

As part of the need to experience isolation and self-reliance all expeditions should avoid villages and populated areas unless that is impossible. This is considered a must at Gold level. All roads must be avoided unless absolutely necessary when linking two sections of route together.

Teams need to be trained to understand the thinking behind this and plan their routes accordingly. It is not about taking the fastest and most direct route.

Long distance footpaths

Teams should not use long distance footpaths, particularly at Silver and Gold levels. Participants should create their own routes based on their own aims and not simply take this easier option.

Depending on the area these routes can provide very little navigational challenge and are often used by many other people, having a potentially negative environmental impact and undermining the sense of isolation. Using small parts of these paths or trails is acceptable to link up other elements of the expedition for the needs of the aim.

Access restrictions

Teams need to check access. Avoid areas where farmers are lambing or field sports are taking place. UK shooting details can be found online and deerstalking information from the Scottish Hill Phones Service. Also be aware of restrictions on MOD land.

TOP TIP...

When planning the expedition try to have more than four team members to start with, it's more enjoyable for the young people and means the expedition can continue if someone has to pull out.

Ana Ireland,
DofE Leader, Supervisor and
Assessor for Girl Guiding UK.

Create natural, logical routes

DofE teams should create routes which are a continuous journey stopping at different locations each night. Routes should be natural, linear routes which have a purpose linked to the team's aim and which are sympathetic to the landscape.

TOP TIP...

Avoid contrived routes that have loops or double-backs in them, unless needed for the team's aim. These types of routes can discourage young people when they think they are close to the finish and then realise they still have a long way to go. Routes should always follow a logical path.

Liz Heaney,
DofE Expedition Advisory Panel

Start early in the day

Teams at all levels should always attempt to start the day as early as possible, particularly towards the beginning and end of the expedition season when daylight hours are restricted. A good way of approaching this is to think about what time participants would like to finish the day's journeying and work back from there. DofE expeditions are not the place for lie-ins.

Make major ascents early in the day

Participants should plan any prolonged period of uphill walking for early in the day when they are still fresh and before any midday sun. It also allows participants to enjoy lunch in high places; taking in the panorama (in good weather) and knowing the most challenging part of the day is behind them.

As problems tend to occur later in the day, it is also good for teams to already be heading downhill, back into the more sheltered terrain and closer to assistance.

Alternative routes

Bad weather, particularly in wild country, should be considered the norm. All teams must identify and record on their route card, easy to follow, non-hazardous emergency escape routes to agreed locations where they can get help.

The DofE recommends that all teams should also create alternative poor weather routes. All teams in wild country must plan alternative, low level (lower risk) routes that can be used in the event of poor weather.

An alternative route is one which enables the team to reach its intended destination, meeting the 20 conditions, and yet avoid the full impact of the weather related hazards which can seriously add to navigation challenges. These alternative routes might be between certain checkpoints or an alternative route for the whole day. Few participants will have the experience to navigate safely and carry on whilst cocooned in mist and cloud.

DofE teams must not feel that using alternative routes is 'not meeting the challenge' or 'letting themselves down'. Managing risk is part of the DofE experience and teams should know when to switch routes and also when to turn back – 'pushing on' can limit options and be dangerous.

Supervisors (and Assessors) will work with participants to redesign routes to still meet the 20 conditions; they are there to facilitate success for the team.

Solitude, not altitude

DofE teams travel and navigate independently through, not over, terrain. While it is naturally tempting to head to the highest peak or a popular ridge – this is not in keeping with the concept or outcomes of DofE expeditions.

DofE teams, with their heavy, high-loaded backpacks, are committed to several days of self-sufficient expedition. As a result, traverses of well-known ridges and ascents of summits such as Crib Goch, Bristly Ridge, Lord's Rake and Striding Edge are unsuitable for DofE expedition teams.

All DofE expeditions are about solitude not altitude. Teams should pass through, not over, expedition areas. Setting the aim to climb peaks is not acceptable.

This should not stop teams wanting to reach some summits, cols or passes, but the amount of ascent should not be more than 500m in a single day.

It is too easy for teams to over-estimate fitness and under-estimate the effort of carrying a full pack. The practice expedition should help participants identify their capabilities.

The Assessor will look upon excessive amounts of climbing with suspicion. Teams looking to reach a summit should do so over multiple days using more sheltered routes, with little height change on the following day.

If participants are inspired to go on and climb more famous ascents in the future, then this should be considered a successful outcome of the section, giving them a lifetime of enjoyment in the outdoors.

Teams must plan their own route and travel independently. Guidance on multiple teams in the same expedition area can be found on page 14.

Use multiple start points

If supporting several DofE teams, ensure they set off from different locations, a few miles/km apart. This helps to ensure personal and independent expedition routes and prevents teams leapfrogging or following each other. This also puts in a natural time gap and reduces the environmental impact or local disruption at a single start point.

Accommodation

Accommodation should be by camping. In almost all cases, DofE teams use lightweight camping as their accommodation as it enhances the sense of adventure and self-reliance.

DofE expeditions are about solitude and independence, so DofE teams are expected to use only very basic campsites. DofE teams may use basic facilities such as drying rooms and toilets/showers. Use of other facilities (usually found on larger tourist sites) such as games rooms, bars, cafés, shops and swimming pools are not in keeping with DofE expeditions. Teams need to remain as isolated as possible while on public or busy campsites.

Teams arriving with all the equipment they need, striking camp and staying in the outdoors overnight, plays a key part in developing the desired outcomes for young people. On rare occasions, to take into account the needs of participants, alternative basic types of accommodation may be considered.

Very rarely, some expeditions in very mountainous areas or completing more unusual expeditions, like cross-country skiing, might need to use mountain huts/refuges. This will need to be discussed and agreed with the team's Licensed Organisation in advance.

Use valley campsites

Most teams use valley campsites, which are not far from a road or track allowing vehicle access for Supervisors, for Assessors and in the case of emergencies. These campsites tend to be more sheltered allowing participants to camp and rest more easily.

Wild camping

Wild camping can be an exciting, memorable and highly rewarding experience for young people. It is well suited to DofE expeditions and can give teams an unsurpassed sense of independence and isolation.

Teams must gain permission, in advance, to wild camp as some wild country areas and land owners do not allow it. Equally, for some teams this may be too challenging and not what they want to do. Teams that want to wild camp will need to build this ambition into their choice of expedition area and route planning. They will need to complete the appropriate additional training, including hygiene and suitable disposal of human waste.

> TOP TIP...
> If the weather forecast is good (dry and warm), try 'bivvying out' for a night rather than sleeping in a tent.
> Ron Verlander.
> Explorer Scout Leader.
> Englefield Green, Surrey

Avoid using the same campsite more than once

The route should be a continuous journey and participants should stop at different locations each night. A campsite may only be used more than once when necessary to meet the team's aim. Teams should still travel to and from the campsite as part of their journeying.

The team will need to break camp and take all their equipment with them. This both ensures team safety and maintains the sense of self-sufficiency and achievement.

Remote supervision

Remote supervision applies to evenings and nights as much as daylight hours. If Supervisors are on the same campsite then they should camp as far away from the participants as they can and have as little interaction as possible.

At Gold level it should not be necessary for any Supervisor to be present on the same campsite as participants overnight. Participants must be trained to this standard.

Hours of planned activity and distance advice

Working out the speed of travel is key to successful expeditions and this should come from the teams undertaking practice expeditions together.

When teams start to plan their route, they should begin by assuming that they will travel for all of the required hours of planned activity, then deduct time for lunch, rests and project work based on their aim.

It may be that additional activity time will be needed above the minimum DofE requirement in order to achieve their aim. For each team, the combination of this project work and journeying will create a unique expedition.

The distance covered by a team will vary greatly depending on their fitness, project, expedition environment, type of route and the weather, which can all influence their speed. A more complex route may require more stops for map reading. Equally some aims will require frequent stops, while others may require fewer, but longer stops.

Every team is different and the nature of their aim and personal situation means that it is hard to give estimates of common distances. However, to help Supervisors, we estimate that a team with appropriate breaks and project investigations will normally achieve total distances of around:

Level	Distance	Usual speeds	
Bronze	24-32km (15-20 miles)	Generally we suggest that an average team might travel between 3-4 km per hour (1.9-2.5 miles).	Some teams may travel much further, while others may put more time into their project and investigation. Whatever they do, it must be an appropriate challenge for them.
Silver	46- 60km (30 to 37 miles)		
Gold	80-96km (50-60 miles)		

Rests and lunch breaks

Reasonable time for lunch and other appropriate breaks can be included within the hours of planned activity. 30 minutes should be considered a reasonable amount of time for DofE groups to plan for their lunch stop.

Try to plan lunch stops in an appropriate location, somewhere with great views; but be flexible to have it earlier or later if the weather is poor and a sheltered spot would be better. All too often groups walk past stunning scenery to eat their lunch in a car park.

Time associated with overnight accommodation and catering is additional to the minimum daytime hours of planned activity.

Walking

When setting out, teams must ensure that there is no rubbish left behind and as little trace left of their presence as possible. Teams need to record their time of departure and adjust their route card if leaving early or late.

They will usually have agreed with the Supervisor when they will next meet them. One of the most likely times to make a navigational error is when leaving the basecamp/campsite;

TOP TIP...
Try to encourage feedback sessions/ forums - Q&As when planning an expedition to share good practice ask participants, 'what advice would you give?' (Silver participants to Bronze participants and Gold to Silver). Use a mentoring scheme to help encourage teams.
        Colin Fagan, DofE Co-ordinator, Alsop High, Liverpool

Supervisors should not step in but allow teams to work out their route, and any adjustments needed, for themselves.

Teams should aim for a steady pace thoughout the day, navigating and checking off landmarks as they walk, maintaining their rhythm, rather than stop-starting. Teams must always travel at the speed of their slowest member. However, they should remember that not walking at their natural pace and gait means that it is often as hard for faster walkers to slow down as it is for others to speed up.

DofE participants must keep together at all times. Unless dealing with an emergency situation, DofE teams must never split up or allow anyone to push ahead or be left behind.

If the route becomes very steep, teams may need to zig-zag to reduce steepness as continually walking on the front of the foot is very tiring, increases strain, reduces boot grip and therefore increases the risk of injury.

Walking down steep terrain often has a higher risk of falls occurring as the tendency is to lean backward out of the normal walking posture, which can lead to feet shooting forward. Teams should zig-zag with bent knees and weight forward.

Teams should never run downhill and should avoid dislodging stones which may injure people below.

Waterproofs should be put on at the earliest opportunity if it starts to rain to keep clothes dry and to avoid any illness/injury due to the cold. Equally, be prepared to remove a layer of clothing before it becomes soaked from perspiration.

Where participants have no choice but to use a minor road as part of their journey, participants should ensure they are visible to drivers. High-visibility vests, clothing and fluorescent rucksack covers will all help them to be seen.

Remind teams to walk in single file keeping close to the right-hand side of the road if there is no path, teams may need to cross over in advance of blind bends.

Equipment

Expeditions on foot use the basic equipment list available from **www.DofE.org/expedition**. However, as all items are carried on the back, equipment should be chosen with care.

Keep weight to a minimum

All rucksacks must be weighed before departure and packs should not be more than one quarter of the participant's own bodyweight.

Keeping the weight down is an essential part of expedition planning and is often a key factor in the expedition success and enjoyment. Take only essential items, other items will slow participants down and increase discomfort, exhaustion and risk.

Participants need to think ahead, plan as a team and balance need with use. There is little point in every team member taking toothpaste, one small tube to share is best, but equally don't cut the toothbrush in half as it makes it difficult to use. Participants are often focused on weight saving in one area, only to use it up with something else (e.g. taking a large towel). Packing at the last minute usually means poor decisions are made, often using whatever is to hand.

Practice expeditions are the best time to learn what to take and what to leave behind. However, participants must remember that this is a team undertaking and that stronger team members may have to carry more of the team equipment and have heavier bags, even if they have been super weight efficient with their personal kit.

Equally, everyone can have bad days and the team needs to come together to support them, perhaps by redistributing the kit. For information about day sacks and pre-positioned equipment, see page 108.

Keeping everything as dry as possible keeps it light. No matter how expensive rucksacks are they are never fully waterproof – they always need waterproofing with inner bags and then all items individually waterproofed in bags.

Packing the rucksack

Modern bags are designed to keep the load near the bearer's centre of gravity. Participants need to maintain this by placing heavy items as close to the body as possible and high up towards the shoulders.

This needs to be balanced with the 'last in, first out' rule, putting items that will be needed frequently at the top of the pack or in the side pockets. This includes the first aid kit, food and water.

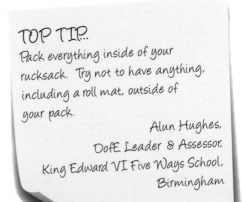

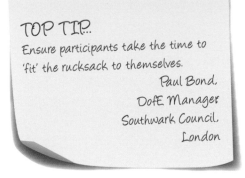

Sleeping bags and clothing, although bulky, are often comparatively light and as they are not needed during the day they should go to the bottom of the pack. Teams should divide up team equipment like the tent, food, stove and fuel equally and these items be placed near the top.

Anything attached to the outside of the rucksack must be securely fastened, so it does not get lost or swing around.

Training

Participants need to complete the DofE Expedition Training Framework to the appropriate level, be competent in the mode of travel and be prepared for the expedition environment. They must also complete any other training required by the Supervisor, on behalf of the LO or AAP, so every participant can be signed off as competent. Information about the training DofE participants need to undertake is set out in Chapter 6.

Supervision and assessment

DofE Supervisors and DofE Expedition Assessors should follow the guidance set out in Chapters 8 and 10. Please note that having an outdoor education qualification like the Mountain Leader Award does not automatically give the right to assess DofE expeditions.

Learning from mistakes

There is nothing better than hiking, but when I first started out, I was very inexperienced at spending time in the woods so I made a lot of mistakes. Some people never go into the woods because they are worried about doing it wrong. However, I found that learning from my errors was one of the best (and most entertaining) parts of backpacking.

It is always important to be prepared and safe, but I learned how to adapt, and how to ask other people for help as well. Those lessons have served me well on and off the trail.

Jennifer Pharr Davis

Jennifer was named National Geographic Adventurer of the Year in 2012 for breaking the overall Appalachian Trail speed record, a trail in the USA of over 2,000 miles, by walking the route instead of running it.

Chapter 5.2

Expeditions outside the United Kingdom

What *The Handbook for DofE Leaders* says...

Expeditions outside of the UK provide varied challenges which can inspire and broaden young people's experiences.

All Expedition section conditions apply equally to expeditions taking place outside the United Kingdom.

Completing a DofE expedition outside of the UK can be an amazing, memorable and inspirational challenge for many participants. The desire to experience completely different environments, from arctic to desert, mountainous to jungle; it drives DofE teams to go almost everywhere on the planet.

Whether created from scratch with their Licensed Organisation or delivered by an AAP, these expeditions can be some of the most rewarding undertakings of a young person's life.

Every year over 2,000 participants embark on their DofE expedition outside of the UK. For most of these participants it is the culmination of their DofE experience, with 85% of expeditions outside the UK undertaken at Gold level. However, participants also head to countries like France, Spain and Germany for their Bronze and Silver expeditions.

The ten most common DofE expedition destinations outside of the UK are France, Ireland, Spain, Morocco, Norway, Italy, Canada, South Africa, New Zealand and Finland; (70% take place in Europe). There are many Supervisors and Leaders who have considerable experience that they are happy to share with DofE teams.

All expeditions outside the UK must still meet the 20 conditions, recommended environments and conform to standard remote supervision and health and safety requirements as normal.

Participants must carefully select destinations which will allow this. Organisers and participants should contact their Licensed Organisation at the earliest opportunity, before money is spent, to ensure the activity will count for the participant's DofE programme.

Although expeditions outside the UK will require more planning, and usually funding, to arrange or participate in, this tends to further motivate the participants who choose this challenge. In some ways they can be easier as countries with lower population densities allow for more low altitude areas and larger expanses of isolated rural, open and wild country. However, documentation, visas, inoculations, additional kit, a lack of established campsites and inadequate mapping can make some countries less accessible.

Remember to consider local restrictions of land use, culture and climate. Ensure that the Supervisor and other staff are appropriately qualified and insured as some countries require them to hold specific qualifications, for example the International Mountain Leader Award, to supervise. Some areas insist on groups being accompanied by armed guards or National Park guides which rule them out as potential DofE destinations.

Opportunities for different modes of travel can also be greatly enhanced. There are often fewer restraints on mountain bikes than in the UK. Novel modes of travel like camel and dog sled can also be considered. The length, breadth and volume of rivers and canals in Europe can offer a new dimension for canoeing and rowing expeditions and the opportunities for sailing are endless.

Expedition routes and areas

Expeditions outside the UK must follow the same recommended environments guidance as all expeditions in the UK. However a more flexible approach is taken with regards to the use of long distance paths, as they can sometimes be the only way of getting access to large areas of remote land or for making progress through very difficult terrain or forests. Careful selection of remote and rarely used long distance paths can allow for an inspiring and challenging expedition.

It is essential that expedition staff have prior knowledge or conduct a reconnaissance of the expedition area. Many areas present such difficulties and hazards that they can only be taken on by experienced and stronger participants. Foothill and lowland areas nearby can provide more suitable

challenges for other teams while still feeling part of the dramatic landscape. As with all DofE expeditions, teams should travel through, rather than over, wild country, it is about solitude, not altitude. Teams can struggle to cover good distances unless they choose their routes with care, considering altitude, daily ascent, descent and temperature. The team must recognise their abilities and choose an area of appropriate challenge for them. The cost and effort of such expeditions means that misjudging this can result in bitter disappointment.

As in the UK, a Supervisor must be located in the area of expedition at all times and participants must have completed all the training requirements of the appropriate Expedition Training Framework and mode of travel. This will need to be evidenced to the Assessor in advance of the expedition.

Most expeditions outside the UK will include several acclimatisation and additional training days as not all areas or conditions can be replicated in the UK practices. This is recommended as best practice.

As part of the progression principle of the DofE, it is assumed that expeditions outside the UK will be the qualifying expedition. However DofE participants must complete an appropriate UK practice expedition before undertaking any DofE expedition outside of the UK.

Local culture and language

When designing the expedition it is important to gain an understanding of the local culture. Participants should take the opportunity before or after the expedition to experience the social and cultural aspects of the country.

Training in the customs, culture and lifestyle of the destination will enhance the whole experience and ensure participants can maintain the high standards of behaviour expected by the DofE and not inadvertently give any offence.

All participants should be sufficiently familiar with the destination country's language, not only to exchange courtesies, but to communicate in an emergency. Some essential phrases should be issued to each participant on paper for them to keep and practice.

Training should include using local telephones to be aware of dialling tones, procedures and costs. Leaders should also investigate local reception for mobile phones; see Chapter 9 on mobile phones.

Some teams have secured funding through establishing an international exchange programme by linking with a DofE team in the destination country. They have then been able to undertake another expedition with them back in the UK for the exchange group's DofE programme.

The isolation aspect of the Expedition section means that cultural experience cannot be used as an expedition aim. Any research, for example visiting a temple or local village, must be undertaken in the acclimatisation period or after the expedition just as in the UK.

Try to find other ways to bring the local culture into the expedition, for example by learning local games to play in the evenings, buy some local music to play and do some pre-expedition shopping at food stalls for the expedition snacks.

Planning

Planning for these expeditions will usually begin early, at least six months in advance. A complete timeline and checklist of all the key steps will be needed to ensure each action is completed in good time.

Build in time to accommodate delays and problems like out-of-date passports or visas.

Arrange a pre-trip meeting to go through all kit, medication, documentation, travel arrangements and emergency procedures. The Leader should have a photocopy of each of the participant's travel documents as well as summary sheets of emergency contacts and any specific needs of group members.

Groups must also be aware of local laws and regulations concerning travel, vehicles, supervision and all their modes of travel used in the country.

When travelling by road outside of the UK, ensure that vehicles comply with the appropriate regulations, are serviced before leaving and are fully insured for breakdown and the repatriation of vehicle and passengers.

Drivers must follow local directives on driving, plan routes in advance for safety and include rests. Road travel can be the most dangerous part of the trip.

International maps

Most of Western Europe is mapped at a 1:50 000 and now also at a 1:25 000 scale. In other areas the quality and availability of maps can vary. The best way to find local maps is either while in the country on the reconnaissance trip or via online shops and support sites.

For remote areas many groups use Google Earth or dedicated mapping programmes as a way to map out the expedition area. It is usually best to provide the Assessor with a prepared map rather than a tracing so that everyone in the area is working from the same resources.

The scale of the maps will depend on what is available.

Safety and emergencies

It is essential that teams clearly understand the emergency procedures in place for the expedition. Many areas of wild country do not have mountain rescue or search teams. Expedition teams, Supervisors and Accredited Assessors will be entirely dependent on their own resources.

Some areas, such as the Alps, have highly efficient, professional rescue teams, but their services are very expensive, often costing thousands of pounds.

Each participant should carry with them a copy of a DofE expedition safety card available from **www.DofE.org/expedition**

Insurance must be in place for all participants and supporting staff which covers search and rescue as well as repatriation of the sick or injured. It should also ideally cover the cost for a parent or guardian to visit participants admitted to hospital while abroad.

Supervisors and participants should have a thorough working knowledge of first aid and prolonged casualty care, proportionate to the risks involved in the country and area to be travelled.

There should be a documented emergency action plan which is familiar to, and practised, by all involved in the expedition, who then also carry emergency equipment which conforms to this plan.

In the event of a serious accident, the restraint exerted by the UK police regarding the release of names to the press until the next of kin have been informed does not necessarily apply abroad. There is a strong probability that parents, carers or guardians may find out about a serious accident by the media, internet etc. unless efficient two-way communications are established beforehand between them and the team.

Participants must be prepared and know how to deal with the weather and temperatures they will encounter as there can be an increased risk of exercise-induced heat exhaustion or frostbite, than in the UK.

Clear precautions must be taken to reduce these risks, for example using strong protection against the sun and preventing dehydration.

Thunderstorms and lightning strikes are more severe and frequent, and wildlife may pose a threat through rabies, malaria and snake bites.

DO NOT ASCEND WHEN LIGHTNING AND THUNDERSTORMS ARE THREATENING.

TOP TIP...

In hot summer days, or in hot climates, start the day very early and enjoy the solitude and lower temperatures found in that space.

Chris Hart,
DofE Assessor,
Yorkshire Dales

Assessor and Supervisor dual roles

In some cases for overseas DofE expeditions, the cost of taking an additional person to be the Assessor can be prohibitive so there is some flexibility in these instances.

For overseas expeditions it is acceptable for the Supervisor to also take on the role of Assessor, if they are accredited by the DofE, while support staff, such as teachers or volunteers, manage the pastoral care of the team.

Even in cases where the Supervisor may have been involved in the team's training programme this is acceptable. If it is possible for an independent person to be the Assessor then this option should always be used as best practice. The team must agree this in advance with their Licensed Organisation.

Notifications

All expeditions outside the UK must be notified to the DofE through the appropriate notification process and in good time, that is several months in advance. This allows the DofE to issue a notification number and support good expedition quality.

Participants must have their expeditions approved by their Licensed Organisation which has the legal responsibility for their safety.

The expedition provider, whether this is the Supervisor on behalf of the Licensed Organisation or an AAP brought in to help, must accept responsibility for monitoring the safety of the expedition. This must be undertaken in accordance with the policies and guidelines of the Licensed Organisation.

Some open expeditions are not run by a DofE Licensed Organisation or centre but by an AAP. In these cases a private contract has been agreed between the participant/parent/guardian and the AAP so the Licensed Organisation is not involved and so may not require

notification. Policies may vary between Licensed Organisations.

It is the Supervisor's/deliverer's responsibility to ensure that it is clear to everyone where insurance and responsibility for health and safety rests, either with themselves, their parents/guardians (if under 18), their Licensed Organisation or an AAP.

Parents, carers or guardians should be kept informed of the details of the general trip, the expedition and other activities.

The team should notify the destination country's National Award Authority, if the International Award operates in that country. See **www.intaward.org** for contact details.

Exploring the world

Travelling and understanding what beauty the world has to offer, and adventuring with friends and loved ones to foreign places is an opportunity that should not be missed.

I have been travelling since I was very young and I have been to some magnificent places around the world and I highly recommend it.

When you plan your expedition, you can choose where to go and explore, whether you want to stay in the UK or go exploring abroad. I have been travelling all over the world including China, Africa, Asia, and America and, although travelling aboard may take a little more time and preparation in research and planning, I believe the sense of adventure, the sights, cultures and new experiences will undoubtedly make the extra effort worth it.

The thought of travelling abroad can be daunting, venturing into the unknown, but if I could give you one bit of advice, it would be to get out there and do it – to travel and explore because travelling and adventuring is about more than discovering new places. I believe when you challenge yourself by doing something like this, you learn a lot about yourself and gain confidence in your abilities. This is true for me – I have become more patient and excited about different countries and cultures and I have learnt to not be afraid of the unknown.

Charley Boorman
An adventurer and actor, best known for his epic world-wild motorcycle adventures including 'Long Way Round' with actor Ewan McGregor.

Chapter 5.3
Open expeditions

What *The Handbook for DofE Leaders* says...

Open expeditions enable independent participants, those who missed their own group's expedition or those unable to form a viable team, to complete practice and/or qualifying expeditions.

They include a familiarisation and planning period followed by a remotely supervised and assessed expedition.

All necessary training and practice expeditions must be undertaken before a participant can take part in an open qualifying expedition.

Open expeditions are DofE expeditions made available to all DofE participants, to join as an individual, and are run at all levels and in all modes of travel. Many Licensed Organisations will run a number of open expeditions. Often they are focussed on supporting mainly their own participants.

Several DofE Assessor Networks also run open Gold expeditions in their wild country areas. Approved Activity Providers offer a range of open expeditions both in many different modes of travel and in many different countries around the world.
A range of opportunities for open expeditions are advertised on **www.DofE.org**.

Participants preparing for an open expedition

It is important for participants to understand what kind of open expedition it is before joining. Some will be expeditions with a project focus whereas others may be very physically demanding. Participants should consider the type of area, local climate and time of year when making a decision on which expedition to choose.

- Participants need to understand that open expeditions require them to get along with people they don't know, so an open mind and willingness to get stuck in is essential.
- Participants need to have the appropriate expedition equipment, level of training and practice expedition experience for the open expedition they are undertaking.

- Participants will need to provide evidence to the Supervisor in advance of the training and practices (if any) they have completed, and when they did them.
- Participants must inform the Supervisor of any medical condition(s) which may affect their performance or supervision needs.
- Information about old injuries and dietary requirements will also need to be provided in advance in the medical and consent forms.

All of the above should be included in the provider's information pack, see page 61.

All open expeditions will have at least one day, probably several days at Gold level, of preparation, planning and training. This allows the Supervisor to evaluate the participants' expedition skills, equipment, competence, fitness and for the group to prepare their route and route cards.

Some participants have to complete all of their Expedition section through open expeditions, in which case they must make it clear to the Supervisor if they are inexperienced.

Not all open expeditions include specific training days, so participants should check in advance that they are on the right open expedition for their situation. It may be necessary for participants to complete a one day first aid course before going on the open expedition.

They may also need to link with another local group to complete some training or short practice expeditions to gain or refresh skills. Participants can also set up practice expeditions with their friends, supervised by an adult approved by their Licensed Organisation.

Organising an open expedition

Open expeditions revolve around a set date and participants need to choose one they can attend. They must be advertised well in advance and are usually best organised during school holidays or Bank Holiday weekends.

Most organisations will run several open expeditions throughout the expedition season, however having one near the start and one near the end of the season often works well for participants who need to finish off their Expedition section.

When promoting the expedition, be very clear what kind of expedition is on offer, where it is and what costs are and are not included, for example equipment hire and expedition food.

Participants should be provided with a full information pack so all information is received in good time and in one place. It should include the following:

- Clear information about the type of expedition, location, description of terrain or water involved, likely physical demands and if it is an expeditions with a project focus or additional needs expedition.
- Clear equipment lists including what will be provided, what may be hired and what participants will have to bring.
- Details of the itinerary including information about accommodation, travel and catering before, during and after the expedition.
- Clear information about the paperwork required from participants, including medical and consent forms, evidence of training and practice expeditions, when they were completed and appropriate emergency contacts.
- Clear information about the costs of the expedition and the responsibilities of the provider/Supervisor.
- Details of how evidence for eDofE will be provided and if the open expedition includes time for the presentation of their aim.

- Information about the expedition area and possible campsites to help teams begin remotely planning routes and aims with the help of the Supervisor.

The organiser and Supervisor take on full responsibility for the young people during the open expedition, so must have in place robust and complete policies and procedures required under UK law and that reflect best practice. Organisers must ensure that appropriate and adequate insurance cover is in place for all open expeditions.

Some open expeditions are not run by a DofE Licensed Organisation or centre but by an AAP. Here participants book onto the open expedition as individuals and not through their DofE centre or Licensed Organisation. In these cases a private contract has been agreed between the participant/parent/guardian and the AAP.

The Licensed Organisation is not involved and so may not require notification; policies may vary between Licensed Organisations. It is the Supervisor's/deliverer's responsibility to ensure that it is clear to everyone where insurance and responsibility for health and safety rests, either with themselves, their parents/guardians (if under 18), their Licensed Organisation or an AAP.

Parents, carers or guardians should be kept informed of the details of the general trip, the expedition and other activities.

To be classed as an open expedition, the expedition must:
- Have been openly advertised, in a way that participants from a number of different centres will have seen the opportunity.
- Include a direct contract between the participants and the provider, rather than being through their centre or Licensed Organisation and the expedition provider.
- Include participants from more than one centre undertaking the expedition.

Managing an open expedition

Organising teams

Open expeditions can be a very challenging experience. A group of individuals or pairs coming together to form an expedition team just a day or few days before undertaking their expedition means that they need to get to know each other and bond as a team quickly.

The participants may have a wide range of expedition experience, skills and physical fitness; all of which the team will have to manage while planning for and completing their expedition.

Supervisors need to carefully balance the advantages of grouping people by physical fitness with personal preferences. Arbitrarily formed teams often work poorly, so participants should be involved in the process and friends should always be kept together.

Always aim for teams of six or seven to account for any participants who may have to drop out. It is always best to have more than one team, it allows for much greater flexibility.

Open expeditions are usually a last chance for participants to complete their Expedition section and often their whole DofE programme. There is often a greater sense of pressure on participants undertaking these kinds of expeditions.

The mixed ability of participants means that organisers and Supervisors must carefully support an expedition, which is an appropriate challenge for each of the participants and also achievable by all the participants.

Open expeditions are rarely the place for highly technical and physically arduous expeditions.

If possible, put participants into groups before the expedition so they can plan their aims and routes in advance. Participants will need to give permission for their contact information to be shared in order to set this up.

While the very nature of open expeditions means that participants undertaking practice expeditions may be mixed with those completing their qualifying expedition, this should be avoided if at all possible.

As all the participants will effectively be completing a qualifying expedition, those doing their practice may then question why they have to do it all again and so lose motivation.

Training, competence and equipment

The most effective way to help teams bond is through the training and planning activities needed in the days immediately before the expedition.

To help facilitate the success of the expedition, use this time as fully as possible to provide training and improve competence for all the participants. These days should always include short training expeditions, so the team can experience walking together and their competence can be observed by the Supervisor.

One of the first tasks, when participants are in their teams, is to do a full equipment check so that if anything is missing or not appropriate there is time to find a solution.

TOP TIP...
Play games using OS. map symbol, menus, calories and equipment cards to help make expedition training more entertaining and into a teambuilding activity.
Margaret Bainbridge,
DofE Supervisor/Assessor,
Buckinghamshire

Make sure there are some scales available to weigh rucksacks (or kit if not on foot) before departure to prevent individuals taking too much equipment.

Keep the evening before the expedition clear so participants can get an early night, prepare their kit (an opportunity to dry/clean it from any practices over the past few days) and ensure they have an up-to-date weather forecast.

Aim and presentation

Allow the participants to agree the aim of their expedition early, several weeks or months in advance if possible. It gives them a focus, provides time for the Assessor to comment and allows them to plan to bring any evidence gathering tools they may need or complete any local research. Ensure that the team is very clear about how they will achieve their aim and complete sufficient research for their presentation.

The presentation may be prepared and delivered back home as individuals. However the DofE recommends that where possible, teams stay an extra evening (either at the base camp, outdoor centre, youth hostel or their usual DofE centre) and complete their presentation as a team in the evening, or morning after their expedition.

It gives time for group reflection, a celebration/presentation 'event' and ensures the section is completed.

To make these presentations a success, plan them in advance. Participants will need time to plan and rehearse, collating their observations and recordings and putting any digital materials into place.

These presentations cannot be rushed or completed in an atmosphere of an impatient driver anxious to head home. Participants will usually need to have kept a written log of their expedition to refer to, as there is unlikely to be time for video editing.

Supervisors and Assessors should help put participants at their ease as they may be tired and nervous. These presentations are a distinct event and separate from the Assessor debrief immediately at the end of the expedition.

Route planning

The route planning process for open expeditions can be difficult due to the amount of time available and newness of the team. Teams should try to plan the route in advance remotely supported by the Supervisor, dividing the work load appropriately. This helps participants to become familiar with both the route and expedition area.

Allocate plenty of time, usually at least half a day, to check and alter routes and route cards with the Assessor before the start of the expedition. Teams can use eDofE Mapping to save time and share

---

An open Gold expedition programme might be:
Days 1 & 2: Preparation, planning, acclimatisation and team building.
Days 3-6: Expedition and debrief.
Day 7: Presentation and travel home.

Friends for life

It's great to go on an adventure with people you don't know, because you discover much more about yourself and you meet a lot more people.

You're tempted to sit down with other people, share experiences with them and get to know their cultures and sense of humour. You know you can actually form relationships, and memories you can keep for the rest of your life in that way.

Russ Malkin

Russ Malkin is a British television producer and director who is best known for completing numerous adventures with Charley Boorman and Ewan McGregor.

routes, particularly if the base camp has an internet connection.

As with all DofE expeditions, the team must come up with their own route, it is not acceptable to provide the team with a ready made route. It is often tempting to book campsites in advance; however this can lead to inflexibility to accommodate for the ability of the team.

Have a range of campsites that participants can choose to use. If going to wild country, always contact the Assessor Network Co-ordinator very early and talk to them about the expedition and ensure that the DofE notification processes are followed correctly, see **www.DofE.org**.

Supervision and assessment

During the expedition the Supervisor and Assessor follow all the normal procedures for their roles with DofE expeditions. Assessors should meet the team at the same time as the Supervisor, as they do not know the team very well so it is good practice to have two members of staff to deal with any situations. For some large multi-team expeditions, Supervisors and Assessors may switch roles with different teams; however one person cannot be the same team's Supervisor and Assessor.

Chapter 6
Training

What *The Handbook for DofE Leaders* says...

Safety is paramount when it comes to the expedition.

Therefore, it is essential that participants undertake expedition skills training using the DofE's Expedition Training Framework.

The Expedition section will stretch participants technically, mentally and physically, so training programmes need to prepare them for these challenges. The excellent safety record of the DofE is largely due to the quality, thoroughness and high levels of training all DofE teams are required to complete before undertaking their qualifying expedition.

Instructors (those who deliver DofE expedition training) and Supervisors will use a range of training techniques, styles and time frames to complete the Expedition Training Framework and prepare teams. However, each should use a systematic approach based on defined learning objectives and outcomes.

DofE qualifying expeditions are unaccompanied, self-sufficient and remotely supervised, therefore participants must have a high level of competence.

During training, participants will require a steadily decreasing level of supervision as their skills, confidence and experience increase, allowing them to remain safe in the outdoors.

Instructors and Supervisors will want to see evidence not only of technical skills, but also of self-discipline, responsibility, good behaviour, positive attitude, maturity and good judgement.

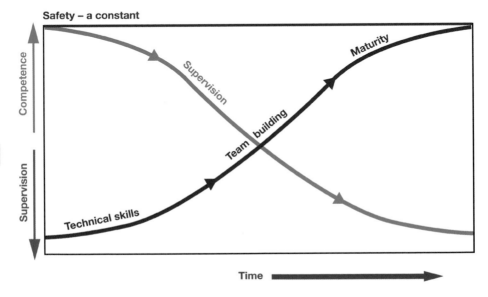

The DofE Expedition Training Framework

The DofE's Expedition Training Framework is designed to provide a structure for training young people undertaking their Expedition section and preparing them to meet the challenges of their expedition.

DofE Expedition training focuses on three key areas: the Expedition section aims and conditions; team building and leadership; and technical expedition skills. The Expedition Training Framework delivers these in nine elements which each participant must complete to the appropriate level and in the chosen mode of travel.

The detailed Expedition Training Framework documents are available for free at **www.DofE.org/expedition**, and in the Resource Zone on eDofE.

The nine elements of the Expedition Training Framework

- First aid and emergency procedures.
- An awareness of risk and health and safety issues.
- Navigation and route planning.
- Campcraft, equipment and hygiene.
- Food and cooking.
- Countryside, Highway and Water Sports Safety Codes (as appropriate)
- Observation and recording.
- Team building.
- Proficiency in the mode of travel.

To allow participants to have ownership of their expedition they must also be informed of the aim, principles, requirements and 20 conditions of the DofE Expedition section, set out in *The Handbook for DofE Leaders* and this *Expedition Guide*. This includes the DofE Environmental Impact Policy (Chapter 6.6) and key behaviour expectations (Chapter 6.10).

EX²

EX² is the DofE's interactive expedition training tool which also contains further details along with practical advice and training support. This is available from our shop at **www.DofEshop.org**.

Forming teams

Each individual participant will depend upon the mutual support and collective experience of their team in order to successfully complete their expedition. Where possible, teams should be allowed to form naturally from the DofE group, with friends remaining together.

It is often beneficial for team members to have a similar level of fitness, however working together and travelling at the pace of the slowest team member is part of the teamwork skills developed through this section.

Teams need to bond and develop trust and respect to cope with the inevitable stresses of an expedition, but also to enjoy the experience. It is the team spirit and their collective commitment which will support individuals through bad weather, blisters, low morale and navigational disagreements. Training that includes team building and leadership development activities is essential, as are team sessions on reviewing and reflection.

Hard/technical skills and soft/people skills

Participants will need training in both the 'hard' technical and practical skills needed to expedition in the outdoors, and the 'soft' or 'people' skills needed to bring the team together as an effective unit. Both are essential and are of equal importance for a successful expedition.

It is usually more effective when the hard skills are used as a basis for teaching and developing the soft skills, rather than teaching them as theoretical concepts. Soft skills should feature specifically in all training sessions and have a special place in the practice expeditions and in the reviews.

The diagram below shows the relationship between hard/technical and soft/people skills:

Safety in the outdoors

In the outdoors there are some situations where there is only one correct way of doing something. Training in these critical techniques to ensure participant safety should involve instruction so that it becomes a drill, an automatic response to follow the correct procedure without need for judgement.

Experience and judgement

Building progressive experience is an essential part of DofE training. Experience develops through time and variety, and so it is beneficial to include activities outside of formal training sessions.

Diverse situations are needed if the greatest benefit is to be gained from the commitment of time and effort

Of all the qualities essential to the safety and well-being of DofE participants, that of sound judgement is the most important. Sound judgement, along with responsibility and maturity, arises from effective training coupled with the development

soft/people skills – the personal skills
Leadership, team building, decision-making, judgement, inter-personal skills.

Hard/technical skills of living out of doors and the mode of travel
Campcraft, navigation, emergency procedures, first aid, conservation, access, observation, recording, reports etc.

The DofE Expedition Guide

of varied experience over time. It can only develop if participants are given opportunities in which to exercise judgement, both as individuals and collectively.

Structured training programmes

DofE Leaders, Supervisors and instructors will carefully plan a training programme to meet the needs of everyone in the DofE group/team.

The timing of the training programme is usually most influenced by the weather conditions and exams. There are several common approaches used but all consist of the core components set out below.

Training sessions

These sessions will cover most of the Expedition Training Framework and are best taught outdoors, although some aspects can be taught indoors during cold weather, over the winter. Sessions are usually regular one or two hour sessions as an expedition team or DofE group.

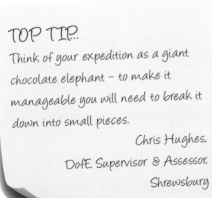

TOP TIP...

Think of your expedition as a giant chocolate elephant – to make it manageable you will need to break it down into small pieces.

Chris Hughes,
DofE Supervisor & Assessor,
Shrewsbury

Sessions will usually focus on one technical skill, working methodically through the framework, but should also include soft skills development at the same time. Begin with the skills that take the longest to learn and when taking on a new mode of travel, ensure the team has plenty of time to gain experience in it.

Training events

Outdoor training sessions, days and overnight camping are used to gauge and refine a team's competence and strengths whilst also identifying areas for improvement. They are great for team building and allowing teams to experience a more prolonged outdoor expedition experience.

TOP TIP...

Encourage the group/team to socialise outside of DofE, for example going ice skating, bowling or having a meal, whatever they enjoy. Getting to know each other away from the DofE centre can really help unite them.

Mary Spanswick,
DofE Supervisor, Marlborough Open
DofE Centre, Wiltshire

Practice expeditions

Practice expeditions are an essential and compulsory requirement of the Expedition section, providing opportunities to develop hard/technical and soft/people skills while in an expedition environment.

More information can be found in Chapter 7.

Practice expeditions often take place in the early Spring or Summer and continue into early Autumn, depending on the training programme.

Several practice expeditions can be needed for teams to gain confidence and competence, particularly when undertaking a new mode of travel.

TOP TIP...

Ask your local orienteering club if they could help your participants learn map reading. They might be able to arrange a couple of local competitions especially for your participants, or let them take part in local competitions.

Sam Bennie,
County DofE Advisor,
Girlguiding UK South West Region

Fitness training

Participants need to plan a fitness programme which will peak just before their qualifying expedition.

The programme should start two or three months before this, depending on the participant and their expedition aim.

Physical training activities should become increasingly strenuous as the qualifying expedition nears.

Qualifying expedition

The training programme should be planned to continue right up to the pre-expedition check in the days before the qualifying expedition, which usually takes place in the summer or early autumn.

Three example training programmes are shown below:

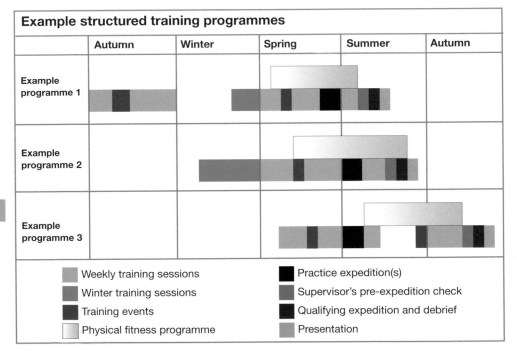

	Autumn	Winter	Spring	Summer	Autumn
Example programme 1					
Example programme 2					
Example programme 3					

Example structured training programmes

- Weekly training sessions
- Winter training sessions
- Training events
- Physical fitness programme
- Practice expedition(s)
- Supervisor's pre-expedition check
- Qualifying expedition and debrief
- Presentation

Key points to remember:
- Take into account the weather, availability of instructors and exams. Make the most of long bank holiday weekends.
- Leave some time between the practice and qualifying expeditions for additional learning and practices, if required.
- Maintain a good pace of learning from the start of the programme to prevent frantic activity as the qualifying expedition approaches.
- Have one person maintain a comprehensive checklist of what needs to be completed and when.
- Be flexible as participants will learn at different rates and have different strengths. This is particularly the case for direct entrant participants.
- Build on the training from previous DofE levels as participants progress to Gold level.
- Teams undertaking project-focused expeditions should identify someone with expertise in the topic area to support and advise them in developing their project and investigations.

Planning training sessions

Each training session should be planned to incorporate these elements:
- Follow a written plan
- Mix the different elements of the Expedition Training Framework
- Focus on the essentials
- Be practical
- Have sufficient equipment
- Review the session
- Record the session.

Focus on sessions being enjoyable, practical and hands-on with equipment. Ensure each participant's learning is recorded to evidence competence to the Supervisor and Assessor, and is signed off in eDofE. Information on sign-off can be found in eDofE. More detail on planning training sessions can be found in EX² and at **www.DofE.org/expedition**.

Reviewing training sessions

Reviewing needs to be built into every training session to enable the DofE team/group to examine and reflect on what they have learnt.

It helps instructors to revise existing training sessions and prepare new sessions. Reviewing does not have to take long, but these discussions and reflections are excellent for reinforcing learning, enabling all team members to consider their progression and contribution to the team.

It helps people identify any weaknesses, share them in a supportive environment and recognise the developing team dynamics.

Team reviewing and reflection should be undertaken both with and without adult support.

Reviewing is a simple process as shown in the 'Plan-Do-Review' diagram. Instructors can help by asking open questions, similar to those below, to initiate a discussion:

- What did we plan to do?
- How well did we achieve these aims and objectives?
- Some of us had *(this issue)*, what should we do differently next time?
- What was our speed of travel today, can we improve it?
- How effective was learning in *(this area)*, is everybody confident?
- Questions should also consider soft skills where more sophisticated team judgements have to be made:
- Why did we argue over *(this issue)*?
- Why didn't we work together on *(this task)*?
- What was each person's role in *(this task)*?
- How can we work together to overcome issues in the future?

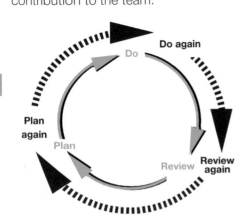

Embracing the adventure

True adventure, capability and success during any challenge lies in working together as a team. A team is certainly stronger than the sum of its individual parts, and with a high performing team you can achieve more.

Whether it's with just one other partner, or a much larger multi-person team, there is a bond of trust linking us which is stronger than any rope. My hardest expeditions have always been when I've been climbing solo: not because of the difficulty or danger, but because I didn't have anyone to share the adventure with or to help motivate me when times were tough.

I've been lucky enough to climb and take part in expeditions with a wonderfully diverse set of teams and relish the company of every member. All the feats that I'm proudest of achieving: it's been down to the teams that I've been blessed with being part of.

When you are on your DofE expedition, remember the importance of your team, and pull hard together to achieve greatness! I can assure you, that the best friends that you'll make in life are the ones that you've travelled through the toughest situations with. Embrace the adventure and cherish the friendship and sense of belonging that teamwork brings.

Jake Meyer

Jake is the youngest Briton to climb Mount Everest and was the youngest man in the world to complete the seven summits, whilst breaking numerous records along the way. He was also part of the British team that broke the world record for climbing the 48 highest peaks of America in the shortest time.

What *The Handbook for DofE Leaders* says...

All participants must complete first aid training to the appropriate level of the DofE Expedition Training Framework as well as the requirements of the team's Supervisor and Licensed Organisation/AAP.

First aid training should only be delivered by people who have been approved by the Licensed Organisation/AAP. Some Licensed Organisations and AAPs choose to define who can deliver first aid training, for example:

- An instructor in first aid who is recognised by one of the voluntary aid societies, the Armed Services or the Health and Safety Executive.
- A qualified teacher or youth leader who holds a valid first aid certificate.
- A State Registered Nurse or Health Visitor (who may not have a first aid certificate).
- An instructor approved by the Licensed Organisation/AAP.
- Licensed Organisations/AAPs will require Supervisors to hold a valid and relevant first aid certificate.

First aid procedures change and develop and it is therefore essential that participants are taught by instructors who are using up to date resources and materials.

There are a number of first aid manuals available and instructors should choose the one that is most appropriate for the abilities of the participants that they are working with, to ensure their participants become competent.

The First Aid Manual, published by St. Andrew's Ambulance Association, St. John Ambulance and the British Red Cross Society, is regarded as being the definitive first aid guide.

First aid kits

Each DofE participant should carry their own first aid kit with them on expedition rather than, or in addition to, a communal kit for the whole team.

Personal first aid kits allow participants to adapt them based on their needs, conditions or allergies. It ensures that each will have their own kit, should they become separated on expedition. When personal kits are combined they will provide sufficient resources to deal with more serious emergencies.

Participants should make the Supervisor, Assessor, other staff and team members aware if they are allergic to an antibiotic or any other medicine or drug.

All first aid kits should carry plenty of disposable plastic gloves to prevent contact with body fluids, especially blood. The DofE recommendations for suitable first aid kits can be found online at **www.DofE.org/expedition**.

TOP TIP...

Ticks are becoming an ever-increasing problem in the Scottish countryside. All teams should carry a tick extractor and know how to use it.

Kath Dickinson,
DofE Supervisor & Assessor,
Cairngorm Assessor Network

TOP TIP...

Blisters can often appear in the same place, so if they are an issue during training or a practice expedition put a blister plaster over that area of skin at the start of the next expedition to protect it, before setting out.

Alex Davies,
DofE Assessor, Wiltshire

TOP TIP...

If you feel rubbing on your feet, then stop and do something about it AT ONCE.

Phil Renold,
DofE Assessor, Yorkshire

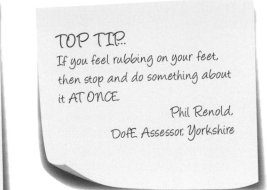

Blisters

Blisters are common on DofE expeditions of all levels and prevention is better than cure, although they may be unavoidable.

Ensure boots are broken in and socks are clean and do not wrinkle when they are put on. Participants should decide if they prefer wearing one or two layers of socks and should bear in mind the expedition route and weather conditions. Boots and, if possible, socks should be removed at campsites so they can dry and to allow feet to dry and harden.

Flip flops or open lightweight sandals are great for this as they are lightweight and protect the feet whilst still airing them.

At the first signs of discomfort participants should stop, remove their footwear and address the area of rubbing or blistering, even if this delays the team.

Sunburn

While participants are often well prepared for the rain and cold, many get caught out by sun and wind burn, particularly over long expedition days, when they may not realise they are being burnt. Teams need to be trained to cover their skin in loose fitting clothing that does not prevent sweating and use suitable, high factor blocking agents. The head and neck should be very carefully protected.

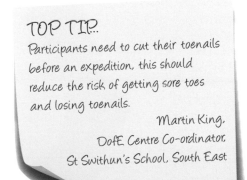

TOP TIP...

Participants need to cut their toenails before an expedition, this should reduce the risk of getting sore toes and losing toenails.

Martin King,
DofE Centre Co-ordinator,
St Swithun's School, South East

Hypothermia, heatstroke and dehydration

The Expedition Training Framework requires all participants and instructors to take a role in preventing hypothermia, heatstroke and dehydration while on expedition. This can be achieved by knowing how to recognise the early symptoms and being able to take preventative action.

Participants need to be aware of the risks of exercise-induced heat exhaustion and ensure they take on frequent and adequate fluid throughout the day. They should be aware of replacing salt lost through sweat and look out for team members feeling light headed or faint. A short rest, lying in the shade with their head down and legs up, and taking on fluids usually remedies the situation.

Every participant should set out each day with enough water to see them though that day; this means usually carrying at least two litres of water with them, more if it is a hot day. If necessary, this can then be topped up by the Supervisors, for example on very hot days where teams are also running late.

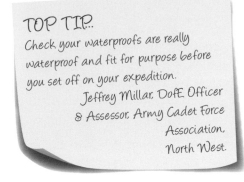

TOP TIP...
Check your waterproofs are really waterproof and fit for purpose before you set off on your expedition.
Jeffrey Millar, DofE Officer & Assessor, Army Cadet Force Association, North West.

Cold-induced numbness and non-freezing injuries

It is essential that participants protect themselves from cold-induced numbness and non-freezing injuries. These can occur in cold, wet weather during long periods of immobility, for example when camping or waiting for the minibus.

Young people who are susceptible to the cold or are of an African or Caribbean descent can be particularly vulnerable. Cold induced numbness and non-freezing injuries are entirely preventable, the best solution is to stay warm and dry.

Spare socks, well fitted boots, a hat, waterproof gloves and covering skin in wind and cold weather, are all simple and effective preventatives. Participants should also eat and drink well and often.

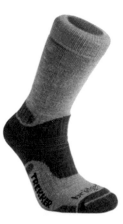

TOP TIP...
By the time you feel thirsty, it's too late. Drink little and often! Don't just stop for infrequent glugs.
Dale Reynolds, DofE Assessor, Lake District

Emergency procedures

Licensed Organisations are required to have in place systems for the health and safety of participants and those who support them. Each Licensed Organisation/AAP must have its own safety and emergency procedures.

Based on these, all DofE expedition teams must have accident procedures and an emergency plan in place, which are understood and agreed by all staff involved in the expedition and approved by the Licensed Organisation/AAP.

More information appears in Chapter 6.2.

Participants must be trained and confident in the agreed emergency procedures. Emergency procedures will usually include:

- A process summary of the actions to complete and the order in which to do them.
- Getting to immediate, relative safety.
- Conducting any first aid needed.
- Deciding who to contact for assistance.
- Deciding how to call for assistance or attract attention and knowing the International Distress Signal and answering signals.
- Deciding how to get help, who will stay at the emergency and who goes for help.
- Redistributing equipment as required.
- Identifying the current locations and planning the route to find help.
- Preparing a written message.
- Going for help and recording how to find the way back.
- Remaining safe until help arrives including finding shelter, using the environment, increasing visibility and remaining alert to attract attention.

For more detailed information, training and advice please refer to the DofE's training resource, EX^2. EX^2 also includes an example process map for participants' accident and emergency procedures.

Chapter 6.2

Awareness of risk and health and safety issues

What *The Handbook for DofE Leaders* says...

Through participation in an expedition, young people learn to manage risk and become more able to overcome both expected and unexpected challenges.

Expedition safety

Through participation in an expedition, young people learn to manage risk and become more able to overcome both expected and unexpected challenges.

All expeditions have an element of risk, so safety must be a key consideration for all DofE expeditions.

Risk is managed and expeditions are made safe through:
- Thorough planning including completing a risk assessment and following the recommendations.
- Thorough expedition training.
- Taking appropriate precautions and treating the environment with respect.
- The attitude of the participants to take control of the situation and be mentally strong.

There are a few basic steps all DofE expedition teams should follow to help ensure their safety.
- **Tell someone the plan:** Always tell a responsible person the names and contact information of all involved, where the team and adults are going and what the estimated time of arrival is. This is achieved through the notification process, route summary and route card system.
- **DofE participants must keep together at all times:** Unless dealing with an emergency situation, DofE teams must never split up or allow anyone to push ahead or be left behind. An Assessor who sees a team allowing this to happen on a qualifying expedition will end the assessment, as condition 10 has not been met. It is also a serious safety issue that the Supervisor will follow up on. The practice expedition(s) should allow teams to become used to walking together at a shared pace.
- **Update everyone:** Always tell the responsible person that everyone has arrived safely and provide an update to all staff involved as to any change of plans or delays.

Here are some other recommendations which can help make the expedition a success:
- Choose campsites with relatively easy access in case of an emergency.
- Limit the amount of ascent to avoid unreasonable physical demands.
- Make any major ascents early in the day where possible.
- Plan natural routes that are sympathetic to the environment.
- Have alternative poor weather routes.
- Select escape routes in advance.
- Start early in the day.
- Be physically fit for the expedition.
- Ensure everyone is trained in first aid.
- Update risk assessments after each expedition and according to different team and individual needs.

TOP TIP...

Remember the six Ps – Prior Preparation and Planning Prevents Poor Performance. This should be the mantra for all DofE activity, especially expeditions.

Mike Spain,
DofE Leader,
Kinross-Shire DofE group

- Keep the weight of backpacks to an absolute minimum.
- Have more than four in the team in case someone has to pull out unexpectedly.

Some advice for preventing potential health issues is set out in Chapter 6.1.

Weather

Weather is the most important factor outside of a team's control which can determine the success of their expedition.

All expedition teams need to have suitable clothing and equipment with them to remain safe in all weather conditions that they may experience during their expedition.

It is possible for the weather to deteriorate to such an extent that a team will need to use their alternative, low level poor weather routes, or even postpone or end the expedition. The weather is always more extreme in upland and exposed areas with stronger winds, higher rainfall and lower temperatures.

TOP TIP...

Remember that, in Scotland, it can feel like winter in the middle of July! Come prepared for the worst, and hope for the best.

Sheila Robertson,
Expedition Assessor Network
Co-ordinator
Grampian & Cairngorm

Supervisors need to ensure they have up to date weather forecasts of the areas where teams will be undertaking their expeditions. For Silver and Gold expeditions in wild country, forecasts may need to be updated daily.

Teams need to:
- Understand how weather will affect them and their mode of travel.
- Know how, where and when to obtain weather forecasts by television, internet, radio, phone and local area services.
- Understand forecasts and relate them to the observed conditions on the ground.
- Be able to look for signs which indicate changes in the weather. This is essential in upland and exposed areas where weather is hardest to forecast.
- Include in their notifications alterative, low level (lower risk) routes to be used in the event of poor weather if intending to travel through areas of wild country. The DofE recommends that all teams plan alternative poor weather routes. This may not be possible for some modes of travel.

TOP TIP...

Ensure foul weather routes are submitted with the initial route trace/map whenever it may be appropriate.

David Hood,
DofE Assistant Manager & Assessor,
The Scout Association,
Dartmoor Assessor Network

Teams need to be able to adapt to changing weather around them. They need to understand the potential risks and know the correct procedures to follow to remain safe in torrential or very heavy rain, flash flooding, thunderstorms, very hot weather and foul weather including high winds and limited visibility.

Participants need to have an understanding of how the following factors interact to affect their expedition and how to plan to manage them effectively:

For more detailed information and advice please refer to the DofE's training resource, EX[2].

Rainfall

Wind

Cloud

Visibility

Air pressure

Temperature

Humidity

Extreme conditions

Third time lucky...

Adventuring is such a difficult undertaking with many challenges, some are unpredictable, like weather on mountains or wilderness trails. But anybody who ventures into adventuring must be fully prepared to fight in spite of all of that.

Reading and getting as much information about an expedition helps one to mentally note what the challenges along the way will be, and that makes the individual prepared to fight. Meticulous preparation before setting off is very vital if one hopes to succeed.

During my Mount Everest climb, a number of times the weather stood in front of us, even though we wanted to summit the mountain we couldn't. But because we knew beforehand that this could happen, we hung in there and motivated each other by encouraging one another not to bail out. A result of which was success after two devastating failed attempts on the mountain!

Sibusiso Vilane

Sibuiso is the first black African and second South African to successfully ascend Everest, taking part in an international team expedition in 2003. The team spent 24 hours at the top of Everest despite the harsh weather conditions with 80 km/hour winds and temperatures as low as minus 30˚C.

Chapter 6.3
Navigation and route planning

What *The Handbook for DofE Leaders* says...

The team must plan and organise their expedition, identifying how they will spend their time to complete it and meet their aim, recording this as a route card.

DofE participants use maps/charts and compasses to navigate during their expedition.

Navigation

DofE participants use maps/charts and compasses to navigate during their expedition.

It is essential that all participants and teams develop, practice and refine their navigation and map reading skills to the level required to undertake their expedition safely.

Participants will need to learn the core skills of map reading, practical skills of using maps in the outdoors and how to navigate with a map and compass. The importance of good navigation skills developed through practice cannot be overstressed for DofE teams.

These skills prevent teams from straying off route and losing time, and help them to stay safe whilst being remotely supervised. Being able to navigate and map read will allow teams to understand and plan their route, navigate it successfully and have the skills to adapt to issues that may arise while on expedition.

All participants need to have completed the navigation and route planning skills to the appropriate level of the DofE Expedition Training Framework and their chosen mode of travel. All participants must be signed off by their

Supervisor as trained and competent. Teams travelling in coastal areas and on open water will need to be competent in the use of appropriate charts and techniques.

Teams undertaking expeditions outside the UK may need specific training based on the maps available of their expedition area.

TOP TIP.

Folding maps can be an issue in the wind and rain. In advance, remove the cardboard cover from an OS map, open fully and lay out flat. Carefully reverse-fold all the long creases and fold the outside rows/quarters over onto the middle rows/quarters. Fold in half lengthways, with the area of map you want to use showing. Fan-fold down the sides to leave the area you want to use. Now as you travel you can follow the route by turning the map like a book.

Mike White,
DofE Supervisor, Wiltshire.

Participants' skills will improve and become more sophisticated as they progress through the DofE levels and undertake their expeditions in more challenging areas.

Teams travelling through wild country will need to be both confident and competent in compass use to navigate in potential situations of poor visibility and areas with few reference points.

For more detailed information, training and advice on navigation and route planning please refer to the DofE's training resource, EX^2.

The DofE Expedition Guide

Route planning

The team must plan and organise their expedition, identifying how they will spend their time to complete it and meet their aim.

DofE teams have complete ownership of their expedition and so will choose their aim, mode of travel, expedition area and their expedition route. More information and advice about the requirements of DofE expedition routes and planning DofE expeditions can be found in Chapter 5.1.

The route card

The role of the route card

DofE participants always plan out and record the details of their expedition route in a route card and route outline/map as a statement of their intentions for their expedition.

The route card is a valuable learning process that encourages participants to recognise the importance of attention to detail and careful organisation. It is

also a key tool in enabling participants to identify and manage risk in their expedition route.

The route card informs the Supervisor, expedition support staff and the Assessor where the team is going and when they will get there, it is the cornerstone of expedition safety.

Route cards act as a log of the journey and are a live document which participants will update as their expedition progresses.

They enable participants to compare their actual times of arrival to their estimated times and so judge their own progress against their original plan.

Building a route card

Participants complete their route cards as a team following this basic process:

1. **Choose departure point:** Using a separate route card for each day, participants record their departure point and the end point for the day's journeying.

> TOP TIP...
>
> Look back from time to time; the views are great and at certain points you may also need to retrace your step so looking back can make it easier.
>
> Nevis Hulme,
> DofE Assessor, Ross & Cromarty
> Expedition Assessor Network

2. **Define route legs:** After planning the day's travel, participants divide the route into natural divisions of roughly equal length ending at an unmistakable landmark. These become expedition 'legs' ending in a 'checkpoint'. A route containing between six and eight checkpoints is suitable for a day's journey.

TOP TIP..

Avoid crossing streams and rivers by walking or wading; always use a bridge. Keep this in mind when route planning.

Ted Tombling,
DofE Assessor,
Methyr Tydfil Borough Council

3. **Estimate timings:** Participants then estimate the time needed to complete each leg. A good team can work out average distances and timings based on their training and practice expeditions. Participants need to take into account additional time needed for height gained using Naismith's rule, rest periods and for undertaking project investigations.

Reasonable time for lunch should be included and it is good practice to identify this as a checkpoint.

TOP TIP..

To aid navigation for each leg, think DOTTT – Direction, Distance, Time, Target, Terrain including tick-off features.

Keith Rodway,
DofE Co-ordinator & Supervisor,
Durham County

4. **Calculate ETA:** Using their estimated timings participants can calculate what time they will arrive at each checkpoint and what time they will set out on the next leg. Participants will also add in their information on bearings (based on the level of their competence) and written details of the route to be followed. These are to allow participants to navigate in the unlikely event that their map is lost or can't be used and to reinforce effective navigation during expeditions.

The DofE Expedition Guide

5. **Identify escape routes:** For each leg there needs to be one or more identified escape routes as a precaution against extreme weather, becoming lost or in the event of an emergency. All DofE groups should also plan alternative poor weather routes to allow them the possibility of continuing their journey on a safer, low level (lower risk) expedition route.

6. **Produce route details:** General information like the team name, participants' names and emergency contact numbers should be added and then several copies made. It is these copies, along with a route map which are used in the notification process. Route outlines/maps are traditionally tracing overlays on to 1:50 000 scale maps (rather than 1:25 000 to make them manageable). More commonly now, they are either drawn onto laminated maps or created electronically and emailed.

Practice makes perfect

Navigation and map reading are key components to any successful expedition because although you want to keep the element of adventure, without good navigational map reading skills, you risk getting lost or getting into potentially dangerous situations.

When I compete in the Patagonian Expedition Race in Chile, we are racing and navigating on our own, the maps are not very good and the terrain is tough but, by really studying the map and the landscape ahead of us, we always reach our goal.

To master navigation, start in an area you are familiar with, equipped with only a map and compass. Take your time and study the map as you walk and pick out the features on the map and match them to what you can see on the ground. Take your time and when you lose concentration have a rest.

Nick Gracie

Nick Gracie is an expedition race champion, athlete and event organiser. He was part of the first British team to win the Patagonian Expedition Race (Chile) – 'the world's toughest race' – in 2011.

eDofE Mapping and digital mapping

eDofE Mapping is a free expedition route submission tool designed to create standard DofE route cards and route summaries. It can be used by anyone using eDofE and helps speed up the route approval process.

The eDofE Mapping system allows participants and Leaders to produce digital files that can be printed, emailed, saved or uploaded onto eDofE. However, for safety reasons, while on expedition, teams must carry full OS maps or appropriate charts with them and not rely on eDofE Mapping print outs. The digital files created can also be used with handheld GPS devices on expedition.

There are a range of other digital mapping products DofE groups may want to use and the mapping files they create can be uploaded into eDofE Mapping.

Global Positioning System (GPS)

The increasing sophistication of GPS and handheld mapping devices make them a good additional safety tool for DofE groups. DofE groups may use GPS devices as a secondary navigation tool, but there must be no reduction in the framework or quality of the navigation training and competence of the team.

The expedition team, Supervisor and Assessor should agree in advance the policy of use during their expedition.

The Global Positioning System (GPS) is a satellite-based navigation system made up of a network of 24 satellites, each sending down radio signals every second to determine a location.

GPS works in all weather conditions and anywhere in the world, 24 hours a day. It is usually horizontally accurate to 15m or better; some also show altitude ascent and descent. However, units can break or be damaged, and accuracy and reliability can also be compromised.

Buildings, terrain, electronic interference, forests or sometimes even dense foliage and the human body can block signal reception to the satellites, causing less accuracy, location errors or possibly no location reading at all.

GPS units will require their batteries to be re-charged or replaced during the expedition and low cloud or poor weather will reduce battery life.

A mobile GPS device can store a predetermined route and provide a continuous display of actual bearings, distance and speed over ground compared to this route. It is essential that the planned route takes into account any possible hazards in advance and is checked to meet DofE requirements.

Anyone involved in DofE expeditions, including Supervisors, support staff, volunteers and Assessors must not use GPS devices as a substitute for the high level of navigational ability required to remain safe, particularly in wild country.

Within a DofE context, GPS should be thought of as additional safety equipment, rather than as a navigation tool.

With all items of equipment, especially those concerned with safety and competence, it is usually the user's level of skill and experience which defines performance.

GPS is particularly valuable when the normal navigation processes have failed

and groups are in the dark, have restricted visibility, in featureless terrain, extreme weather conditions and when the team is lost, anxious and stressed.

It is essential that in these conditions, the user can feed in the correct data and interpret the

> *TOP TIP...*
>
> *Take GPS as a route recording tool. It can give a great summary of where teams went which can help with further training and evidence for their presentation.*
>
> *Paul Taylor,*
> *Co-ordinator & Assessor,*
> *CIAdventures OA,*
> *Yorkshire & Humber.*

information coming out of the instrument accurately to select appropriate routes or escape routes, which are as free from hazards as possible.

In such conditions, if considerable distances have to be covered, GPS can help by supporting pacing or reducing the uncertainties of 'dead reckoning' when carried out by those who are less experienced. It may be possible to pre-programme escape routes to speed up route selection in an emergency situation.

GPS devices can be very useful when outside of the UK where less accurate maps exist. The GPS device may need its settings changed to reflect the maps being used, units for distance, time zones and the north reference should reflect the magnetic variation of the international location.

GPS as secondary navigation tools

GPS devices may be used as an additional, secondary navigational tool by DofE expedition teams, however the DofE stipulates the following requirements:

- There must be no reduction in the training framework or quality of the navigation training and competence of the team, signed off by the trainer/Supervisor for each participant. The level of competence must be checked by the Supervisor and Assessor during the pre-expedition check.
- Teams carrying GPS devices must remain aware of their surroundings and be able to navigate to the same standard as teams not carrying GPS. Teams must be fully prepared should the GPS malfunction and must not be allowed to fall into a false sense of security.

- **DofE teams are required to navigate using a map and compass, this is an essential skill for all team members. A DofE team must not simply follow the directions of a GPS device nor use it every time they want to check where they are.**

- GPS allows teams to make informed decisions if a situation threatens to deteriorate and to navigate to avoid hazards. A GPS device should not be used simply to avoid making navigational mistakes, as getting lost and sorting it out for themselves is a valuable learning experience and is an important part of their DofE experience.
- Decide how the GPS device will be used and plan ahead to carry an ample supply of spare batteries or method of recharging. Spare batteries may not be carried by the Supervisor/Assessor as DofE teams have to be self-sufficient. If there is

an available power outlet then the device may be recharged by the team at their campsite.

- Extra training will be required for teams:
  - To develop their understanding of the OS national grid system, use ten figure grid references and the map indexing of 1:50 000 and 1:25 000 maps. For example, it may be necessary to key in the sheet index letters before a six-figure reference.
  - Abilities to plot positions, bearings and routes provided by GPS onto the relevant maps. Then, like all DofE teams, to choose the most suitable routes, alternative routes and escape routes which pose the least hazard.
  - To practice using the instrument's functionality to store a series of way points so as to reduce the amount of map work needed in extreme weather conditions.
  - Expeditioning outside the UK, to be able to establish their location using latitude and longitude, plot positions, bearings and routes on foreign maps of the appropriate scale and to communicate such information to Supervisors and Assessors.
  - To gain an understanding of the terminology of GPS and the ability to utilise quickly and accurately all the information and data which the instrument is capable of supplying.

GPS devices can add an additional level of safety, particularly when outside the UK or during poor weather conditions; however they are not a necessary piece of equipment for DofE teams.

Case study: what about unmapped areas?

One expedition Supervisor taking a team to Borneo created a sketch map of the area and used aerial shots to mark up areas of movement, planning on the GPS the various campsites. The team could then create a 3D fly-by plan with contours to mark up the route and potential dangers. For their aim the team made detailed records of their route and, back in the UK, plotted their route as part of their project and created a detailed map with descriptions.

Charlie Richards, DofE Supervisor, South West

TOP TIP...

make sure the GPS device has sufficient memory to store all the information you want.

Charlie Richards
DofE Supervisor,
Gloucestershire

GPS tracking systems

GPS tracking systems can be used by DofE groups as an additional safety tool. However great care must be taken to ensure that they do not compromise either the number of supervising adults or the team's feeling of isolation and self-reliance.

There must be no reduction in the framework or quality of the emergency training and competence of the team, nor any compromise of the Supervisor's emergency planning/procedures. The expedition team, Supervisor and Assessor should agree in advance the policy of use during their expedition.

A GPS tracking device can be placed in a participant's rucksack which can then transmit location information to a GPS receiver and then on to a (usually encrypted) secure server. This data can then be transmitted securely to a computer via an internet connection or a hand held device. Supervisors, Assessors, Leaders, Licensed Organisations and emergency contacts can then monitor the team's location and progress.

Using tracking systems can be an effective way of supporting team safety. Most systems have a panic button or some (editable) emergency phone numbers that can allow the group to call for help in the event of an emergency.

The tracking systems provide an accurate indication of a team's location, reducing the time taken to find them.

Tracking can help Supervisors and Assessors with effective remote supervision. Knowing where expedition teams are, or are not, can help save time and money for Supervisors and Assessors.

Working out where and when they are likely to meet their teams can reduce the amount of driving and environmental impact of expeditions and prevent waiting long periods at checkpoints. Such systems can also involve other people in the Licensed Organisation, allowing them to keep up to date with their team's progress.

DofE expeditions are an opportunity for participants to be independent; so allowing parents to be able to monitor progress can undermine this, and delays or travelling off route may potentially worry parents unnecessarily. Therefore

it is not recommended that parents have access to GPS tracking systems.

Care must be taken to work out how Supervisors and Assessors will have access to the tracking information while supporting expeditions and to ensure all involved are trained in using the tracking device and the accompanying software. Tracking systems that use the mobile phone networks should not be used as reception is too unreliable.

Within a DofE context, tracking should be used with some caution. Whilst it can enhance remote supervision, giving teams more space and less adult contact, a tracking system does not tell Supervisors how the group is feeling or how individuals are coping.

Tracking systems must not allow a false sense of security to set in with the Supervisors responsible for the young people.

Tracking systems must not be used to reduce the number of Supervisors supporting DofE expeditions. Ratios of Supervisors to young people are based on the needs of emergency situations and not day to day monitoring of the team(s) progress.

For participants, knowing they have a tracking device can undermine the spirit of isolation and self-reliance felt by their DofE team and themselves.

For example, getting lost and sorting it out for themselves is part of many DofE expeditions and knowing that they are being monitored may reduce the feeling of having to get themselves back on route.

TOP TIP...
Using the route card, agree with your group before leaving them, the next checkpoint and meeting time when you will meet them, it gives them an aim to focus on.

Karen Gribbin,
DofE Leader, Supervisor & Assessor,
Cheshire Border
Girlguiding UK

Tracking systems are not there to stop teams making mistakes, but are there to help if a situation deteriorates or if help is needed. Supervisors must ensure, through training, that GPS tracking devices have no more impact on this feeling than groups with mobile phones in their rucksacks in case of an emergency.

While the DofE allows DofE groups to use tracking systems to support the safety of their expedition teams, it is not a requirement, nor is it a substitute for the required emergency training and competent supervision.

Chapter 6.4
Campcraft, equipment and hygiene

What *The Handbook for DofE Leaders* says...

All participants must be properly equipped.

Teams should carry all their equipment and food to allow them to operate in a self-sufficient way.

Expedition equipment

Having the right equipment is essential for expedition safety and well-being as well as comfort and enjoyment. A lot of the expedition equipment can be borrowed from friends, family and Licensed Organisations, allowing participants to save money and test and use a wide range of equipment.

All participants should have their own clothing and boots and may also want to buy some items of personal and emergency equipment like their rucksack and sleeping bag.

All equipment must be checked by the Supervisor before being used for DofE activities.

The DofE recommends a basic equipment list available online at **www.DofE.org/expedition** for participants and Supervisors to use.

However, additional equipment may be needed depending on the personal requirements of those involved, the expedition environment and the mode of travel chosen.

Expedition equipment can be divided into five categories:
- Clothing.
- Personal and emergency equipment.
- Personal camping equipment.
- Team camping equipment.
- Equipment related to the mode of travel.

For DofE qualifying expeditions participants will also need equipment related to their aim, project and investigation methods. Please refer to Chapter 6.7 for more information.

Advice on equipment and clothing relating to alternative modes of travel can be found in the chapter specific to the mode, in this guide.

TOP TIP...

Include in your planning an expedition kit talk where parents and participants are both invited along, and clothing and equipment can be exhibited.
Trevor Smith,
DofE Leader & Assessor,
John Cleveland College, Hinckley

The DofE works hard to secure excellent discounts and deals for adults and participants involved in the DofE. Details of current offers can be found on the DofE website, the DofE shop and in eDofE.

Clothing

There is an element of personal preference in expedition clothing, but here are three key principles for dressing in the outdoors:

1. Use multiple layers:

Wear layers of clothing to provide more insulation and to allow better regulation of body temperature by adding or removing them. This is particularly important in cold climates where clothing must transfer moisture away from the skin, provide warmth and provide protection from the wind and rain.

2. Stay dry:

If clothing becomes wet, through rain or perspiration, it loses its ability to insulate. Waterproof clothing will protect against the rain and using breathable fabrics or removing layers will protect against soaking by perspiration.

3. Choose suitable materials:

Synthetic fibre clothing offers very good insulation while being lightweight, absorbing less water, being less heavy when wet and drying quickly.

Expedition clothing is often categorised according to the layer in which they are worn. To work well all expedition clothes will need to be kept clean and looked after.

- **Outer layer:**
  The purpose of the outer layer is to act like a shell, providing protection against the wind and rain. Even the most modern water and windproof trousers and jackets, using breathable fabrics, have difficulty coping with sweat from working hard in severe weather climates. It is important to be able to open vents and zips to allow for ventilation. The best items are flexible, a hood that goes over a hat or that can be removed, a double zip to allow for ventilation, zipped trousers to go over boots and so on.

- **Middle layer:**
  These are insulating, lightweight, windproof and quick drying long sleeved tops/fleeces. Fleeces are popular as they absorb little moisture and remain light even when soaked. Trousers also need to have all these attributes and give freedom of movement, so jeans are not suitable for expeditions. Lightweight trousers are often preferable to shorts as they provide greater protection from sunburn, insect bites and grazes. In hot conditions loose-fitting tops with long sleeves and long lightweight trousers are good to wear to keep cool and also provide good protection against the sun.

- **Inner layer:**
  The inner layer needs to draw sweat away from the skin into the next layers. More expensive items tend to be made of synthetic materials as they dry out quickly and transfer moisture faster than cheaper cotton clothes which are better used in the middle layer.

Headwear

This should help to retain heat and keep participants warm. On hot days and in strong sun, a light, wide-brimmed hat can help protect the head, neck and face.

Gloves

Choose gloves depending on the environment and mode of travel, for example for water based expeditions they would need to be waterproof. Gloves should be long enough to protect wrists and to tuck inside sleeves.

Socks

Socks perform three functions; they cushion feet, absorb perspiration and provide insulation against the cold. Participants on expedition should carry at least one spare pair, preferably several, ideally one set for each day.

Gaiters

Gaiters help to keep feet warm and dry in wet and windy weather and when conditions are soggy underfoot. They can be useful even on hot days when dew is still on the ground.

Boots and footwear

No other equipment will have a greater impact on the enjoyment of an expedition than a participant's footwear.

The DofE policy on footwear is as follows:

- Licensed Organisations and AAPs will have policies on footwear which participants must follow and which Supervisors will enforce during training and equipment checks.
- Footwear must be suitable for the expedition environment and mode of travel. The final decision on what is suitable footwear rests with the participant's Licensed Organisation or AAP.
- The DofE expects, and considers it essential, that participants at Gold level and those in moor and mountainous areas and wild country, wear waterproof boots with ankle support.
- The DofE recommends that expedition boots with ankle support, rather than hiking shoes, are used on all DofE expeditions.
- The DofE suggests that if participants are going to spend money on footwear they should buy boots rather than shoes, as boots adequate for Bronze and Silver level can now be bought very cheaply.

Participants should:

- Ensure their expedition boots are well fitted and should spend time wearing them to break them in before using them on expedition. This helps to reduce blistering.
- Wear waterproof boots or use waterproofing products to improve water resistance.

TOP TIP...

Wear the expedition socks you will use on expedition when trying on boots to buy. Try on a whole range of makes to find the one that is best for you, as they all have different fits.

Tess Osman,
DofE Instructor,
Woodrow High House, Amersham

- Carry a pair of flip flops or lightweight sandals/trainers to wear around the campsite. However, these should not be worn whilst journeying.
- Not borrow someone else's boots if they can avoid it, as they will be moulded to that person's foot.

TOP TIP...

Take spare laces - it's not a good thing to face halfway through a hike, having the lace snap on your boot.

Katrina Gadsby,
DofE Leader,
Crawley Open DofE Centre,
West Sussex CC

Personal and emergency equipment

In addition to clothing, each individual must carry the personal emergency equipment as listed on the DofE website. This is usually the same for all environments, although there are some additional items for wild country expeditions and those using alternative modes of travel.

Map and compass

Every UK expedition team must take with them full OS maps or appropriate charts for the area(s) in which the expedition is being undertaken. All teams undertaking a DofE expedition should have with them sufficient compasses, route cards and maps to allow for effective navigation and to ensure the safety of all participants, should the team split up for any reason. Map cases are also really helpful to protect maps and route cards.

First aid kits

Each DofE participant should carry their own first aid kit with them on expedition rather than, or in addition to, a communal kit for the whole team. A first aid kit list is available online at **www.DofE.org/expedition**. More information is available in Chapter 6.1.

Emergency rations

Participants should each take some rations to be eaten in an emergency only. Chocolate bars, nuts, dried fruit, jelly, mint cake and cereal bars all work well and are usually then eaten by participants as a post expedition treat. Participants should also pack hot chocolate, tea, coffee or soup to be able to make a hot drink.

Notebook and pencil

To record experiences and note down emergency information.

Torch with spare batteries and bulb

A head torch can be useful as it leaves hands free.

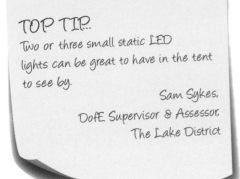
Survival bag

An emergency 'bivvy bag', large enough to fit inside, is a proven life-saver in an emergency.

Water bottle(s)

A strong plastic water container(s), usually totalling around two litres of capacity. Some people like to use a plastic bladder which fits into the top of the rucksack, allowing a steady intake of water without needing to stop journeying.

Pocket knife/pocket tool

Helpful in an emergency and can also have a range of other useful accessories.

Whistle

Every participant should carry a plastic whistle to attract attention in an emergency.

Matches or a lighter

Essential to light the stove to make hot drinks and cook food. Make sure they are kept in a dry container; waterproof matches can also be bought.

Spare clothing

This should be appropriate for the expedition environment and be kept waterproofed and dry.

Personal camping equipment

Every member of the expedition team will need to carry their own personal camping equipment.

Rucksack

The rucksack needs to be big enough to contain all the equipment and be tested for fit and comfort. The shoulder straps should be wide and well padded and it is essential that there is a padded hip belt to take the weight off the shoulders. A chest strap is also beneficial. It is recommended that participants take a rucksack liner and high visibility rucksack cover to improve water resistance and help keep all kit dry.

Sleeping bag

Choose a sleeping bag that is appropriate to the expedition environment and is suitable for use in the expected night time temperatures. Using one that is too warm can add weight and make sleeping at night uncomfortably hot. Use a stuff or compression sack to reduce the bulk and a waterproof bag to put it all in.

An inner bag can add a layer of flexible insulation and is useful when using a borrowed sleeping bag.

Sleeping mat

Lightweight and inexpensive, these add insulation, are useful in an emergency and make sleeping much more comfortable. Self inflating sleeping mats can also be used but are more expensive.

Changes of clothing

As well as emergency clothing, participants will also need a complete change of clothes for an expedition lasting more than one day. They will also need some appropriate dry clothing for wearing in the tent.

Eating utensils

Lightweight mug, knife, fork and spoon and something to eat from; a flat based bowl can often work for all meals.

Wash kit and towel

Take the essentials only: soap, lightweight towel, antiseptic hand gel, toothbrush, toothpaste, toilet paper and wet wipes. Some items like toothpaste can be taken by one person to be shared amongst the whole team.

> TOP TIP...
> Include a luxury item particular to you. I always have a tiny hot water bottle.
>
> Irene Bews,
> DofE Supervisor,
> Scotland

Team camping equipment

Every team member should carry their share of the team's camping equipment.

Day sacks, equipment drops and pre-positioned equipment at campsites

There may be some cases when a participant has circumstances that make it inappropriate for them to carry full camping and cooking equipment and so do not meet condition 2.

The rest of the team may be able to help so that they remain self-sufficient. However if it cannot be carried by the rest of the team, in these cases only, some items may be deposited at the campsites or pre-agreed checkpoints. This must be agreed between the LO and the Assessor.

Each individual must still carry their personal emergency equipment, typically in a day sack (see page 105).

TOP TIP...

Always have a roll of bin bags – they have a multitude of uses!

David Snowden,
DofE Manager,
Leicester City Council

Tents

There are dozens of lightweight tents to choose from and Licensed Organisations and AAPs usually have a selection that participants can use rather than having to buy one. Practise putting up the tent before the expedition, preferably in the dark or blind folded. Extremely lightweight pegs can also be bought to save on weight.

Cooking stoves

The most popular stoves are those fuelled by gas or methylated spirits. Participants need to be well trained and experienced in using cooking stoves in the outdoors before going on expedition. This includes handling fuel, fuelling and refuelling the stove.

DofE participants and adults must follow the instructions and safety guidance given by the manufacturer of the stove they choose to use.

More information about gas stoves, spirit stoves and stove safety guidance can be found on page 120.

Fuel bottles

Liquid fuel needs to be kept in specifically designed bottles which have a secure screw top. Fuel bottles need to be easily distinguished and kept separate from water bottles.

TOP TIP...

Keep track of any equipment you lend by getting participants to sign a form detailing what they took and committing to return it in good condition.

Louise Mills, DofE Development Worker/ Expedition Supervisor,
Wiltshire OA
& Court Mills Open DofE Centre

Use the practice expedition to work out how much fuel will be needed on the qualifying expedition.

Cooking set

Teams will need a suitably sized, lightweight cooking set for each cooking group and their food choice.

Washing up materials

Teams will need a small amount of ecological liquid washing detergent, abrasive pads/a nylon scouring pad and a tea towel. Take plastic bags to put wet items into and to use as rubbish bags.

Watch and stop watch

This is an important tool to support navigation and keep to route card timings.

Other items

There is also a whole range of other optional items that teams might take with them including cameras, sun block, a collapsible water container, tin opener, money, a football, pack of cards etc. String is also enormously useful and can make a handy washing line.

Expedition campcraft and hygiene

Campcraft can be understood to be the ability to provide food and shelter under all conditions likely to be encountered in the outdoors.

The skills and confidence to do this are developed with practice and experience and the DofE expects high standards to be maintained at all times, by all participants.

Campcraft is divided into two parts:
- The provision of shelter (e.g. tents, bivvies and so on).
- The provision of food.

Campcraft has at its centre, the care of the environment in which participants are camping.

Preparing equipment for a DofE expedition

Camping equipment should be divided into personal equipment and team camping equipment that is shared between the occupants of a tent. Two or three people should usually be considered as the basic unit occupying each tent, with two or more tents forming a DofE expedition team. Participants and teams should follow some basic steps when preparing camping equipment. More information is given in each chapter on the different modes of travel.

Choose containers

Successful camping begins at home by planning what equipment is needed and deciding what containers should be used to hold and carry it in. These containers will range from rucksacks for expeditions on foot to panniers for cycling expeditions or waterproof containers used by those engaged in expeditions on water. It is essential that all equipment is waterproofed, even during the summer months.

Minimise the load

Irrespective of the mode of travel, participants must keep the weight of the load to a minimum. For expeditions on foot, packs should not weigh more than one quarter of the participant's own body weight. All rucksacks must be weighed before departure.

Packing equipment

All equipment and gear should be inside the chosen container(s), with the possible exception of sleeping mats, due to their bulk. Anything carried outside of the container needs to be securely fastened and waterproofed. Participants may want to dry clothing while they travel by securing clothes to the container to expose them to the sun and wind.

All wet or damp clothing and socks which have been washed should be dried as soon as possible so as to lighten the load and make them useable. Participants need to keep an eye on their own and other team member's equipment attached to the outside of containers, to ensure it does not become loose or lost.

> TOP TIP...
> Compass, stove strap, peg bag and all the other bits and pieces that go astray on the campsite put them in a rucksack top pocket.
> Jane Dickson,
> DofE Co-ordinator & Assessor
> St. Mary's School,
> Calne

The DofE Expedition Guide

Hygiene

Hygiene is the most important aspect of campcraft and is of major concern to Supervisors when they visit a campsite. Personal cleanliness should always remain at a high level throughout the expedition.

Participants need to make every effort to keep feet clean and dry; removing wet socks at the end of the journeying, and airing them and feet in the evenings is usually advised.

TOP TIP...

Take wet wipes and flip flops – they are the top two most recommended items from every Gold expedition I've ever seen.

Jamie Reach,
DofE Assessor,
Dartmoor Assessor Network and
Clayesmore School,
Dorset

Try to plan in advance what toilet facilities are available at a campsite, or if a pit latrine will need to be dug.

Water supplies must be kept clean. No washing should take place in streams and never throw dirty or greasy water into a stream or river. Pour dirty water into a hole in soft ground, well away from any water courses, made by removing a piece of turf with a trowel.

Information and advice about food and cooking hygiene can be found on page 121.

Campsites and camping

DofE participants need good campcraft skills to enable their enjoyment and comfort, allowing them to remain safe while being remotely supervised.

For more detailed information, training and advice please refer to the DofE's training resource, EX[2].

Information about accommodation is set out on page 42.

Choosing a campsite

A campsite suitable for mobile, lightweight camping should be:
- Sheltered from the wind.
- Permissible to camp.
- Free from danger.
- Within reach of water.
- Able to provide privacy.
- Reasonably level.
- On solid ground.

Setting up and leaving campsites:
- DofE teams should set up their tents as soon as they arrive at their campsite. Drive tent pegs in at an angle of 45 degrees. One team member may take charge of setting up a stove to start cooking.

- While cooking participants need to keep their area clean and litter free, washing and packing away equipment after use.
- Participants will need to agree who does what in their tent team and how they will share the small living space.
- Participants should make every effort to keep their tent dry, leaving all wet clothing and boots in the porch. Participants need to keep a set of dry clothing for sleeping in, even if this means putting on wet clothes the next morning to journey in.
- If no toilets are available participants can dig a pit latrine following the training from their Supervisor.
- When leaving the site:
  - Ensure it is clean and free from litter, leaving the site as if a team had not camped there. More information is set out in Chapter 6.6.
  - Wipe clean and dry (if time allows) the underside of the groundsheet and wipe mud off tent pegs. Shake tents to remove moisture before packing.

TOP TIP...

Always keep a dry set of comfortable, lightweight clothes for use overnight in your tent. Put wet clothes back on to walk in, you'll soon warm up!

Alistair Beeley,
DofE Assessor,
Cairngorm Assessor Network

  - Pay any bills due to the campsite owner.
  - The Supervisor and team should agree at what checkpoint they will next meet.

Camp fires

The DofE does not encourage the lighting of camp fires on expeditions. Camp fires might be used by participants when faced with a hazardous situation or using a camp site which allows the lighting of camp fires. Participants must follow Licensed Organisations' policies.

DofE Assessors

As part of their contract with the participants, agreed in the Assessor's pre-expedition check (page 189), DofE Assessors will want to see the participants showing a respect for the outdoor environment in line with:

- The DofE's behaviour expectations (Chapter 6.10).
- The DofE's environmental impact policy (Chapter 6.6) including the Countryside Code.

If the Assessor feels there are any issues, they will follow the guidance set out in Chapter 6.10 on behaviour expectations.

Ed avoided taking any short cuts...

Don't be scared about going abroad for your expeditions.

I've spent seven of the last ten years in South America and much of that has been in the jungle. It's an environment most people think of with dread - but they are missing out.

Sure there are snakes, spiders, scorpions and jaguars - but they don't bother you all the time and very soon you realise that it's just a big wood full of amazing creatures and beautiful rivers!

Ed Stafford

Ed is the first known person to walk the entire length of the Amazon River. For this adventure Ed walked over 4,000 miles, and it took him two and a half years to complete, making it the longest jungle expedition ever recorded.

Chapter 6.5
Food and cooking

What *The Handbook for DofE Leaders* says...

A substantial meal should be cooked and eaten by participants each day. This is optional on the final day.

Good expedition catering is one of the best team building activities of the Expedition section. Getting teams to cook from scratch, prepare meals themselves at home, manage a team budget, choose and agree a menu and share meals are all excellent for team building and developing life skills.

Whilst individual participants can simply use lightweight and high energy dehydrated food packets or boil in the bag meals for their expedition, these can miss many of the potential benefits and personal development opportunities of expedition catering.

Participants should not be taught to think of expedition food as dull, functional or unpleasant. It is an opportunity for them to be creative, show off and use it as a core part of a positive expedition experience.

The key principles of expedition food

Participants should design an expedition menu which considers the following:

- As the length of the expedition increases, so does the need to ensure participants eat a balanced diet, designed for physical activity in the outdoors.
- The key task is to pack as much energy (or calories) into the least weight and volume as possible. Depending on the activity and the participant, three, four or even five thousand calories may be needed each day. Choose foods high in sugars, carbohydrates and fats.

- Take food which participants like and enjoy, which are quick and simple to cook and that will keep for the duration of the expedition, even in hot weather. Dried, cured, smoked or vegetarian foods will usually last well.
- Think about keeping weight and litter down by removing packaging and cooking as a team.
- Make sure all food is packed and waterproofed so it will stand up to the inevitable squashing into rucksacks, being sat on and being dropped that will happen during the expedition.
- Try and pack each meal together in a container or bag for each day so that it is in one place and easy to find.

For more detailed information and advice please refer to the DofE's training resource, EX^2.

Example expedition recipes are available through the DofE Outdoor Eating app (**www.OutdoorEating.org**) and at **www.DofE.org/expedition**

> ### TOP TIP...
> Make up your own porridge before you go with oats, nuts, fruit and muesli, then add milk powder. Once on expedition simply add hot water to make quick porridge.
>
> Caroline Hague,
> DofE Supervisor,
> The Windsor Boys' School,
> Berkshire

Expedition meals

Breakfast

It is good practice to start the day with a substantial breakfast. This can include cereals, muesli, porridge, noodles or even a full English with tea, coffee or hot chocolate.

Lunch

There is a wide variety of options for expedition lunches, but the usual approach is for picnic or larder style foods that don't need to be heated or kept chilled. A lunch break might

consist of a hot drink with sandwiches, pitta bread or wraps with other high energy foods like flapjacks, cereal bars, nuts, dried fruit, biscuits, chocolate bars, dried sweets, jelly, mint cake and so on.

Some participants prefer to have only a short rest and 'drip feed' high energy snacks continuously whilst journeying, it's up to them to decide as a team.

Evening meal

Most participants choose to cook and eat their substantial daily meal in the evening at the campsite, when they have more time.

With practice and planning, even on one stove, it is quite easy to produce a hot three course meal in a short amount of time.

Soup, curry, stews, pasta, bangers and Smash or noodle stir-fry are all great expedition meals and can be followed up with a hot or cold pudding like hot chocolate cake or crumble and custard.

Training and preparation

Expedition teams or tent groups don't have to cook shared meals or share menus and they can use ready prepared individual expedition meals. However the DofE recommends that teams work together as much as possible to design their menus, buy the food and then cook and eat as a team while on expedition.

To get the most out of cooking a substantial meal, teams need to practise preparing and cooking meals in expedition conditions. Techniques can be honed on the final practice expedition, but it is beneficial for participants to have had several training sessions or practices at home to help decide what food they want to use.

> ## TOP TIP...
> A parent volunteered to teach cookery skills in a fun way. This led to great expedition menus and a newly developed skill for many.
>
> Judy Middleton,
> DofE Network Assessor & Supervisor,
> Meams Academy,
> Grampian & Cairngorm,
> Aberdeenshire Council.

A taster day is often a good way to get teams interested in their expedition food. Have a selection of cheap and easy meals for them to try and then ask them to have a go at cooking them at home in their kitchen. The next step is to practise cooking on stoves as a team, developing skills and learning how long different food takes to prepare and cook through. Weigh out meals to see how they compare and think about how to make them lighter.

Teams should work out that the more they can get ready in advance, the faster they can have food ready to eat on expedition. For example, having a homemade pasta sauce with vegetables and meat/vegetarian alternative all mixed in, ready cooked and only needing re-heating.

For shared evening and breakfast meals get participants to design their menus to a budget and then decide as a team who will buy and carry what. It helps to ensure everyone will eat well, includes everyone and shares the responsibility. Most participants will prepare their own lunch meals.

Encourage teams to be creative, but keep them focused on getting enough food, energy and liquids into the menu, rather than just a wide variety of meals. Ask them to think about their favourite foods and how they could adapt them so they could be used during their expedition.

> ## TOP TIP...
> Teams, especially those travelling on water who can carry more kit or those travelling outside the UK, might like to try and base their menus on the regional specialities for the area of their expedition.
>
> Gemma Nash,
> DofE Leader, Marlborough
> Open DofE Centre, Wiltshire

Breakfast on day two of a Silver DofE expedition; it doesn't have to be just soup or noodles!

Cooking and cooking stoves

The most popular stoves are those fuelled by gas or methylated spirits. Participants need to be well trained and experienced in using cooking stoves in the outdoors before going on expedition. This includes handling fuel, fuelling and refuelling the stove.

DofE participants and adults must follow the instructions and safety guidance given by the manufacturer of the stove they choose to use.

Gas stoves

Gas stoves are clean, reliable, easy to operate and heat water very quickly. Butane cartridges do not vaporise very well in cold weather, but propane cartridges or butane/propane mixes are available. Gas stoves are a safe cooking option but teams must be trained to use them safely.

Spirit stoves

Spirit stoves are robust, easy to use, light and compact, often consisting of the stove and pans packed together into a single unit. They are stable with a broad base, burn with a moderate heat and do not damage the ground.

Clean and free from oil, they are also fuel efficient. Methylated spirits is cheap to buy in bulk and does not have the storage restrictions of oil or petrol. Treated with care, spirit stoves will last a long time and so remain a popular choice for DofE centres to buy and use year on year.

The DofE spirit stove safety instructions should be followed and can be found at **www.DofE.org/expedition** and in EX².

Stove safety guidance

Location

- Take some time to pick the cooking location. A firm level surface at ground level where the stove will not be knocked over is ideal and it must be at least two metres away from flammable items/tents.
- Consider the weather conditions and wind direction.
- Make it clear to other people that stoves are lit/hot and get everything needed together before starting to cook. Have somewhere safe nearby to put hot pans.

General safety

- Always be familiar with the stove and fuel before setting out.
- Be confident in how to use the stove and what dangers are associated with it and the fuel, for example gas canisters.
- Have water and a wet tea towel nearby, ready to use as a fire blanket. Always be careful to check if there is a flame or not, especially in bright sunlight.
- Never leave a lit stove unattended or unwatched.

Gas stoves

- DofE teams must never use a gas stove that does not use self-sealing cylinders or cartridges.
- Remove cartridges from the stove for journeying and replace part used cartridges for full ones before the start of the expedition.

- It is best to use a gas stove that is low, stable and easy to shield from the wind.
- For exposed areas participants can use wind shields made of aluminium foil which can be bent into shape.

Methylated spirits stoves

- Fill the stove from a small container, never from a bulk container.
- Fuel should not be handled near tents or any naked flames; it is good practice to have a 're-fuelling' area where fuel is handled away from the designated cooking area.
- Take great care when re-fuelling the stove, make sure that the flame is completely extinguished (the flame can be invisible, especially in sunlight) and the stove/burner has cooled before removing the burner to re-fill it (take the burner to the fuel, not the fuel to the burner).

The DofE Expedition Guide

Fuel bottles

Liquid fuel needs to be kept in specifically designed bottles which have a secure screw top. Fuel bottles need to be easily distinguished and kept separate from water bottles.

Use the practice expedition to work out how much fuel will be needed on the qualifying expedition.

Basic cooking safety and hygiene

It is essential to maintain good food hygiene while on DofE expeditions. Some basic considerations and tips for your participants are set out below:

Do:

- Wash hands at least as often as if at home. Antibacterial wipes or gel can be helpful.
- Make sure, if cooking on a stove outside, that it is level, easy to see and use.
- Plan menus before setting out and take into consideration the cooking facilities and the environment.
- Make sure food is properly packed or wrapped to prevent cross-contamination.
- Make sure hot food is hot and cooked all the way through and that cold food stays cold.

- Dispose of all waste responsibly.
- Clean up and wash up after every meal.
- Be aware that, at altitude, water boils at a lower temperature, but food will take longer to cook.

Don't:

- Be tempted to cook in or near the tent if the weather is bad, a tent fire can be horrific.
- Wash up in streams or under campsite taps.
- Use the same utensils or containers for raw and cooked food.

- Let everyone crowd the cooking area, that's how accidents happen.
- Cook more than can be eaten, leftovers will attract all sorts of pests.
- Leave cooking food unattended.
- Try and cook in the dark, always have plenty of light.
- Let accidents occur, remember that everything used will either be hot, wet or sharp.

Drink

Participants need to ensure they take on frequent and adequate amounts of fluid throughout the day, particularly in hot weather.

Participants should 'tank-up' with fluid before leaving the campsite each morning and drink as much as possible as soon as they arrive at their campsite in the evening.

While participants may start expeditions with energy drinks, assume that water is what they will drink for the majority of the expedition and plan routes accordingly.

Having sufficient fluids and topping up

Running out of fluids must be avoided on expeditions so take more than is likely to be needed and keep an eye on how much fluid the team has with them.

As well as the water they carry, participants can get additional water as needed during their expedition. The best places are from their campsite, their Supervisor or other expedition support staff.

Every participant should set out each day with enough water to see them though that day; this means usually carrying at least two litres of water with them, more if it is a hot day. If necessary, this can then be topped up by the Supervisors, for example on very hot days or where teams are running late.

It is not recommended that participants take water from streams, as there is a high probability that it may be contaminated.

Participants will need to boil the water or use some kind of filtration device/ sterilisation process before they can drink or cook with it.

This should only be needed on the most remote and high level of expeditions and should not be relied on as the team's water supply.

> **TOP TIP...**
> As a team, boil a pan of water and use it to make soup as the starter or a hot drink, then use the rest to cook a boil-in-the-bag pudding. Don't throw the leftover water away as this can be used to do the washing up!
> Rikki Rutter,
> DofE Co-ordinator,
> The Windsor Boys' School,
> Berkshire

Chapter 6.6
Care for the environment, Countryside, Highway and Water Sports Safety Codes

What *The Handbook for DofE Leaders* says...

All DofE participants must follow the Countryside, Highway and Water Sports Codes, as appropriate. These are available online at **www.DofE.org/expedition**.

Participants undertaking expeditions in Scotland should follow 'The Scottish Outdoor Access Code', available at www.DofE.org/expedition.

The DofE Leader and Supervisor both have a key role in ensuring that the impact of the Expedition section is a positive and sustainable one, for both the participants and the local communities, wherever it takes place. Everyone participating in the DofE should follow the DofE's environmental impact policy.

Supervisors should review all of the expedition plans and routes to make sure that the impact on the environment and rural communities is as minimal as possible.

Expeditions often take place in popular areas visited by tourists and day visitors; DofE participants and Supervisors need to be aware of their responsibility to protect the good image of the DofE.

Supervisors are responsible for the behaviour of their teams at all times, even when they are not directly supervising them.

Issues to be aware of include:
• Noise on campsites, especially early in the mornings or late at night.
• Inconsiderate car parking – blocking roads or farm entrances.
• Excessive use of public facilities.
• Litter, especially uncollected 'dead-letters' completed by teams.
• Failure to adhere to the Countryside Code/Water Sports Safety Code.
• Overuse of particular footpaths or areas.
• Walking abreast on narrow paths rather than walking in a line.
• Not following access laws and rights of way.
• Excessive disturbance for the local community at the start and finish of an expedition when participants are dropped off or collected by parents or the minibus.
• The expedition's carbon footprint.

From the local people's and landowners' perspective, these issues can occur frequently as many DofE groups often use the same area for expeditions and have the same sorts of expedition plans.

Litter

All litter created during an expedition must be removed by the participants; it must not be buried, hidden or burnt, but must either be carried away or may be disposed of in appropriate bins.

Participants should leave areas as they would wish to find them and should be willing to remove other litter they find as well as their own.

If teams and Supervisors are using a 'letterbox', 'dead-letter droppings' or 'dead-letterbox' system for remote supervision then these must be collected and never left behind.

TOP TIP...
On arrival at the campsite, the first task is to put up the tent. Remember to do a 'line search' (like police) for litter, tent pegs and so on when clearing the site.

Gerald Richardson,
DofE Leader &
Lomond and Argyll
Network Assessor

DofE environmental impact policy

(as set out in *The Handbook for DofE Leaders*)

Care for the environment:

The Duke of Edinburgh's Award aims to provide a programme of development for all young people, long into the future. Therefore, sustainability of our environment is essential. In light of this we have developed an environmental impact policy, which we all commit to.

The environmental impact policy aims to:

- Promote sustainable use of the outdoor environment.
- Enhance partnerships with the wider community.
- Educate participants about the natural environment and local area.
- Conserve global resources.

Promoting sustainable use of the outdoor environment

- Exercise care and concern for the environment in line with the Countryside Code/The Scottish Outdoor Access Code.
- Monitor locations used for environmental damage.
- Consider modifying the use of locations to reduce damage.
- Consider assisting with the repair or maintenance of sites, especially if DofE activities have significantly contributed to that damage.

Enhancing partnerships with the wider community

- Respect the interests of others, especially those who live, work, manage or carry out their recreation in the environment of DofE activities.

TOP TIP...
Learn from Chief Si'ahl: Take nothing but memories [and photos!], leave nothing but footprints.

Ross Grant,
DofE Leader,
Grange Academy,
East Ayrshire.

- Comply with bylaws and access agreements.
- Liaise with landowners, local communities and other organisations over any activities which may affect them or the land over which they have control, or an interest in.
- Be sensitive to the potential and actual impact of the DofE's operation on an area or community.
- Follow the Countryside Code/The Scottish Outdoor Access Code.

Educating participants about the natural environment and local area

- Promote awareness and respect for the natural environment.
- Encourage a greater understanding of the natural world and the cultural setting of their surroundings.
- Educate participants as to the appropriate way to enjoy, explore, move or live in the countryside.

Conserving global resources

- Reduce use of global resources and recycle waste products.
- Use products and materials that support the ethos of the DofE.
- Use materials from sustainable sources and recycled materials.
- Using environmentally efficient methods such as eDofE and other online resources.

Chapter 6.7
Observation
and recording

What *The Handbook for DofE Leaders* says...

The post-qualifying expedition presentation will be based on the aim so it must allow for the team's own observations and investigations during their expedition.

Time spent exploring is determined by the team to meet their individual needs.

The aim and investigation methods

Participants should base their investigation methods on their aim and the needs of their intended presentation. To get the most out of their expedition, participants will need to do some initial research about their aim and how best to practically investigate it on an expedition, be it academic, scientific or artistic.

Their own investigation must be new to them. If the information can be found on the internet or locally, then the expedition loses its meaning. For example, if participants are interested in environmental impact projects, then they should investigate what has been done previously and then plan how to add to this through their project.

Their own practice investigations on the expedition should be set in the context of this relevant material, literature or art and culture.

As part of preparing for their qualifying expedition, teams will often test out their investigation methods on their practice expedition and complete other research before and after their expedition.

Supervisors and Assessors should keep up to date with how the investigations are progressing during the expedition, based on the team's plans and their ability.

Observing

Teams should consider that they observe though all of their senses and think about how they can utilise them all to enhance the experience. Solitude from the rest of the team can help

participants to really look around and observe the surroundings in more detail.

Observation should include the emotions experienced by participants during an expedition and how they impact on the individual and the team.

Recording

Routes must be planned with the aim and investigation in mind. Participants will be able to identify areas where the investigation can take place in advance, for example based on the location of stone circles, streams, observation points or woodland.

Teams should always be ready to add in additional investigations if they come across an unexpectedly good location or source of inspiration.

TOP TIP...
Take lots of photos. They'll make people laugh when the expedition gets tough and they'll be useful as evidence and for the presentation.

Phil Bond,
DofE Manager,
Millfield School,
South West

Most methods are built around some simple observations, measurements or experiments using basic home-made equipment, or are focused on being flexible to allow the development of artistic images and creativity. Recording equipment can be kept very simple, lightweight and inexpensive, no more

than pencils, notepads and measuring or drawing equipment. However more expensive scientific measuring equipment, cameras or digital video recorders are also often taken, although the risk of damage must be considered. Teams need to consider how much memory space will be required and how they will keep them powered.

Refer to Chapter 9 on mobile phones for their use as evidence gathering tools.

It is important that teams record not just the project observations of the day, but also their thoughts, feelings, attitudes and amusing or anxious moments. The disappointments and feelings of accomplishments as individuals and as a team are invaluable for participants to gain an insight into themselves. This, far more than online or tourist book research, will have a lasting impact on them as an individual.

For advice on how to create a digital video of an expedition please refer to page 30.

Chapter 6.8
Team building and leadership

What *The Handbook for DofE Leaders* says...

Through participation in an expedition, young people learn the value of sharing responsibility for success, through leadership, teamwork, self-reliance and co-operation; as well as recognising the needs and strengths of themselves and others.

DofE teams make decisions and accept their consequences.

Teamwork is a cornerstone of the Expedition section. It is the collective strength and unity of the team, working together, that will see it through any difficult and challenging elements of their expedition. Developing good personal relationships is an essential part of the process and it takes time for teams to develop their own identity and style.

The DofE Leader/Supervisor should be able to recognise the abilities and strengths of all those involved in the expedition and help them to do the same with each other.

DofE Leaders, Supervisors and expedition support staff need to ensure that all participants have an opportunity to develop their leadership and teamwork skills. This cannot simply be left to the most assertive, dominant or loud character in the team.

To make this happen successfully:
- Delegate and rotate realistic opportunities to practise the roles of leadership and teamwork throughout the section.
- Give opportunities to build up skills and confidence in leadership and teamwork over time.
- Allow participants to review the processes and approaches to leadership themselves.

Leadership and teamwork theories

There are many theories of leadership and teamwork which DofE Leaders and Supervisors can draw upon to help train their team and develop their understanding and experience. These are easily available online or in team management books.

Some good authors to consider are:
- **Tannerbaum and Schmidt** (1968) – who looked at styles of leadership from authoritarian behaviour along a continuum of increasing freedom in decision making to democratic styles of management.
- **Bruce Tuckman** (1965, 1977) – who looked at stages of teamwork theory and team forming, usually summarised in five stages as: Forming, Storming, Norming, Performing and Adjourning.
- **Meredith Belbin** (1981) – who looked at team inventory which includes nine roles within a team and considers how an individual behaves in a team and how they may have multiple roles.
- **John Adair** – who looked at a task led and action centred leadership model, based on the overlapping needs of the task, the group/team and the individual.
- **Bernard Bass** (1985 and others afterwards) – who looked at transformational (and transactional)

TOP TIP...
Try to get teams to take five minutes together at the end of the day to think about their teamwork; what worked, what didn't and new ideas for the next day.
Chris Dine,
DofE Assessor,
Army Cadet Force Association

leadership where the leader: considers the individual; considers people's intellectual stimulation; inspires the team and is a role model.

For the purposes of the DofE, an inclusive group decision making and democratic approach is most appropriate, both between participants and with expedition support staff and volunteers. However, authoritarian styles are not wrong and these can be appropriate in certain situations such as emergencies and where time is very limited.

Leadership and management

DofE Leaders and Supervisors are usually both a 'leader' of the Expedition section, inspiring, motivating and leading their DofE group and expedition teams, whilst also being a 'manager' to facilitate the trip, submit the required paperwork and manage the processes of the Expedition section.

To do this DofE Leaders and Supervisors should have these key skills to allow them to be both an effective leader and efficient manager.

These key skills, listed below, should also be developed in DofE participants to help prepare them for their expedition:

- Develop technical competence to inspire confidence and respect in the team.

TOP TIP...

Happy staff and volunteers make for a smooth running expedition; take time to plan for staff needs as well as participants'.

Helen Pickett,
DofE Leader,
Therfield School
South East

- Develop practical experience over time and discuss with others to develop best practice.
- Carefully plan and prepare for all of the Expedition section to build in the capacity to absorb issues, support people effectively and empower participants.
- Communicate clearly and consider the audience while making sure other people understand what has been said and have the chance to contribute.
- Have an awareness of the team, of the individual and of the environment. Consider the needs, concerns and dangers for/in each.

- Exercise good judgement to inspire trust and confidence in people, analysing and anticipating situations and working in a collaborative way for the best of the team.

TOP TIP...

An expedition should be a life-changing experience your goal is to ensure it is a positive one.

Peter Barker,
DofE Leader & Assessor,
Buckinghamshire County Council

It all started with the DofE...

Growing up, I was not what some might consider the 'typical' explorer. It wasn't until I started my DofE when I was 14 that my passion for adventuring began. I went on an expedition in the Brecon Beacons which really inspired my love of adventure. The DofE provided me with a chance to grow both physically and mentally and I still consider my Bronze Award one of my best achievements.

My many adventures have taught me some great lessons about both physical and mental strength. Good leadership is crucial to the success of any expedition and I have come across many different styles of leadership. It is always important to judge when to lead and when to take a step back and give your team mates that chance.

Leadership can be a daunting role to undertake but as long as you have great communication, an understanding of the individuals within your team and the belief that you can take the lead, you are sure to succeed.

I led the first unsupported group to the Geomagnetic North Pole and whilst the responsibility for the safety of my team members was daunting and frightening at times, the pride I felt, safe in the knowledge that I had led a team to victory, was fantastic. Good leadership and teamwork enabled us to reach the Geomagnetic North Pole and return home safely.

David Hempleman-Adams LVO OBE CStJ DL

David is a Trustee for The Duke of Edinburgh's Award and a Gold Award holder. In 1998 he became the first man to reach the Geographic and Magnetic North and South Poles as well as climb the highest peaks on all seven continents. In 2000 David became the only pilot to fly a balloon to the North Pole and has set numerous ballooning records since.

Chapter 6.9
Proficiency in the mode of travel

What *The Handbook for DofE Leaders* says...

The Supervisor must ensure that all participants are capable of undertaking the planned expedition.

Participants must be properly prepared and competent in their chosen expedition mode of travel, to allow them to safely complete their planned journey. Each Licensed Organisation and AAP will stipulate the level of competence they require from the participants under their care. Some Licensed Organisations will have their own training frameworks they follow to ensure and evidence competence.

The DofE sets out the minimum levels of training that participants need to complete. These requirements are set out in this *Expedition Guide* and detailed in the DofE Expedition Training Framework.

The DofE Expedition Training Framework includes required competencies at each DofE level (Bronze, Silver and Gold) and also includes several specific training documents for modes of travel. These documents are listed below and are available at **www.DofE.org/expedition**, and in eDofE's Resource Zone:

- Training framework for boatwork.
- Training framework for paddling skills.
- Training framework for sailing expeditions.
- Training framework for horseback expeditions.

In addition participants need to follow the Countryside, Highway and Water Sports Safety Codes, as appropriate to their mode of travel. All training must be signed off by the team's Supervisor. Some modes of travel, for example sailing, require participants to complete national governing body competence certificates or awards. More information about each mode of travel can be found in the appropriate chapter in this guide.

Multiple modes of travel

While the DofE is not against the use of multiple modes of travel, it should be noted that participants must be trained to the required standards in all the modes of travel they use. They must also still be capable of journeying unaccompanied and being self-sufficient. Minimum adult intervention and the concept of a journey must still be embraced.

The *DofE* Expedition Guide

Teams considering using more than one mode of travel should consider:

| **Safety** | Choosing more than one mode of travel can erode the margins of safety that must be in place for all DofE expeditions as there are more areas of risk and safety for participants to focus on, review and manage. |

| **Training** | There must be no drop in the level of competence expected for each mode of travel from all participants in the team. Teams will need to complete extra training, increasing their workload and that of their instructor. This can also increase the expedition cost as additional instructors, equipment and expedition support staff may be needed. |

| **Self-reliance** | Choosing more than one mode of travel can increase participants' dependence on adult support and interference. Teams must still be self-sufficient and this will require them to plan very carefully how the different modes of travel interact and in what order they are used. |

| **Journey** | The expedition needs to remain as a journey using the recommended expedition areas for the appropriate DofE level and mode of travel. Using more than one mode of travel can end up with the expedition being contrived and unnatural to the environment. |

| **Aim** | To remain in the spirit of the Expedition section, there must be a very clear aim which explains why more than one mode of travel is needed. These expeditions should still meet all of the 20 conditions of the Expedition section. |

Where might more than one mode of travel be used?

Teams which use multiple modes of travel to fulfil a carefully thought out aim and who design an expedition which is sympathetic to the expedition environment, may be able to create a successful DofE expedition.

For example, an expedition where a team paddle into a remote area, climb a Munro and then paddle out again can remain entirely self-sufficient and fulfil all of the 20 conditions.

Multiple modes of travel can also work well for some participants who have additional needs and who want to explore a range of environments otherwise inaccessible to them.

Portaging is quite common in some expedition areas and is perfectly acceptable as long as it is not motorised.

Expedition fitness

Every training programme needs to include physical training. The most common reasons for expeditions being aborted arise from the weather, poor navigation leading to tiredness and loss of motivation, overweight rucksacks, deterioration in team relationships and a lack of physical fitness.

Being physically prepared can help overcome many of these issues and enhance the enjoyment of the challenge. It can be hard and time consuming for individuals to become physically fit for their expedition and it will require some discipline.

TOP TIP...

For teams inspired to try more than one mode of travel why not spread this across different DofE levels. E.g.: a group from St Helens walked for Bronze, canoed on a canal for Silver and, for Gold, cycled from Liverpool Anglican Cathedral to York Minster.

Paul Griffiths, Operations Officer, DofE North West Office

Team fitness

Participants need to understand that their expedition(s) will test them physically and that they will need to consider their fitness both in terms of their team, route and their training programme.

It can be difficult for a team to support someone who is struggling physically with their expedition, so undertaking an expedition with people of a similar fitness is usually beneficial. It can be as hard for team members to slow down as it is for others to speed up, but this is all part of expedition teamwork.

Participants who are less fit than others in a team should be prepared to work on their fitness so their team know effort and progress has been made by them.

The enjoyment and success of expeditions can be jeopardised by a team member lagging 100 metres behind, who only catches up with the rest of the team when they are ready to leave from their rest. Mutual support and encouragement is as important in physical training before the expedition as it is during the expedition.

Fitness training and timing

Gauging the levels of fitness needed for an expedition is a personal judgement, and is often best observed during a short practice where participants carry a full rucksack.

The key is to start early, building up fitness and stamina levels over two or three months to coincide with the start of the qualifying expedition.

The most strenuous and intense activity should be in the weeks immediately before the expedition.

Each participant's fitness programme will be different, but regular activity totalling about three and a half hours of strenuous exercise a week that leaves participants out of breath, tired and sweaty is usually sufficient.

Participants should focus on aerobic exercise, which builds stamina and strengthens the cardiovascular and respiratory systems. A mix of walking, running, swimming and cycling works very well and should not be particularly expensive.

Getting fit is not complicated; it requires effort, perseverance and discipline. However, listed below are certain precautions which should be taken:

- Exercise should always be preceded by a gradual warming up period.
- There should always be a cool down period after the exercise session.
- Suitable clothing should be worn, including high visibility items if out on roads.
- Exercise should be tailored to account for any medical conditions or restrictions.

TOP TIP..

Suggest participants agree a team training programme and set personal targets for improvement. The best way to prepare for walking expeditions is walking, and cycle expeditions by cycling etc. Participants might use their Physical section to prepare themselves for their expedition.

Martin Curtis, Scout Leader & Head of Centre at Woodrow High House Residential Centre

Participants need to consider their mode of travel and build a training programme which develops the physical fitness needed. Foot and cycle expeditions will place demands on the lower part of the body, while rowing and canoeing will require strength in the upper body. Participants should consider the kit they will be carrying on expedition when designing their fitness regime.

Seek advice from people with experience in the mode of travel, as to how best to prepare. Participants need to gain experience in their mode of travel and they can develop this into a physical training programme by adding weights and increasing speeds. Training in this way will strengthen and harden the right parts of the body for the expedition.

Chapter 6.10
Codes of behaviour for participants

What *The Handbook for DofE Leaders* says...

Key behaviour expectations
Through participation in an expedition young people gain an appreciation of and respect for the outdoors.

Personal music players, speakers, radios and games
DofE teams can take personal music devices with them on expedition but they should not be used during the hours of activity and especially when journeying. The expedition team, Supervisor and Assessor should agree in advance the policy of use during their expedition.

Key behaviour expectations of DofE participants undertaking the Expedition section

The DofE expects to see high standards in terms of attitude and behaviour from all those taking part in a DofE programme. It is essential that participants respect the interests of others in the countryside, particularly those who live or work in that environment.

The Supervisor, as the representative of the Licensed Organisation, is responsible for the behaviour and conduct of their participants.

The DofE expects every DofE participant while on expedition, to adhere to and comply with:

- The code of conduct and behaviour expectations agreed between the expedition team, Supervisor and Assessor.
- Their Licensed Organisation code of conduct and/or behaviour expectations.
- The Countryside Code, available at **www.DofE.org/expedition**.
- The law of the country where the expedition activity is taking place, including access rights.
- The Highway Code and, if undertaking an expedition on water, the Water Sports Safety Code.
- The DofE Care for the environment policy, set out in Chapter 6.6, with specific attention given to the area and environment visited.

- The expectations of the DofE to avoid disturbing rural communities, to have regard for others enjoying the countryside, especially at campsites, and not to act in anyway that may damage the reputation of the DofE or bring the DofE into disrepute.

Very occasionally participants do not meet these expectations in terms of attitude, behaviour or training. Teams not complying with the above whist on training or practice expeditions should expect to be asked to complete additional training and practices. This is to demonstrate that they can comply before undertaking their qualifying expedition.

On qualifying expeditions, the Assessor should draw attention to these matters immediately with the individuals concerned, and consult with the Supervisor, to negotiate a way forward. This should allow the team an opportunity to improve, comply with the 20 conditions and successfully complete their expedition.

The Assessor will wish to highlight the issue to the DofE Leader to prevent a similar situation happening again.

However, if the Assessor feels that the team then goes on to persistently and deliberately flout these requirements, they should consult with their Licensed Organisation or Assessor Network Co-ordinator and may, reluctantly, remove their services and end the assessment.

Any individuals or teams that are identified as causing damage to the countryside and/or causing difficulties for landowners, such as releasing livestock or ruining crops, are subject to the laws of the country in which they are journeying and as such may expect to have to pay compensation for damages.

The Code of Behaviour for all adults involved with the DofE Charity and DofE programme activities, is set out on page 172.

Personal music players, speakers, radios and games

There is a view that if a participant is prepared to carry it, then they are allowed to take it. However, this general rule of thumb needs to be measured against the principles and outcomes of the Expedition section, most fundamentally that it is a team activity. An expedition is an opportunity for participants to have a unique and memorable outdoor experience, different from their normal routine, which will stay with them their whole lives.

The basic approach should be that the device is for the team and not for an individual to isolate themselves. Any items taken must enhance the team experience and not detract or reduce the feeling of isolation and adventure while on a DofE expedition.

Participants should always think very carefully before taking any expensive or personally valuable electronic equipment, which is not designed for the outdoors, with them on expedition. Some Licensed Organisations do not allow this kind of equipment to be taken on DofE expeditions, so teams should check with them first.

Personal music players can now not only hold tens of thousands of songs and music videos, but also TV programmes, films, games and live streaming. While participants can take these devices with them, and take the risk of damage or loss, they should not be used during the hours of planned activity.

It is unacceptable for participants to use these devices while journeying as they can greatly increase the risk of accident or injury by drowning out sounds around them or by not paying as much attention to where they are going. Equally, it is not acceptable for a team to sit down and watch a film or TV.

> TOP TIP...
> My group's rule the only permitted music is live music. This prevents the personal music player 'plug-in and tune-out' team fragmentation.
> Nick Neve,
> DofE Leader,
> Oakham School, Central England

Even in the evenings, using such devices should be discouraged. The Expedition section is about being in a team and communicating with that team. So while it may be acceptable for participants who want to get a few minutes of time to themselves to listen through their headphones; this should in no way lead to them being isolated frequently, or in a prolonged way, from the rest of the team.

Being in the environment is part of the experience, so they should also not be used to drown out the night time noises. The Supervisor and Assessor should agree with the team what is and is not acceptable use before the start of the expedition.

A much better use is to take small speakers so the team can have some music in the evening, set at an appropriate volume considerate to other people around and to any rules at the campsite. Often sharing music and agreeing the playlist can be a very positive experience. Most teams will develop a team song and this interaction (volume allowing) is all part of an enjoyable and engaging expedition.

Games

Most DofE teams will take some ball games, board games or a pack of cards with them to have something to do in the long light summer evenings or while huddled in their tent with their torches out of the rain or away from midges.

Some participants are now asking what is the difference between a group playing a game of cards and a group playing a board game on a computer pad? Apart from the obvious limitations of battery life, risk of damage or loss, cost and weight, there isn't much difference. As long as it is used for multi-player, social games which can include all of the team, then this can be acceptable for DofE groups.

However, remember that the DofE expedition is meant to be an outdoor experience which is different from a participant's normal routine, so a physical or tactile, rather than an electronic, game is almost always a more appropriate choice.

Case studies

- **Members of an open DofE group from Leeds** all found that they were cricket mad so took a radio with them and listened to the Ashes test match while having their lunch on a peak in the North York Moors. They all told the Assessor it was a magic moment and 'a memory that will stay with them forever'.
- **A group of apprentices were gutted** at the prospect of missing an England World Cup game whilst away on expedition. Their expedition Assessor told them in advance that they would not be allowed to watch the game at a pub local to their campsite. So the group decided to take a radio and everything they needed for a BBQ on their campsite and had a fantastic evening listening to the match.

TOP TIP...

A pack of cards, fold-up Frisbee or ball is more sociable than a personal music player and won't run out of batteries.

Adrian Allsopp,
DofE Assessor, Solihull School
Central England

Chapter 7
Practice expeditions

What *The Handbook for DofE Leaders* says...

Both enjoyable and essential, practice expeditions must replicate as closely as possible the conditions of the qualifying expedition. This includes mode of travel, accommodation and terrain.

Participants must complete at least one UK practice expedition at each level. This must include sufficient experience of being unaccompanied and remotely supervised so the Supervisor can confidently sign off their ability to undertake an unaccompanied, qualifying expedition.

Good practice expeditions prepare participants for the challenges of their qualifying expedition, allowing them to avoid problems like poor time-keeping, overweight packs, lack of fitness and blistered feet while under assessment.

Practice expeditions should be an enjoyable and rewarding learning experience where participants can make mistakes and learn from them.

Whilst participants may complete several practice day walks or training expeditions, every DofE participant must complete a practice expedition which is evidenced in eDofE and meets all the requirements set out here. The practice expedition should be considered as important as the qualifying expedition.

- Practice expeditions must not be over the same route or be in the same vicinity as the route planned for the qualifying expedition.
- Any team undertaking a qualifying expedition in wild country must have completed a practice expedition, of the appropriate duration, in wild country.
- The last practice expedition should not be immediately before the qualifying expedition as time is needed for reflection and recovery. Several weeks, at least, should separate the final practice from the qualifying expedition.
- All normal and Licensed Organisation requirements for the safe supervision and/or remote supervision of expedition teams must be followed.

The requirements

- Participants must complete sufficient journeys to confidently and competently undertake their unaccompanied, qualifying expedition.

- **All participants must complete at least one UK practice expedition at each level for the appropriate duration.**

- The practice expedition must replicate as closely as possible the conditions of the qualifying expedition. This includes: mode of travel, 4-7 team members, accommodation, terrain, hours of journeying and self-sufficiency.
- At Bronze level a minimum of one day and overnight practice expedition is required.
- At Silver and Gold levels, a practice of at least two days and two nights away, consecutively, is required.

Verifying competence

Teams will need to complete a variety of training days, some of which might include an overnight stay, before they are ready to undertake their practice expedition.

During this training, as the Supervisor gains greater confidence in the team's abilities, they can reduce the level of close supervision. This ensures that during the practice expedition the team is able to demonstrate their ability to journey unaccompanied.

The practice expedition must be structured so that it allows the Supervisor to be completely satisfied, and able to verify, that before the start of their qualifying expedition participants have the expedition skills and fitness levels appropriate for their unaccompanied, remotely supervised, qualifying expedition. This must be signed off within eDofE.

For Silver and Gold groups who have expedition experience this may mean just one practice expedition which is several days long where the first day is accompanied but the other days are remotely supervised.

For other teams, this process of decreasing direct supervision may take place over several training expeditions and then their practice expedition, as their skills, confidence and experience increase.

Accompanied training expeditions and day walks allow the Supervisor to delegate navigation and leadership roles to individual team members. Rotate these roles to give all participants the chance to learn and improve their skills. This direct, *in situ* learning is extremely effective and teams can quickly improve

TOP TIP...

Physically practise first aid scenarios rather than just talking them though. Mock emergency scenarios are a good way to test group skills while on an expedition. By initiating emergency procedures to test first aid training and the identification of escape routes with timings, you can help participants see how they cope as a team under pressure.

Dr. Keith Horsted,
DofE Assessor, Lincolnshire

from this approach. This can aid the Supervisor in making the decision of knowing when to remotely supervise and also to identify areas for further training.

Changing the mode of travel between DofE levels can provide great additional engagement, excitement and challenges to participants, extending both the

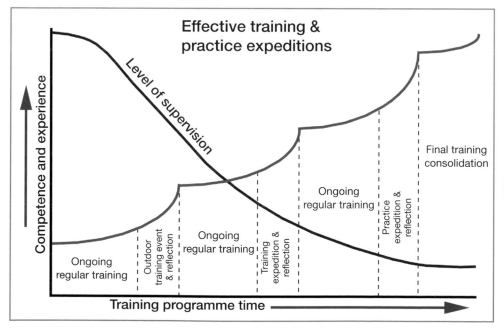

Effective training & practice expeditions

Competence and experience →

Level of supervision

Training programme time →

Ongoing regular training

Outdoor training event & reflection

Ongoing regular training

Training expedition & reflection

Ongoing regular training

Practice expedition & reflection

Final training consolidation

experience and level of skill. This usually requires additional training and practice expeditions.

Practices undertaken some time ago

Some participants come back to their DofE programme after some time, looking to complete their qualifying expedition. The Supervisor must decide if their practice expedition was too long ago to adequately evidence competence and must agree with the participant how they will prove they are capable of safely undertaking a qualifying expedition.

Getting the most from practice expeditions

Consider what the practice expedition aims to achieve and involve the participants to clearly establish the learning outcomes before planning each one. While helping with team building and confidence, they bring together all the skills and techniques learnt by the team so they can be practised under realistic conditions.

TOP TIP...

Deliver as much of the training outdoors as possible and always include at least one day for navigation and campcraft practice.

Pam Martin,
DofE Supervisor,
Brecon, Powys

Common learning outcomes for participants

- Practising expedition skills with an emphasis on the mode of travel, navigation and campcraft.
- Determining their average speed of travel for their qualifying expedition.
- Testing the suitability of their clothing, footwear and equipment.
- Considering the weight of their packs and the need for every item they carry.
- Identifying how much food, drink and fuel they will need during their expedition.

The DofE Expedition Guide

- Understanding the levels of physical fitness required for the qualifying expedition.
- Testing their planned menus and the amount of food they need to take.
- Provide an opportunity to practise the skills of investigation, observation and recording to use in their qualifying expedition.

- Developing their team dynamics essential to complete successfully a challenging, physical endeavour in a demanding environment and possible adverse weather.

Common outcomes for Supervisors and other staff

- Providing opportunities for individual and team tuition in expedition and travelling techniques.
- Evaluating the competence of the team and the individuals to undertake an unaccompanied, self-reliant expedition.
- Observing and, where necessary, facilitating the team-building process.
- Considering if any individuals would be better placed in a different team.
- Gauging participants' respect, behaviour and attitude to the outdoors.

TOP TIP...

After their practice, ask participants to empty their packs, grouping everything that was used and everything that wasn't. Ask them to add what would have been used in different weather conditions and then consider what could be left behind next time.

Alasdair Offin,
DofE Assessor, Lowther Hills

Practice expeditions are essential for accurately determining a team's speed of travel and giving them the chance to develop how they work together under genuine expedition conditions.

At Silver and Gold level, to make up the required consecutive two days and two nights away, practices are usually planned over a bank holiday weekend, school holiday or a Friday night to Sunday afternoon.

It is essential that teams at these levels learn the lessons of multiple night expeditions; coping when tired, possibly with wet camping equipment and clothing and having to use it again the following night.

Always consider carefully how long it will take to get to and from the expedition location and think through what impact this will have on the participants.

Remember the importance of participants knowing what to do if bad weather closes in.

Timing and reflection on the practice expedition

The majority of training, including all essential skills, will need to be completed before the practice expedition to ensure participants are properly prepared and not put off by a bad experience.

The Supervisor must ensure that the qualifying expedition happens soon enough after the last practice so participants do not lose their fitness, competence and confidence.

The DofE strongly discourages, at all levels, teams planning to complete their practice expedition immediately before their qualifying expedition. It rarely facilitates success and can mean participants starting their expedition feeling exhausted, with blistered feet and wet clothing.

The impact and benefits for participants must be considered carefully and prioritised over saving time or money.

Reflection and reviewing is essential in a young person's DofE programme and the Supervisor should facilitate this throughout the practice expedition. So as not to intrude on the team's isolation and self-reliant learning experience, use checkpoints, the campsite and a planned debrief session.

Teams and individuals need to reflect on their equipment, skills, training and fitness; while considering the aims and learning outcomes of their practice and how they have progressed overall. The discussion should lead to new strategies and techniques that the team

The difference between success and failure

The amount you would plan depends on whether you would like as close as 'guaranteed success' as you can or to deal with things as they pop up. By nature I am quite impulsive and enjoy the spontaneity of unplanned travel, but if you're responsible for other people in a team then it is imperative to plan meticulously to ensure safety.

If you're fixed on achieving a specific goal – as I was with the Seven Summits, for example – then thorough planning and plenty of practice can be the difference between success and failure.

Rebecca Stephens MBE

Rebecca was the first British woman to have climbed Everest, an achievement recognised around the world. She is the first English-speaking woman in the world to climb the Seven Summits and also holds several other records.

can test out during the remainder of the practice expedition and qualifying expedition.

Teams should consider their performance both as a team, and as individuals, what their team roles were and the leadership dynamics. Teams should also be encouraged to reflect on their expedition independently of the Supervisor. Participants can record these reflections in eDofE as part of their development.

> ### TOP TIP...
> Share the leadership amongst the group during the practice; give all participants the chance to lead.
> Matthew Shiells,
> DofE Leader,
> South Gloucestershire

Chapter 8

Supervising DofE expeditions

What *The Handbook for DofE Leaders* says...

All expeditions, including practice expeditions, must be supervised by a suitably experienced adult who is competent in the chosen mode of travel and who will be based in the area where the expedition takes place. Supervisors accept responsibility for the safety and welfare of the team on behalf of the Licensed Organisation.

Additionally, Supervisors should be familiar with the team, their individual strengths and weaknesses and their knowledge of the chosen route. An understanding of the aims, principles and requirements of the Expedition section is also essential.

The role of the Supervisor

The role of the DofE Expedition Supervisor is a crucial one, both in ensuring the safety of the participants whilst on an expedition and in maintaining the standards of the DofE. There is a specific DofE course for Supervisors.

Supervisors must have a sound knowledge of *The Handbook for DofE Leaders* and this *Expedition Guide,* EX² and the Expedition Training Framework.

Where expeditions are taking place using modes of transport other than on foot then Supervisors must be aware of the DofE guidance for that mode

Is the focal point for communication before, during and after the expedition, keeping everyone informed.

Checks all training and practice expeditions have been completed and evidenced in eDofE and that the Expedition Assessor has also provided evidence of the completion of the qualifying expedition.

Has the legal responsibility for the safety and welfare of young people on their practice and qualifying expeditions.

Ensures that the team's expedition will meet the 20 conditions of the section.

The Supervisor

Ensures that all appropriate expedition approvals have been received.

Carries out a risk assessment of the route and the expedition.

Is responsible for the supervision plan and for co-ordinating other expedition support staff.

Ensures that the teams are properly equipped to do their expedition.

To do this the Supervisor must be:

Appointed and approved by the Licensed Organisation/AAP

Familiar with the aims, principles, requirements and 20 conditions of the Expedition section

Experienced and competent in the appropriate mode of travel

The *DofE* Expedition Guide

of travel. The guidance is set out in this Guide and the required training is available at **www.DofE.org/expedition**.

Note that it is up to the Licensed Organisation or AAP to decide how many young people, split into expedition teams, a Supervisor is responsible for. Where there are multiple teams, there are often multiple Supervisors, each with designated young people/teams they are responsible for.

There are usually expedition support staff, who are approved by the Licensed Organisation or AAP, who help their Supervisor to deliver an expedition safely, using remote supervision. More information about the roles in the Expedition section and expedition organisations are set out in Chapter 3.

Who can supervise?

Each Licensed Organisation/ Approved Activity Provider (AAP) has the responsibility for ensuring that those who supervise expeditions are appropriately trained and qualified. Each Licensed Organisation/AAP will have their own requirements for the approval of Supervisors.

Registering with a Licensed Organisation/ Approved Activity Provider (AAP)

Every Licensed Organisation/AAP will have a register of those people who are approved to supervise DofE expeditions. Anyone wishing to become a Supervisor must contact their Licensed

Organisation/AAP to find out the requirements. Supervisors must register with each Licensed Organisation/AAP they intend to supervise for.

Some Licensed Organisations/AAPs will require Supervisors to have national governing body qualifications; others will have arrangements for an internal verification system. The DofE suggests Supervisors obtain national governing body qualifications where possible, as these are transferable to other Licensed Organisations/AAPs.

Licensed Organisations/AAPs will also require Supervisors to hold a valid and relevant first aid certificate and to have undertaken the relevant safeguarding checks.

Supervisors must understand the operating procedures of their Licensed Organisation/AAP including the notification and emergency procedures. Failure to follow these requirements may have serious legal consequences.

The skills needed by a Supervisor

It is the role of the Licensed Organisation/AAP to ensure that anyone appointed as a Supervisor has the correct range and balance of hard, soft and supervision skills (see below).

Supervision skills

Knowledge of Expedition section, planning skills, understanding of remote supervision, knowledge of Licensed Organisation procedures.

Hard skills

Navigation, campcraft, mode of travel skills, experience, qualifications.

Soft skills

Listening skills, empathy, communication, understanding, leadership, teambuilding, interaction, inter-personal skills.

The Supervisor's tasks during the expedition process

Each of these stages is set out in greater detail in the dedicated chapters found elsewhere in this Guide.

Training	• DofE participants must complete the DofE Expedition Training Framework for the appropriate level and mode of travel. Full information can be found in Chapter 6. • The training can be delivered by the DofE Leader, Licensed Organisation staff, volunteers, AAPs or the Supervisor. • Training should only be provided by those who have the necessary skills and experience and are approved by the Licensed Organisation.
Preparation	• Check notification and variation forms, route cards and outlines. • Undertake a team and route specific risk assessment. • Check the accident and emergency procedures for their Licensed Organisation/ Approved Activity Provider and gather all relevant safety information. • For qualifying expeditions make arrangements for a team meeting with the Assessor just before the expedition for the Assessor's pre-expedition check.
Verify training	• Verify that the team have all been trained appropriately. • Carry out a pre-expedition check and ensure that all of the team are properly prepared and have the correct equipment for their expedition. • Know the accident and emergency procedures for their Licensed Organisation/ Approved Activity Provider. • Collect all relevant safety information including medical and consent forms with any alterations.
On expedition	• Carry out the agreed flexible supervision plan. • Undertake an ongoing, dynamic risk assessment. • Respond to hazards by changing the supervision plan, where necessary. • Be responsible for communications and keep everyone informed of any changes of plans. • All relevant safety information must be carried by Supervisors. This includes the names, addresses and emergency contact numbers for all participants, the Assessor, the home contact, a nominated person in the LO and the DofE's Head Office emergency telephone number (01753 727400).
In addition, for practice expeditions	• Check on the team as required. • Where necessary intervene to provide additional training. • Decide if further practices are required. • Confirm the competence of the team to move on to the qualifying expedition and provide evidence for eDofE. • Debrief the team and decide on any further training needs.
In addition, for qualifying expeditions	• Check the Assessor's DofE Accredited Assessor photo ID card to confirm their identity, level of accreditation and its expiry date. • Check the team at least once a day or as the needs of safety make necessary. • Attend the Assessor's debriefing, if invited by the team. • Receive the expedition presentation if requested by the team or check on its progress if it is to be received by someone else.
Assessment	• Ensure that the Assessor has provided evidence of the completion of the qualifying expedition. • Review the supervision plan as part of the expedition review and note any learning for next time. • Report any near misses/incidents/accidents to the Licensed Organisation/ Approved Activity Provider.

Carrying out a pre-expedition check

The Supervisor's pre-expedition check is intended to prevent participants travelling to an expedition area only to find that their equipment or training is inadequate.

It should take place at the team's home base, normally between seven and ten days before departure for the expedition, to enable teams to bring all their equipment together but still have time to make any necessary changes.

This check, near the end of the expedition preparation process, is completed by the Supervisor and can be attended by the Assessor (usually only at Bronze level when the Assessor may live locally).

Teams will often have already contacted someone with local knowledge of their expedition area, at the start of the planning process, who could be helpful at this check. More information about the Assessor's pre-expedition check is set out in Chapter 10.

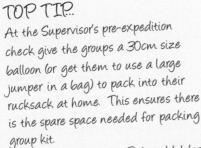

TOP TIP...

At the Supervisor's pre-expedition check give the groups a 30cm size balloon (or get them to use a large jumper in a bag) to pack into their rucksack at home. This ensures there is the spare space needed for packing group kit.

Robert Holder,
DofE Assessor &
Supervisor course tutor,
Suffolk County Council

TOP TIP...

At the start of the day, make a note of the colour of the clothing of the individuals in a group. This makes them easier to identify at a distance from other groups.

Rod Webster,
DofE Development Worker,
Derbyshire County Council

Levels of supervision

The way in which an expedition is supervised will have a substantial effect on the outcomes for the young people involved.

The key is always to use the minimum level of supervision possible whilst still ensuring the participants' safety. Supervisors must always be able to deal with team emergencies.

'Over-supervising' expedition teams is a common mistake made by inexperienced Supervisors or those who are not confident in the team's ability. This can frustrate participants who feel they are being constantly watched and could lead to them questioning their own abilities.

There are three levels of supervision:

Direct

- Where the Supervisor is in direct contact with the team and is accompanying them.
- Used for training expeditions and journeys.
- Used for certain parts of practice expeditions.
- It may also be appropriate at a particularly hazardous section on a qualifying expedition, such as a dangerous rapid or crossing a railway line.

Close

- Where the Supervisor is close enough to intervene if necessary, in order to offer support and guidance and/or to stop mistakes from being made.
- Teams are usually aware of the Supervisor's presence and are normally in visual or hearing contact at all times.
- Close supervision may be appropriate for the first part of a practice expedition, for some young people with additional needs, or for identified hazards at a particular point on a route.

Remote

- Where the Supervisor remains out of sight and hearing of the team and allows them to get on with the expedition without any intervention.
- The Supervisor will have a good idea of roughly where the team are and how they are progressing.
- This is the norm for the majority of practice expeditions and all qualifying expeditions. It allows the Supervisor to:
    - Periodically observe the team without intervening.
    - Allow the team to make mistakes and to recover from them without outside intervention.
    - Support the team by remaining remote yet in the expedition area and able to intervene if absolutely necessary or if requested.

Ensuring the appropriate level of supervision on qualifying expeditions

All qualifying expeditions must be unaccompanied and self-sufficient. The team must be unguided and supervision must be carried out remotely. The Supervisor must be satisfied that participants are capable of undertaking the planned expedition. Contact with adults should be kept to a minimum.

It is important to remember that all DofE expedition teams have undertaken a rigorous training programme. By the time the qualifying expedition takes place, all of the training and practices will have been completed, ensuring all the participants are competent and capable.

At this point it is time to stand back and let them get on with it. Remember that the greatest amount of learning will probably come from the difficulties that the team encounter. If the Supervisor is too quick to smooth the difficulties teams encounter then little learning will take place.

If the team does not have the necessary training and skills to operate safely in an area or environment unaccompanied for the duration of the expedition, then they should not be there. Either the expedition is taking place in the wrong environment or the team has not been sufficiently trained.

Supervisors may supervise teams more closely for short periods of an expedition when travelling through potentially hazardous environments. This must be kept to an absolute minimum and used to allow a team to overcome an unavoidable hazardous area in their expedition route.

Remote supervision at campsites

Remote supervision applies to evenings and nights as much as daylight hours. If Supervisors are on the same campsite then they should camp as far away from the participants as they can and have as little interaction as possible.

At Gold level it should not be necessary for any Supervisor to be present on the same campsite as participants overnight. Participants must be trained to this standard.

If the only campsite available insists on the Supervisor's presence or the participants have additional needs then Supervisors may use the same campsite following the advice above.

At Gold level it is unacceptable to use low levels of training or poor behaviour as a reason for using the same campsite as participants.

The use of mobile phones by Supervisors and Assessors

A mobile phone is an extremely useful tool for Supervisors and Assessors supporting Bronze and Silver teams in normal rural and open country, but is more limited in wild country, coastal waters or outside of the UK.

An expectation of mobile contact in unreliable areas of reception can increase the anxiety of Supervisors or Assessors. This has led to unnecessary call outs to mountain rescue for teams who are in fact in excellent condition and needing no assistance. This is an inexcusable waste of the mountain rescue team's time.

Establish the Supervisor or a base contact as a hub for all phone communication, ensuring they have mobile reception with a landline back up available. This ensures fast and accurate information updates and allows the team to call for emergency assistance. This hub can get updates from staff and Assessors as they see participants, relay information in an emergency situation and let parents know if teams are running late to the pickup point on the last day.

It is unacceptable, at any DofE level, for Supervisors and staff to rely on text messaging or phone calls with participants for updates rather than seeing the team.

A text or phone call cannot provide the same level of understanding of a team's morale, attitude or physical ability as a face-to-face discussion and observation during a Supervisor's visit.

Supervision planning

Every Supervisor should have a supervision plan for every team that they supervise.

A supervision plan is:
- An informal, written plan to empower the Supervisor with the strategy and confidence to successfully fulfil their role.
- Essential to ensure the team enjoys a safe and successful expedition.

Supervision planning is about being pro-active and having a plan, rather than just reacting if something goes wrong.

Supervisors are responsible for the behaviour of their teams at all times, even when they are not directly supervising them.

They must all be aware of their responsibility to maintaining the good reputation of the DofE.

A good supervision plan should consider the:
- Planned route and any possible alternative routes.
- The expedition environment.
- The planned mode of travel.
- The expedition team.

The supervision plan should assess the potential risks of an expedition in terms of:
- Specific hazards along the route.
- The mode of travel.
- The expedition environment.
- Weather conditions.
- Campsites.
- Team dynamics and leadership.

The supervision plan should define the Supervisor's proposed:
- Levels of supervision during the expedition.
- Meeting points.
- Route that will be taken between these meeting points.
- Alternative plans.
- Communication plan.
- Licensed Organisation/AAP's emergency procedures.

Consider the environmental impact by:
- Referring to Chapter 6.6 for the DofE Environmental Impact Policy.
- Ensuring that the impact is kept to a minimum.
- Ensuring that a positive image of the DofE is presented to local people. This will include:
  - Removing all litter.
  - Parking sensibly and never blocking entrances, gates or rights of way.
  - Reducing noise.
  - Using footpaths correctly.
  - Correctly using local facilities.
  - Following the Countryside Code
  - Giving a bit back to the local community.

The supervision plan should be flexible enough to cope with:
- Teams moving ahead or behind schedule.
- Changes to the expedition route taken.
- Changes in weather conditions.
- Emergency situations.
- External factors such as road closures, traffic congestion or accidents.

For information on supervising young people with additional needs, please refer to Chapter 12.

TOP TIP...

Get participants to make their own campsite code of conduct and all commit to abiding by it. This way you should not have behaviour problems.

Steve Chandler,
DofE Manager,
Wiltshire OA

Equipment for the Supervisor

It is helpful for the Supervisor to carry the following with them:

Essential paperwork:
- Copies of route cards and tracings for each group.
- Copies of health/permission/contact forms as required by the LO/AAP.
- LO/AAP emergency contact details.
- Campsite details.
- Phone numbers of all staff and Assessors, as well as a back-up landline number.

Essential equipment:
- Waterproofs and warm clothing
- Food
- Water (and some spare for the team)
- Flask
- Shelter
- Comprehensive first aid kit
- Mobile phone and loose change/ phone card
- Notebook and pen
- Map, compass and any other navigational aids
- Torch and whistle.

Optional equipment:
- Binoculars
- Survival bag
- Sit mat
- Repair kit
- Reading book
- Sweets
- Camera
- Walking pole.

TOP TIP...

Always carry binoculars with you for remote supervision.

Victoria Squire & Ben Ford,
DofE Supervisor & Assessor,
Pembrokeshire County Council.

TOP TIP...

Keeping equipment dry can make the difference between completing an expedition or dropping out. Keep a supply of strong plastic garden sacks to give to participants at the start of the expedition if needed.

Peter Smith,
DofE Expedition Advisory Panel

Safety and emergency procedures

The Expedition Supervisor is legally responsible for the safety and welfare of the young people whilst they are on their expedition. The Supervisor can ask for help and support from the Assessor but can never hand this responsibility over to them.

There are many factors that can affect the safety of a team but the main ones are:
- The mode of travel.
- The team's choice of route.
- Team equipment.
- Communications.
- Weather conditions.
- Fitness.

Taken individually each of the above factors can usually be dealt with by a team; it is often when there is a combination of factors that difficulties arise.

Some of these factors can be mitigated by good planning before the expedition starts. A team who are fit for the challenge they have set can often cope far better with other problems than teams who are struggling even in good weather when everything is going well.

Weather conditions in the UK will always be an unknown factor. In recent years substantial flooding has occurred in July and August, whilst earlier in the year the conditions have been mild and dry. Always be prepared for the unexpected.

All teams should plan alternative poor weather routes – the importance of this cannot be over emphasised. Those

> **TOP TIP...**
>
> Create a 'supervisor folder' with clear pockets labelled for essential paperwork – consents, route cards, approvals, emergency procedures, alternative poor weather routes, staff contact numbers and so on.
>
> Mary Harper,
> Dartmoor Assessor Network Assessor.

doing expeditions in wild country must plan alternative, low level (lower risk) routes that can be used in the event of poor weather.

A well planned alternative route will allow a team a much greater degree of flexibility if conditions deteriorate. It also means that everyone is working to an agreed plan, rather than to ad-hoc decisions.

Each Licensed Organisation/AAP must have its own safety and emergency procedures and it is essential that Supervisors have this information to hand throughout the expedition.

The expedition team(s), Supervisor, support staff and Assessor will all have agreed an emergency plan based on these procedures. If things appear to go wrong then the Supervisor needs to allow the team to put the plan into action before rushing to see if anything is wrong.

All expedition teams must be trained in how to identify an emergency and respond correctly.

A well trained Gold team who are two hours behind schedule may simply give the Supervisor an opportunity for another break; whilst the same delay by a novice Bronze team on their practice may give greater cause for concern.

Whilst Supervisors may fear teams getting completely and hopelessly lost, there is really very little danger that they can get into even if they are lost. Remember that they have all of the equipment and training they need to survive quite happily, without adult supervision, out in the countryside overnight, including tents, food, sleeping bags, stoves and fuel.

Rightly, many mountain rescue teams will not contemplate looking for a DofE team at night, unless they know for a fact that someone is injured. Participants are well equipped and well trained with an emergency plan that they know will work.

All minor and major incidents must be reported to the DofE. Please go to **www.DofE.org/go/emergencies** for more information.

Dealing with the press

If things do go seriously wrong and the emergency services have been called then Supervisors may find that the press become involved.

Local authorities and national youth organisations usually have a policy for dealing with press enquiries. In many LOs only their own press or public relations officer can make comments to the media. It is essential that Supervisors have and follow the correct Licensed Organisation/AAP emergency procedures with regards to the press.

The press have their job to do but it is important that:
- The enquirer's name, organisation and contact number are recorded and then tell them that they will be contacted with an answer as soon as possible. Never say 'no comment'.
- Supervisors must not speak to the press without the permission of the Licensed Organisation/AAP.
- Young people must be protected from press attention and should not be allowed to talk to the press. No names may be given out until the parent/guardian has been informed and the Licensed Organisation and emergency services have authorised staff to do so.
- Licensed Organisations/AAPs ensure that the DofE Region/Country or DofE Head Office Duty Officer has been informed. All media enquiries must be referred to the DofE's Marketing & Communications Team at Head Office (or the Duty Officer out of office hours) on 01753 727400. Further information can be found at **www.DofE.org/press**.

Duty of care

Licence requirements

Under the terms of a Licensed Organisation or Approved Activity Provider licence, there must be in place the following:

- Systems for the health and safety of participants and those that support them. These must be in line with relevant legislation as amended from time to time.
- A system for the approval of staff, including Leaders, Supervisors and Assessors, which ensures they are appropriately qualified or experienced and acceptable for their roles.
- Safeguarding policies and procedures.

Code of Behaviour for adults

All adults involved with the DofE Charity and DofE programme activities should follow the DofE Code of Behaviour to support the safeguarding of participants.

Supervisors and staff must be familiar with the steps to be taken in the event

---

The DofE Code of Behaviour (set out in *The DofE Handbook for Leaders*):

- Treat everyone with respect.
- Act as a good role model of appropriate behaviour.
- Ensure at least one other person is present when working with a participant or at least be within sight or hearing of others.
- Provide separate sleeping accommodation for DofE Leaders and participants during expeditions and residential activities.
- Remember that actions, remarks and gestures can be misinterpreted, no matter how well intentioned.
- Provide access for participants to talk through any concerns they may have.
- Encourage participants to feel comfortable and care enough to point out attitudes or behaviour they do not like.
- Recognise that caution is required, particularly in sensitive moments.
- Not permit abusive youth peer activities (e.g. initiation ceremonies, ridiculing, bullying, cyberbullying, harassment, etc.).
- Not have any inappropriate physical, verbal or electronic/online contact with others.
- Not jump to conclusions about others.
- Not react to inappropriate attention-seeking behaviour such as tantrums or crushes.
- Not exaggerate or trivialise harassment or child abuse issues.
- Not show any favouritism.

In addition, Supervisors should also follow the DofE Environmental Impact Policy set out in Chapter 6.6 and the Licensed Organisation/AAP policies on behaviour and safeguarding. Any individuals or teams that are identified as causing damage to the countryside and/or causing difficulties for landowners, such as releasing livestock or ruining crops, are subject to the laws of the country in which they are journeying and as such may expect to have to pay compensation for damages.

of becoming aware of, suspecting or receiving allegations of harm or risk of harm to young people.

These may include physical, sexual or emotional abuse; neglect, harassment or bullying.

Care of the participant

Supervisors and staff need to comply with Licensed Organisation/AAP guidelines and procedures and have a duty to look after the physical and emotional welfare of the young people, and act as any reasonable adult would.

Points to consider are:
- The age and maturity of the participants.
- The team's wishes with regards to decisions.
- Parental wishes.
- Cultural issues.
- Team numbers and gender mixes.
- Relationships within the group.
- Team and individual training/fitness.

Remember it is the responsibility of the Supervisor to know their Licensed Organisation's/Approved Activity Provider's safeguarding and health and safety policies.

Insurance

All Supervisors, as adult volunteers, are covered by the DofE's Personal Accident policy.

The policy does not cover personal effects, camping equipment and valuables. Individuals who require more information or consider that they might be eligible to claim should contact DofE Head Office.

Challenging times

In some of the far-flung adventures I have completed with my husband, including climbing the Seven Summits and skiing to the Poles, there have been some incredibly challenging times.

Climbing Mount McKinley, we had to negotiate dangerously crevassed glaciers, while coping with the deteriorating weather and dwindling food supplies. We accepted that things wouldn't all go to plan and that's what's exciting about venturing into the unknown. You can achieve anything when you are in a team of people you know and trust – the encouragement and support can make all the difference.

We knew that by thorough planning and preparation, training hard and pushing ourselves outside of our comfort zone, that our adventures would stand the best chance of being safe, successful and enjoyable.

Jo Gambi

Jo entered the Guinness World Records for the fastest female ascent of the Seven Summits. She is the second British woman to ever climb Everest's North Ridge.

Chapter 9
Mobile phones

What *The Handbook for DofE Leaders* says...

Using mobile phones on an expedition can destroy the sense of isolation and solitude core to the learning and self-reliance of the Expedition section. While useful additional safety tools, and in many cases a useful means of capturing evidence, the DofE strongly recommends that mobile phones be used for emergencies only.

The expedition team, Supervisor and Assessor should agree in advance the policy of use during the expedition, for example, their use as a camera to record evidence for eDofE and not as a means of communication.

Mobile phones must always be considered an unreliable safety tool due to possible lack of reception, battery failure etc.

The Expedition section is designed to develop self-reliance and self-confidence through isolation and remote supervision, overcoming challenges and managing risk as an independent team of peers.

Mobile phones can seriously undermine these outcomes and compromise the team's attitude and approach to the decision-making processes during their expedition.

The more advanced mobile phones become, the greater their potential impact on effective expeditions, so it is vital that the expedition team, Supervisor and Assessor agree well in advance how they may be used by the team.

Increasingly a DofE expedition is one of the very few times that young people will experience isolation away from mass media and instant communication, working only with a team of their peers. This must be embraced as one of the core principles of the Expedition section.

Policies

Licensed Organisations and Supervisors can select one of the following three policy options to agree in advance with the expedition team and Assessor.

1. No mobile phones will be carried by the team and so the emergency procedures (and evidence gathering methods), must be carefully thought out and designed to take this into account.

2. Mobile phones may be taken by the team for emergency use only. These phones must be switched off, kept in sealed bags and packed with first aid kits. Teams should make allowance for this when planning how to gather evidence.

3. As for policy two, but additional mobile phones without sim cards or satellite internet access may be taken by the team for use as cameras, digital video recorders and alarm clocks etc.

Mobile phones should always be thought of as a team kit item and not as an individual kit item.

Mobile phones may never be taken for navigation or GPS purposes.

The expedition team, Supervisor and Assessor must agree their mobile phone use policy well in advance of the expedition.

Emergency mobile phones should be kept switched off to remove the temptation to answer incoming calls and to protect their battery life.

The DofE Expedition Guide

The emergency phone is there to allow the participants to raise the alarm if there is reception. Supervisors and staff must use alternative means to contact teams as part of remote supervision. See page 167.

Radios

Radios can provide an effective alternative for teams, Supervisors and Assessors to contact each other in wild country or outside the UK, where there may be poor mobile phone reception.

Radios with a pre-arranged frequency can work well over a radius large enough for most expeditions; test them in the area to ensure they work. Radios can be combined with Leaders having sat-phones to allow a communication line to the outside world.

The guidance given here for mobile phones also applies to the use of radios. They are for emergency purposes only and must be kept in sealed bags.

Behaviour and misuse

In the DofE context, mobile phones must be thought of as either additional, unreliable, team safety equipment or as a team evidence gathering tool. It must be made very clear to participants that it is not acceptable to use them for general communication.

Persistent or deliberate misuse of mobile phones may lead the Assessor to conclude that the team cannot fulfil condition two of the 20 conditions: to be isolated, unaccompanied, self-sufficient and remotely supervised.

When agreeing their policy, DofE groups should consider the following factors to get the most effective use from mobile phones.

Mobile phones as emergency equipment

For many teams mobile phones are a normal part of their emergency equipment and emergency procedures. As well as being used to raise the alarm or seek advice in an emergency, they can also help save Supervisors and Assessors time by training teams to send texts if they have fallen well behind their schedule and/or are significantly off route. They can be an excellent support tool when used correctly and thought is given to minimise their limitations; accommodating them appropriately into emergency procedures.

Key requirements:

- Mobile phones must always be considered unreliable as there are several potential problems which can make them useless. Teams carrying mobile phones can feel a false sense of security and they must not assume they will have reception throughout all their expedition. Everyone must know what to do if their mobile phone fails as a means of contact.

TOP TIP.
Register the team's mobile phones to be able to text the emergency services on 999. Text messages requires less reception than a voice communication but should only be used as a last resort as the system is slower than phoning 999. Information about registering can be found at www.DofE.org/expedition
Dawn Scott, Operations Manager,
DofE Central England
Regional Office

- Carrying mobile phones must not change the way expeditions are planned, supervised or assessed. For example, the Supervisor must still visit the team at least once a day.
- Teams must be trained in the correct use of mobile phones, both technically and as part of emergency procedures. There must be no reduction in the quality of emergency training or equipment used by the team.
- Leaders must locate themselves at night where they have access to incoming and outgoing calls; this also applies to any base camp location in the area, so mobile phones must always be backed up by a landline 'fall-back'.
- In wild country and outside the UK, mobile phones will frequently have no reception and therefore have limited use for the majority of terrain used by land-based Gold expedition teams.

Getting the most out of mobile phones on expeditions

- Create a safety list of pre-programmed emergency numbers in the mobile phone, including the Supervisor(s), base contact, Assessor, Licensed Organisation and emergency services (999 and 112) etc. The Supervisor and base contact will also need participants' home contacts.
- It may be better to agree to text rather than call as this requires less reception, prevents being misheard, will not break up or be cut off, can be stored for future reference and uses less power.

- Ensure all phones in the safety list are not withheld numbers so callers can be identified.
- Ensure that everyone is trained in the technical use of the phone so they can set the volume to loud, set up the personal greeting or call diverts to other numbers.
- Ensure that voicemails are turned on and users know how to retrieve messages.
- Ensure that any 'pay as you go' phones have sufficient credit on them to remain active in a prolonged emergency situation, or the user is able to add more credit.
- Do not be tempted to hold or use a mobile phone during a thunder storm as evidence suggests that they increase the danger of lightning strikes.
- Try to identify in advance where mobile phones will/will not work in the area and where they can be recharged.

Mobile phones as evidence gathering tools

Mobile phones can help gather excellent evidence for eDofE and presentations of a participant's expedition and aim. Many participants will not own a separate camera, digital video recorder or even alarm clock/watch. However, using mobile phones for these purposes should be treated with caution and the following guidance followed:

- Mobile phones taken for use as evidence-gathering tools are considered team equipment and as tools for the evidence function they are intended for, such as a team camera, and not as personal mobile phones. The sim card must be removed and the phone must not be used for general communication. If this stops the phone from recording evidence then it cannot be used on the expedition and other arrangements will have to be made.
- Mobile phones are often very expensive and make up a huge part of a young person's social life. Most phones are not designed to survive the kinds of conditions and robust use that expeditions inevitably include. Participants should carefully consider if they really want to risk damaging their phone by taking it with them. If they do decide to take it, they should take steps to protect it with covers, insurance and back up any important information.

- It is highly recommended for participants to keep an expedition diary or log in a variety of formats. However, keeping an online blog or posting online updates to social networking sites during an expedition is not acceptable.
- Many phones include mapping, GPS and navigation features, which appear very sophisticated. These must **not** be used by the team as they are wholly inadequate for the remotely supervised expedition environment.
- Using features like cameras and digital video recorders can quickly drain a mobile phone's battery and memory, so teams should plan how to manage this, particularly if participants want to be able to phone family or friends on the way home.
- Most mobile phones include games and music; please refer to page 148 for guidance on personal music and games players.

When D*of*E teams can use mobile phones for communication

It is often tempting for a team to use a mobile phone if they have it. Clear training is the most effective way of ensuring that teams understand what the role of a mobile phone is during their expedition and when they should use it.

TOP TIP...

Participants need to remember to wear a watch on expedition as they won't be able to use their mobile phone to tell the time.

Catherine Corfield,
DofE Manager,
East Sussex

Communicating with expedition staff and emergency services

It is a core part of the Expedition section that participants take responsibility for their decisions, manage risk or unexpected challenges and learn through experience.

When a team gets into difficulties, or is lost, it is up to the team alone to work out what to do and how to solve the situation. Having a phone has, in the past, led to teams calling out mountain rescue teams just for being lost. If there is a serious accident, illness or injury within the party, it is a different situation and rescue teams expect to be involved.

Teams need to be able to establish emergency communication with their Supervisor or other staff at a base camp using either their mobile phone or a public phone box or house. If there is a need to call the emergency services with a mobile phone it is important that teams remain stationary. There can be a loss of signal by moving even a few metres and it is important that the rescue team is able to remain in contact.

If teams decide to carry mobile phones for communication purposes then they should be used sparingly for essential supervision and safety/ emergency purposes only.

A timely text from a team to their Supervisor to say that they were lost but are now at a given grid reference and are running two or three hours behind schedule; or they are running late and will arrive after dark, can be a good way to help effective supervision. However, repeated texts to Supervisors for advice should be considered as demonstrating a similar lack of competence as a team that needs to be shadowed.

Communicating with the outside world

As part of the pre-agreed mobile use policy it is just as important for parents and friends, as well as participants, to understand that while on expedition they should not expect to have any communication with each other. If any communication is required it should be through the Supervisor.

Participants with care responsibilities should make arrangements before leaving or ask contact to be made through the Supervisor if necessary. Participants should not plan expeditions for times when they may need to take urgent action, such as applying through clearing following the release of A-Level results.

The Supervisor should use good judgement to decide if direct contact is appropriate. For example, a new parent may want to talk to their partner in the evening, or if there is an accident involving a relative or an incident which requires urgent action from the participant. A phone call home by a participant might be the difference between them dropping out or keeping going. This can be permitted, but should be a last resort as the team and Supervisor should be providing this encouragement.

It should be made very clear to parents that no news is good news and that they should expect no contact at all from their child during the expedition.

Chapter 10

Assessing DofE expeditions

What *The Handbook for DofE Leaders* says...

All qualifying expeditions must be assessed by a competent adult who is approved by the Licensed Organisation and accredited by The Duke of Edinburgh's Award.

Assessors are the guardians of the DofE's high standards; they protect the interests of the DofE and ensure that the 20 conditions of the Expedition section are fulfilled.

This chapter provides a summary of what to expect from a DofE Accredited Assessor.

The role of the Assessor

The Assessor is a member of a partnership consisting of the participants, the Supervisor and the Assessor, formed to bring about a successful outcome to the team's expedition.

The role of the Assessor is to confirm that the 20 conditions of the Expedition section have been met.

There is no testing, no marking, either the 20 conditions have been fulfilled or they have not.

Ensure that the aim of the Expedition section is met.

Protect the interests of the DofE.

Ensure that the 20 conditions of the Expedition section are fulfilled.

Assessors are the guardians of the DofE's high standards.

Their role is to:

Provide, as appropriate, local expedition area information to teams to help them decide how best to meet the 20 conditions.

Be a fair, impartial and positive person who adds to the expedition experience, supports the team and sees a successful outcome.

The DofE Expedition Guide

To carry out their role effectively, all Assessors will be familiar with the conditions of the Expedition section and should have access to the latest edition of *The Handbook for DofE Leaders,* this *Expedition Guide* and the Expedition Training Framework. It is beneficial for the Assessor to know the expedition area(s) they are assessing DofE teams in.

As representatives of the DofE, Assessors will take interest in the participants' other sectional activities. They should encourage them to continue on to complete their Award and progress to the next DofE level or become DofE Leaders and Assessors.

Giving information to aid safety

The Assessor has no responsibility for the safety of the DofE participants they are assessing.

Responsibility for the health and safety and the welfare of participants while on their expedition rests entirely with the Supervisor who is the representative of the Licensed Organisation, which has the legal responsibility for their safety and well-being.

The Assessor may provide local information about the expedition area to help the team and Supervisor decide how to best meet the 20 conditions.

Whilst Assessors can provide information and check routes and teams against stated DofE standards, they have no responsibility for the appropriateness of training or expedition equipment.

If the conditions of the Expedition section are not being met, or there are serious safety concerns, the Assessor will highlight their concerns and talk with the Supervisor and participants, at the earliest opportunity.

Both Assessor and Supervisor should consult with their Licensed Organisation/AAP/Assessor Network Co-ordinator if needed. As a last resort, Assessors may withdraw their services. This will bring the expedition to an end or turn it into a practice expedition.

If the Assessor takes this course of action, they will make it clear to the Supervisor the reasons for doing so and provide a written report to their Licensed Organisation/AAP/Assessor Network Co-ordinator to follow up.

Emergencies

In the event of an emergency, the Assessor may assist the Supervisor, at their request, following the emergency procedures agreed with the Supervisor and set out by the Licensed Organisation/AAP.

An expedition team must always follow their first aid training and emergency procedures regardless of an Assessor being present at the time. Where an Assessor cannot contact the Supervisor and the emergency needs immediate action, the Assessor may act to ensure the safety of the participants.

As with any member of the public with formal first aid training, Assessors who have first aid training may use it to help save lives or help participants in immediate danger, but will need to then defer to the team's Supervisor and their emergency procedures as soon as practically possible.

Assessors will maintain a written record of incidents including what happened, to whom, where, when, what has happened since and the times of phone calls, etc.

Who can assess?

All Expedition Assessors must be accredited at the appropriate DofE level through The Duke of Edinburgh's Award Expedition Assessor Accreditation Scheme (EAAS). For details, contact the LO or visit **www.DofE.org/training** Note that not all Assessors can assess in areas of wild country.

At Bronze and Silver level, Assessors should not have been involved in any training or instruction of the team. At Gold level, the Assessor must be independent of the DofE group and not associated with the team in any way.

Although a member of a partnership, the Assessor at Gold level must always be totally independent of the DofE group and not associated with it in any way. It is the responsibility of the Licensed Organisation, communicating with the Supervisor/AAP, to ensure that this condition is satisfied.

All the advice and procedures provided in this guide apply equally to all modes of travel. In some situations for specialised modes of travel, it may be difficult to find an Accredited Assessor with competence and experience in that area. In these cases it may be appropriate to use an Assessor who works alongside another adult with the specific mode of travel skills, this might be the Supervisor.

The assessment process

The foundations of a successful expedition are established by the Leader, the Supervisor and the Licensed Organisation or AAP many weeks before the expedition commences, by ensuring that the expedition is correctly set up in accordance with the 20 conditions. The assessment should be regarded as a continuous process with several significant steps:

> **Send expedition information to the Assessor.**

> **Make initial contact with the Assessor and discuss their review of the expedition plan.**

> **With the team, meet the Assessor in the expedition area for the Assessor's pre-expedition check.**

> **The Assessor will meet with the team en-route.**

> **The Assessor will debrief the team and sign off the expedition.**

> **If requested by the team, the Assessor may receive expedition presentations.**

The Assessor's contribution can be greater than this, however, and each year many expeditions owe their success to the support inspiration and encouragement of their Assessor.

Sometimes, the Assessor's knowledge of an expedition area enables them to make a valued contribution, such as guidance on the aim of the expedition and how to investigate it.

Guidance will always be encouraging and enrich the experience being offered at an appropriate moment; it will never be intrusive or time consuming.

Assessors will always consult with the Supervisor and remember that the expedition belongs to the young people.

Send expedition information to the Assessor

The Assessor checks that the proposed expedition meets the 20 conditions and suggests any essential modifications.

Many of the 20 conditions can be checked at this stage, from the notification form, route outline (or tracings), route cards (including information about their project and planned investigations), supervision plan or through future enquiries.

Assessors will often pass information and comments back to the team to help them get the most from their expedition.

Details of the 20 conditions, other requirements and considerations relating to the mode of travel are set out in chapters 2 and 13.

Make initial contact with the Assessor and discuss their review of the expedition plan

After checking the basic expedition information, Assessors will:

- Phone or email the team's Supervisor/Leader to introduce themselves and approve the submissions or make comments.
- Confirm with the Supervisor that all the training and practices have (or will have, by the time of the expedition) been completed. Agree how this will be evidenced to the Assessor.

- Confirm that a pre-expedition equipment check will be undertaken by the Supervisor.
- Arrange to see (unless they have already been received) the team's route cards, equipment lists, menu plans and further details of the expedition's aim, project theme, investigation methods and presentation ideas.

Assessors cannot change a proposed route but may provide information to help the team adjust their route to manage risk and comply with the 20 conditions. The preparation of the route outline and cards represents a major undertaking by those concerned and involves many hours of hard work.

The Assessor will talk with the Supervisor to understand the ability of the team based on their practice expedition and assess if the proposed expedition will be a sufficient personal challenge. The Assessor will review and approve the balance in activity time between journeying and investigation as appropriately challenging for the team.

Assessors will bear in mind that, while some routes may appear short, the route and distances will be based on the aim and ability of the team.

Assessors will need to agree with the Supervisor any requested variations to the 20 conditions through the DofE variations process available at **www.DofE.org/expedition**.

The Assessor will tell the team their route has been approved as meeting the 20 conditions.

The Assessor, the team and the Supervisor will need to arrange a first meeting where they can all get together. Usually this is at a pre-expedition check during the acclimatisation period in the expedition area on the day, or evening, before the start of the expedition. Agree where to meet, provide a postcode/grid reference where possible, share contact phone numbers and a way to identify each other and vehicles.

The Assessor will bring their DofE Accredited Assessor photo ID card to this first meeting to prove their identity and level of accreditation to both the team and the Supervisor.

An example of this ID card is shown here.

With the team, meet the Assessor in the expedition area for the Assessor's pre-expedition check

This is the most important meeting where the Assessor, Supervisor and team agree their 'contract'. At Gold level this is usually in the acclimatisation period, lasting between one and two hours.

At Bronze and Silver levels it is usually shorter, often being in the morning of the expedition, when teams are keen to start their expedition. An Assessor local to the team might do this a few days early or during the Supervisor's pre-expedition check.

The Assessor will:

- Establish friendly relations and remove any fears or apprehensions the team may have of the Assessor. Ensure the team sees the Assessor as a positive person who wishes to support the team in their expedition and see a successful outcome.

TOP TIP...

Assessors love small photos of the team members, it makes accessing and writing the reports afterwards more personal and remembering names easier. The Supervisor needs to have the team members' permission to do this.

Katie Hall,
DofE Centre Co-ordinator,
Horsham Open DofE Centre,
West Sussex

- Set clear expectations and explain the role of the Assessor as the person who simply ensures that the 20 conditions are complied with.   The young people establish a 'contract' on what is involved and agree to the DofE's requirements, behaviour expectations (see Chapter 6.10), environmental impact policy (see Chapter 6.6) and the 20 conditions (see Chapter 2).
- Discuss with the team the Assessor's plans for visiting them during the expedition. They will:
  - Explain that if all is going well, one visit a day will probably be the norm, except at the beginning of the expedition.
  - Tell the team it is their expedition so they should not wait for the Assessor at checkpoints.

- Explain that Assessors are (usually) volunteers and so may support more than one team or are balancing other commitments, travelling large distances. Assessors supporting more than one team will plan carefully how they will see each team.
- Discuss and give advice on the team's aim and confirm how, and to whom, they wish to make their presentation. If participants want their Assessor to review their presentation then arrangements must be made in advance to book a suitable location and allow enough time.
- Discuss and examine the detail of the route on the map with the participants. They will confirm with the team and Supervisor if the supervision plan allows participants to leave checkpoints early and then adjust their remaining route times accordingly.
- Review alternative routes for foul weather and emergency escapes and the associated consequences of their use including actions to be taken by the team, Supervisor and Assessor.

- Tell participants that many teams make mistakes or get lost (or maybe become temporarily unsure of their position) at some stage on their expedition, this is acceptable and part of the learning process. Providing the team manage to sort themselves out in an appropriate way to reach their destination, it should not present any problems other than being late and tired.

- Ask the team to talk through their equipment and pack weights, although the opportunity for the Supervisor to correct shortcomings at this late stage is limited.

- Agree the supervision plan with the Supervisor i.e. how many visits will be carried out and when. The Supervisor has the responsibility for the team's safety and will make contact with the team as and when necessary. An Assessor will have concerns when a Supervisor tracks a team or makes contact at every checkpoint. It is usually an indication of inadequate training, a lack of confidence in the team or little experience of the expedition area.

- Establish with the Supervisor (and other staff) where they will be based and the means of communication for daily use, updates after meeting the team(s) and in case anything should go wrong. This is usually achieved by phoning an agreed staffed mobile number with land line backup.

- Ensure all of those involved in the expedition, particularly participants, understand and agree the emergency procedures, deciding the action which would be taken if there was an emergency or unexpected end, through illness or impossible weather conditions.

- Agree with the team and the Supervisor the expedition policy on mobile phones (particularly for emergencies), GPS, GPS tracking, personal music, speakers and radios. Please refer to the appropriate chapters in this guide.

Topics to cover during an Assessor's pre-expedition check

What to expect from an Assessor's pre-expedition check

The pre-expedition check allows the Assessor to verify with the team many of the 20 conditions including, but not limited to, condition 4 (aim and project), condition 5 (properly equipped), and conditions 6 and 7 (training and practices):

- **The objective is to find out what the participants know**, not to lecture or demonstrate what the Assessor knows. Assessors will make every effort to involve all of the young people together at each stage of the check, although individuals in the team will be able to demonstrate their own competence.
- **The Assessor will use supportive oral questioning and visual inspection**, never using written tests or in an examination atmosphere. The tone will be encouraging, where the young people can speak freely about any problems or apprehensions before embarking on what is, for many, one of the greatest challenges of their lives.
- **Assessors will usually start by asking the team to talk through their equipment choices** as it puts participants at their ease. They will talk about personal clothing, emergency equipment, personal and team camping equipment and the team's plans to keep their equipment dry, especially the sleeping bags and spare clothing. Many young people may have borrowed their equipment; it does not need to be top of the range and it will have already been checked by the Supervisor in the team's equipment check.

If the Assessor thinks there are shortcomings in any equipment, they will consider this in relation to the overall level of provision and bring it to the attention of the team's Supervisor.

- **Next they will check participants' training**, covering the Expedition Training Framework to the appropriate level and for the mode of travel. The Assessor willl ask the participants to talk through their route, describing their strategies, recognising hazards and discussing what it will actually mean to journey from point to point. Attention will focus on evidencing practical navigation skills like setting the map, finding positions, identifying and locating places from the map.
- **Assessors won't need to discuss planning skills** as these are evidenced through the route card/ outline. Awareness of the dangers associated with the various types of stoves and fuel to be used may be reviewed.
- **There may be wide variations in ability** so Assessors will consider the overall competence of the team. The Assessor will accept support given to individuals as long as they have the basic necessary competence to carry out the expedition without being a danger to themselves or a hazard to the rest of the team or the environment. If the Assessor feels there is a problem, they will discuss it immediately with the Supervisor.

The Assessor will meet the team en-route

During the expedition, the Assessor will make contact with the team as often as is necessary to ensure that the 20 conditions are being fulfilled. They will keep meetings to a minimum and as short as possible, as all meetings represent an intrusion into the team's expedition and undermines their sense of remoteness, self-sufficiency and self-reliance.

The timing of the visits will be varied. Expect the Assessor to meet the team en-route, at the campsite in an evening and at the campsite in a morning.

The Assessor may meet a team at lunchtime, or when they are undertaking exploratory work. This can work well as it can be undertaken quickly and may help to avoid delaying either the team or the Assessor.

TOP TIP...
Supervisors: help Assessors by making notes about individual participants after every meeting with the team, but not in front of them. Record anything funny, impressive, memorable and personal – it makes writing the feedback and providing evidence much easier.
Emma Simon,
DofE Supervisor & Assessor,
Birmingham

Often, some teams don't have the experience to set reliable journey times so they will frequently be late at checkpoints and at their campsites. Assessors will be used to this and be very patient.

TOP TIP...
If the Assessor is assessing more than one team out at once, help them with copying their route cards on to different coloured paper so that they can see at a glance which team is which.
Zoe McLean,
DofE Supervisor and Assessor,
Brecon Beacons, Wales

Teams can be several hours late and the Assessor will have the resolve and patience not to be panicked into unnecessary action and work closely with the Supervisor to get updates on the team's location. Guidance on the use of mobile phones is set out in Chapter 9.

Equally, some teams may be very early to checkpoints. The Assessor and Supervisor can work with teams to re-plan their routes and timings to ensure the expedition remains an appropriate challenge for the participants.

The Assessor will debrief the team and sign off the expedition

This is the second most important meeting between the team and their Assessor and comes immediately at the end of the expedition. This is the opportunity for the Assessor to share in the team's success and congratulate them. The Assessor will help the young people review their expedition and express their feelings and reactions.

The Assessor's debrief will:
- Start by confirming the successful completion of the expedition.
- Draw out overall impressions and achievements.
- Help participants to recognise their learning and personal development as individuals and as a team.
- Remain positive and informal.
- Encourage participants to complete their Award, progress to the next level and stress the value of the DofE on their CV and future endeavours.
- Normally last between 20-30 minutes.

The Assessor's debrief is separate to a presentation given to the Assessor. Where an Assessor is debriefing multiple teams at the end of the day, try to ensure that the finish times are staggered so that each team has time for a proper debrief.

The Expedition section is about developing teamwork and success is dependent on the whole team completing the expedition. If a team finishes their expedition and meets the 20 conditions, they have successfully completed their expedition. Assessors cannot pick out individual participants as being unsuccessful if they have made it to the end of their expedition. Issues with individual participants need to be resolved during the expedition, not after it.

> **TOP TIP...**
>
> Assessors, do not be rushed by waiting parents or bus drivers, the debrief is an essential part of the expedition experience. Use this time of high spirits to encourage all participants to complete their DofE and progress to the next level. The Supervisor needs to build this time into the expedition schedule.
>
> Norry Barber,
> DofE Manager, Kent

Some suggested questions for the Assessor's debrief

Assessors will facilitate the expedition debrief by asking open-ended questions to the team, enabling the team to reflect and learn effectively.

Supervisors can also use these questions to help participants reflect and learn at the end of the Expedition section.

Reflecting on themselves (reflecting on performance)

- Now you have finished, how do you feel?
- What were the best and most challenging parts of the experience?
- What do you think you learnt about yourself and others in your team?
- Has the expedition experience given you more self-confidence/self-belief?
- Did you discover any hidden abilities during your expedition experience?
- What did you do differently/better than your practice and what would you do differently next time?
- What do you think the benefits were of being on your own away from other friends, family and social media?

Reflecting on the team (teamwork, leadership, self-reliance, co-operation)

- Why do you think it is important to work as a team on an expedition, and how did you get on with each other?
- Were there any factors which helped the team work together?
- Were there any factors which prevented the team from working together?
- Give an example of a problem that arose on the expedition and how you overcame it

- If you made the wrong decision, what happened and what did you learn from the experience?
- Did people take on different roles (leader, navigator, motivator, helper, chef) or did you all share the different roles? What role do you think you would take on in a different team environment?

Reflecting on the expedition (route, menu, kit, managing risk)

- Was your route plan accurate and how closely did you follow it and your timings?
- In the light of experience, are there any other preparations you would make for future expeditions?
- Were you able to find the balance between keeping safe and having an adventure and where would you want to do your next expedition?
- What advice would you give another DofE team setting out on their expedition?

Next steps (completing the section and Award)

- Are you going to do a written report or will you create a performance, video presentation or an online report for your presentation?
- When will you deliver your presentation and what work do you need to do?
- What else have you got to do to complete your programme?

Signing off evidence

At the end of the debrief the Assessor will provide positive feedback to each participant which they can use as evidence in eDofE to show that they have completed their expedition. This can be written directly into eDofE through an Assessor's Report. Assessors' Reports can be made on **www.DofE.org/assessors**.

The feedback will be personal, usually be several short paragraphs, and reflect and capture the memorable and major achievement that completing a DofE expedition represents.

In the event of an expedition team not meeting the 20 conditions, the Assessor will inform them and their Supervisor of the reason.

If requested by the team, the Assessor may receive expedition presentations

To complete their Expedition section participants must deliver a presentation in any format to any suitable adult. Many choose their Assessor and they should agree when and how this will be completed.

If the Assessor is to be sent the presentations at a later date, ensure that they have the participant's and Leader's correct contact details.

Refer to Chapter 1 for more information on presentations.

Assessing expeditions with a project focus

It is helpful if Assessors have had experience of assessing DofE teams before assessing those with a focus on exploring and their project. It is also helpful to use Assessors who have a good understanding of the exploration subject to give relevant advice, understand the appropriateness of the investigation methods used and the balance between investigation and journeying.

It may be necessary to have two Assessors – one to deal with the 20 conditions and one with the necessary knowledge and experience to assess the results of the aim.

The second Assessor could be a local expert in the aim, rather than a DofE Accredited Assessor, and can also be the person who receives the presentation.

It is essential that all concerned, the two Assessors, the team, the Supervisor and the Leader co-operate right from the initial stages of preparation and planning to ensure a successful outcome of the expedition.

For more information about expeditions which have a project focus, please refer to Chapter 4.

Problems

The 20 conditions are designed to help Assessors, and all involved in DofE expeditions, work to the same requirements, so new rules are not inferred or created.

Assessors will always exercise great care not to advise hasty or ill-considered actions which would prevent the 20 conditions from being fulfilled. For example, placing an overdue team in a vehicle and taking them to their campsite would immediately invalidate their expedition. Here, it is better that they camp where they are, if safe to do so, or take the most direct route to a campsite.

Problems will still arise during expeditions from uncontrolled factors, such as the weather, injury, illness, fatigue or being very overdue. The Assessor and Supervisor should use their common sense to ensure the safety of the young people and to try to allow the expedition to continue.

The Supervisor must liaise with the Assessor and agree any changes, variations or actions advised or requested to allow participants to still meet the DofE requirements. Conditions such as those relating to time or team size cannot be modified, while certain requirements such as cooking can be interpreted far more liberally to meet individual needs. Assessors have the discretion to discuss modifying routes in consultation with the team and Supervisor, and will ensure that the new route still meets the 20 conditions.

Occasionally it may be difficult for an Assessor to decide whether or not a team has complied with the 20 conditions or if a team's inability to meet the 20 conditions was due to omissions or inadequacies of a third party.

The Assessor will then reserve judgement and seek the support of their Licensed Organisation/AAP/Assessor

Network Co-ordinator who can discuss the matter with the DofE.

Please refer to Chapter 6.10 for the key behaviour expectations of DofE participants undertaking the DofE Expedition section.

Ensuring an observance of the Countryside/Water Sports Safety Codes during the expedition and maintaining good relations with the farmers who provide the campsites are all part of this task.

Protecting the interests of the DofE

The DofE relies on Assessors to look after its interests in the Expedition section.

This is largely achieved by Assessors using their local knowledge to inform teams of possible sensitive areas or issues, such as existing friction with certain landowners or overburdened communities.

TOP TIP...

When assessing or supervising in popular areas, keep a note of all the teams you meet, not just your own. You never know when it might be useful.

Steve Beaven,
DofE Supervisor & Assessor,
Yorkshire.

Sharing the pains... and the gains

Surely the best role in the whole of DofE has got to be that of the Expedition Assessor. For starters it gives you the excuse, should you need one, to get out into the countryside you know and enjoy.

Second, it gives you the opportunity to play a small but significant part in the best youth development programme in the world. Most of all, it gives you the opportunity to meet some great young people, from all backgrounds and of all abilities, who allow you the privilege of observing them as they bring together all their training and plans for their assessed expedition.

You sense their feeling of excitement and a little apprehension at the first meeting; you share their highs and lows as they journey through their proposed route; you remember how you first felt when they come across something new; you recall how you first felt when the path you were looking for wasn't there; you sense the feeling of camaraderie as they make camp for the night and finally you experience their elation when they arrive at their final destination, their task accomplished.

No two teams are the same; all experiences are unique to them and how each team deals with the challenges they are confronted with is wonderful to observe. I've been assessing DofE expedition teams for almost 40 years and can honestly say it has been a real joy and privilege to meet so many excellent young people, their Leaders and Supervisors and to play my small part in the successful outcome of their expeditions.

Lister Baynes
*North York Moors Network Assessor
and Chair of the DofE Expedition Advisory Panel.*

Chapter 11
Expedition presentations and reflection

What *The Handbook for DofE Leaders* says...

All participants must deliver a presentation, related to the expedition's aim, in order to complete the section; it is entirely up to the team how their presentation is delivered - it could be in any format.

The presentation should also include an account of the journey to encourage participants to reflect on their experiences.

Reflecting on, summarising and telling others about their expedition experience is a key part of the DofE Expedition section.

Like the aim, the presentation needs to be considered very early in the planning as they will be closely integrated together.

Participants are free to give their presentation in any format and this will often direct how the aim will be researched, investigated and recorded.

It is the responsibility of the participants to choose an aim, research and organise a presentation which represents a genuine effort and contribution from all members of the team, be it arts or academically focused.

The almost unlimited choice of presentation styles is designed to accommodate all aptitudes, abilities, interests and resources.

Participants should be encouraged to use their imagination and take the lead, be it written, oral, photographic, audio or video, drama, song, artistic or any other appropriate form or combination of forms.

The presentation

The presentation should provide a permanent record of a major achievement for each participant. Whatever the method it must be agreed in advance with their DofE Leader, although it may be later changed, if needed.

The presentation should bring the expedition aim to life and be more than just a report of their project. It must be based on the participants' own first hand experiences, observations and investigations during their expedition and be in a format which inspires them.

Presentation ideas...

- **Written/document:** Printed booklet, written formal report, holiday brochure, statistical report, environmental report, story book, I-spy book, 'top tips' or accessibility guide.
- **Images:** Portfolio/scrapbook of photos, paintings, sketches, comic book, collage of colours or textures seen, annotated map and photo wall display, expedition poster, create own map of expedition area, comparative map/photo book between land use/panoramas now and 100 years ago.

- **Oral presentation:** PowerPoint, speech, comedy, story, drama, team song or sea shanty, poetry, music from sounds/catch phases recorded on expedition.
- **Video:** YouTube video diary, documentary short film, 'how to' expedition guide, music video.
- **Mixed:** Advice on mode of travel report, navigation skills guide, market a selection of new games, a fashion show of jewellery made of litter and their own rubbish collected on expedition, present local myths and legends, expedition master chef or expedition experience evening for parents.

The DofE Expedition Guide

The presentation may be produced and delivered as a team or as individuals. Whichever is chosen, it must reflect the contribution and involvement of each participant during the expedition and afterwards in the preparation of the presentation. The person(s) receiving the presentation will need to know who is responsible for what.

Most Expedition sections which are not achieved are because a presentation was not completed. Build it in at the earliest planning stages and set a date for the presentation soon after the expedition to make sure it happens.

Reflection and recognising achievement

Through creating a presentation and communicating their experiences publicly, participants have to think carefully about what impact the expedition had on them and what they have achieved. For this reason the presentation should be more than a simple display of research results to complete the aim, it should be an account of their journey and adventures.

Much of the value of the Expedition section comes from participants considering their thoughts and feelings, reflecting on what they have undergone, the positives and negatives and gaining an insight into themselves. Their presentation should reflect this.

Many of the experiences, both the highs and lows, will be easily remembered and add an extra level of interest for the presentation viewers.

Not every participant will want to keep a full log of their experiences but they can be an invaluable way for participants to manage their thoughts and anxieties.

Some participants may prefer the idea of producing a digital video log of their experiences, which can then be edited after the expedition and easily shared online with the presentation Assessor as well as staff, friends and family.

Alternatively they could record one sentence statements about themselves and the team every few hours.

Oral presentations

Most teams will use a range of presentation styles, but the most common is an oral presentation given at an open evening for parents, friends and supporters, or a school assembly. Oral presentations must be backed up with other materials such as photos, video and written research in addition to the usual observations and recordings.

Oral presentations can be given to the Assessor at the end of the expedition, providing this has been planned in advance to allow for sufficient time.

Refer to Chapter 5.4 on open expeditions for guidance.

Who assesses the presentation?

It is up to the participant/team to decide who will receive and assess their presentation. It can be any suitable adult. Often it is their DofE Leader, their Supervisor, Assessor or an expert they received advice from, but it could also be a teacher, tutor, youth worker or social worker.

It is usual for the person chosen to know the team and their individual abilities so as to properly assess their contribution and effort. For this reason there are no guidelines for the length, quality or scale of a presentation.

TOP TIP...

If the participants agree, a presentation given to younger, potential DofE participants can be a great way to inspire them to take up the challenge. Presentations from Gold participants can be particularly effective in sowing the seeds of ambition in potential participants of all levels.

Phil Treleven,
DofE UK Services Director

Something to shout about...

Throughout my life I have constantly burned for adventure, for knowledge and for new experiences – probing the unknown for new mental and physical thresholds. Oh! Adventure! Adventure! Dear God in Heaven! Give me adventure unlimited and oh my, what a wonderful blue orb we live on.

I have a deformed right foot. From my earliest days certain people maintained that I would never be able to realise my dreams and go on adventures. I will have none of it!

Over the past 60 years I have proved them wrong, scaling the highest mountains of the Himalayas, sweating through the jungles of Africa, Asia, ascending the summit of mighty Aconcagua in South America in dreadful katabatic winds and reaching the glowing freezing pulse of the magnetic North Pole. Nothing daunts me! I will not be constrained! The greatest danger in life is to not take the adventure. I urge you all to go for it and fulfil your dreams!

Brian Blessed

Brian is an actor, mountaineer and explorer who is renowned for his Shakespearian portrayals and blockbuster movies. He is the oldest man to reach the North Pole on foot and has attempted to climb Everest three times.

Success story

A DofE group from the South East Region chose to do something a little different as their aim for their Bronze canoeing expedition. Andrew Burdett, a participant in the group, had a keen interest in photography and filming and therefore decided to document their journey on film. Other members of the group created a music video.

Whilst canoeing on the River Thames from Lechlade to Eynsham Lock, Andrew filmed the highs – and lows – of their two day expedition, documenting the group's challenging journey.

Having already had experience with filming, this project was ideal for Andrew and the rest of the group as they could not only gain the benefits from completing a DofE expedition, but also build on an existing skill.

The film was a success and made for a great presentation evening at which the group received their Bronze Awards. It has also been used as an advertisement tool to show new DofE participants what to expect on their expedition, and the group are now well on their way to achieving their Silver Awards.

Chapter 12
Additional needs

What *The Handbook for DofE Leaders* says...

A Duke of Edinburgh's Award is achievable by any young person who chooses to take up its challenge, regardless of ability, gender, background or location.

A DofE programme is a personal challenge which can be tailored to suit personal circumstances.

Every participant's programme is tailor-made to reflect their individual starting point, abilities and interests.

The personal and non-competitive nature of a DofE programme means that participants from different and diverse starting points can be equally proud of achieving a certificate based on their personal challenge and journey.

The Expedition section can be one of the most challenging, but also the most rewarding sections of their programme. By planning their own expedition, participants can ensure it is based upon the interests, skills and different abilities of the individuals within their team.

Adults working alongside participants who have additional needs will find that there are considerable rewards in extending the breadth and scope of the young people's experience through the Expedition section.

The participant's sense of fulfilment and feelings of achievement may alter their whole perception of their own strengths and abilities.

DofE Leaders, Supervisors and Assessors supporting young people with additional needs through their Expedition section for the first time may need some supplementary support and guidance.

There is a wealth of experience available in this area and the DofE strongly recommends that Leaders and Supervisors contact their DofE Regional/ Country Office or their Licensed Organisation for advice and support at the earliest opportunity.

There is also a huge amount of information, ideas, suggestions and resources available online at www.DofE.org/go/additionalneeds

Advice on inclusion

Some young people may wish to undertake their expedition with participants who have similar needs. Others may wish to undertake their expedition with their friends and peers from their group, despite any difference in ability and need.

Young people should be encouraged and empowered to undertake their expedition with a group that they feel comfortable with and be appropriately supported through their chosen challenge.

This *Expedition Guide* puts great value in young people taking ownership of their own expeditions and forming their own teams. The Expedition section is highly valued by young people and inclusive teams need to be formed and agreed at the earliest stage of expedition preparation.

Each member of an inclusive team needs to challenged, it may be that the physical aspect of the expedition is reduced for some but the other benefits such as teamwork, cooperation, planning and recognising the strengths of others are greatly enhanced.

For those with mobility disabilities, an expedition on water, horseback or cycle may create an exciting, accessible and challenging journey. This can be an opportunity for the whole team to learn new skills in their chosen mode of travel and participate on an equal basis. Participants, Leaders and Supervisors should consider and explore the best options for the group, acknowledging the individual needs of each participant.

Parents and carers

Parents and carers should be kept informed of the details of the expedition, as some may have concerns about the perceived challenge and barriers of journeying in the outdoors.

Parents and carers are a good source of information and can often provide advice and support during the planning stages of the expedition.

Success story

For a DofE group in Cambridge, their route planning and mode of transport were key to ensuring their Gold expedition was a success. The five participants, including two who had physical disabilities, chose cycling as their mode of travel to ensure they could complete their DofE expedition as a team.

Cycling helped to create this equal setting as all five participants had similar levels of cycling experience and fitness.

DofE Leaders, Duncan and Sue, assisted the group in finding an accessible route on the Liverpool to Leeds canal from Cargrave to York, which avoided hills.

By cycling an appropriate route, the Gold expedition could be an equal challenge to all of the participants which would not have been possible had they chosen to walk. It was also crucial for the DofE Leaders to understand the capabilities of the participants.

By taking part in an inclusive expedition with young people who have a mix of abilities and needs, the group have developed many teamwork skills.

The participants needed to understand and adapt to the differing needs of the group in order to successfully overcome challenges and achieve their Gold Awards.

They may also be willing to assist in teaching the participant a particular skill in their own time, in a familiar and comfortable environment for the participant.

The Expedition section pushes participants' abilities and can lead to the participant achieving more than they, or their parents or carers, thought possible.

Help and advice

DofE Leaders, Supervisors, volunteers and instructors are encouraged to share good practice through networking with other groups working with young people with similar needs and abilities.

Licensed Organisations and DofE Regional/Country Offices will be able to identify other DofE groups and Leaders. This can prove invaluable when exchanging contacts for off-road wheelchair hire, route planning, recommending campsites and sharing expedition kit.

There are numerous DofE Award holders who could act as excellent role models for inspiring participants and other young people thinking about doing their DofE. The DofE also has specialist staff around the UK who can help provide advice and guidance.

Supervising young people with additional needs

For general guidance on supervising expedition teams please refer to Chapter 8.

Supervisors of teams with participants who have additional needs should consider the nature and level of supervision. Levels of remote supervision should be aligned to the group's individual requirements.

The DofE Expedition Guide

As with all expeditions, teams will benefit from the feeling of remoteness and independence and the intrusions by adults should be kept to a minimum.

There are now more accessible routes such as disused railway lines, cycle paths and towpaths which can help to allow effective remote supervision. A pre-visit with a thorough review of proposed routes will assist in the planning process.

Leaders and Supervisors must respect the wishes of participants if they do not want to declare their needs to others. However, the Supervisor needs to be aware of the range of needs of all the young people whom they are supervising. It should not be assumed that all young people with additional needs will require extra supervision, support or a variation to the 20 conditions.

Advice on expeditions with wheelchairs

When planning a wheelchair route, acknowledge the independence of the participant in a wheelchair. Always investigate the necessity of pushing and lifting by others. Where intervention is required, Leaders and participants should consider potential dangers as part of their risk assessment process.

It is essential that routes are visited in advance, ideally checking the route with a wheelchair, to identify barriers and obstacles that might be easily overlooked when just walking. Often expeditions where participants are

using manual wheelchairs will proceed more slowly than those on foot. Integration to a common pace and careful scheduling of the group's project investigations are needed for group success.

TOP TIP...

If a team includes a participant who can walk but may struggle to cover the distance, ask them to take a wheelchair as an extra team member. Give it a name to make it a member of the team and rotate who pushes it. If the participant needs to use it then they can do so without feeling 'different' from the rest of the team.

Sue Emmerson,
Operations Officer,
DofE Yorkshire & Humber Office.

If powered wheelchairs are to be used, ensure adequate battery power or recharging facilities are available together with rain covers.

Larger tents may be required for sleeping and toilet facilities must be suitable for people using wheelchairs.

Wheelchairs may need to be repaired and maintained whilst being used for expeditions and this should be covered as part of the pre-expedition training, for both team members and expedition support staff, to ensure the participants remain as self-sufficient as possible.

For expeditions using hand powered bikes, much of the advice in the cycling expedition's chapter (Chapter 13.1) may be relevant.

Taking the challenge

It's a huge challenge to go on an expedition in a wheelchair, especially because they aren't really designed to go anywhere adventurous and because it takes so much more effort.

Since I was paralysed I've been to places most other people will never see. I've climbed mountains and skied back down, I've dived to the bottom of the sea and swam with sharks, I've flown my paraglider all over the world and I've kayaked between icebergs – all without using my legs!

They're different adventures to the ones I'd go on if I could walk, and I get frustrated sometimes that I can't go everywhere, but I accept that and I've found ways to explore without being able to walk.

I use ways that work for me and focus on what I can do, which lets me get away from the boring pavement and feel the amazement of being somewhere new!

Andy Campbell

Serving in the British Army from 17, Andy was paralysed from the waist down following an accident. Not easily deterred, he set out to become the first wheelchair user to paraglide from 6,000ft off Babadag Mountain in southern Turkey. He has gone on to set numerous records and is currently undertaking a record-breaking wheelchair journey around the world.

The 20 conditions and advice for supporting participants who have additional needs

Introduction

The overriding principle and objective is to ensure participants recognise that they have achieved the same standard as all other participants. The expedition should always be centred on a participant's abilities and not on their additional needs. The DofE encourages the use of carefully thought out variations to allow for these aspirations.

All participants should endeavour to meet the DofE requirements and the 20 conditions. There are a number of variations to the 20 conditions, which DofE Leaders and Supervisors can use to support their young people with additional needs.

The variation application process has been created for DofE Leaders and Supervisors to seek guidance and to obtain approval for their expeditions. This should be submitted as soon as possible, at the start of the section, with the guidance of the Licensed Organisation.

The appropriate application form can be found at **www.DofE.org/expedition**.

This chapter will set out a range of options available to DofE Leaders and Supervisors to enable all participants with additional needs to undertake an expedition, in both inclusive and additional needs teams.

Some young people with additional needs are closely supported throughout their day-to-day lives. Their DofE expedition can provide a new opportunity for them so Supervisors should not try to remove all the challenges.

Condition 1: *All expeditions must be by the participant's own physical effort, without motorised or outside assistance. Motorised wheelchairs may be used where appropriate to the needs of the participant.*

Use careful route planning and effective practice expeditions to prepare participants for the challenges of navigation, journeying and carrying equipment.

The steady growth of accessible routes for wheelchairs, for example towpaths, disused railway lines and the creation of national cycle tracks, are creating exciting new environments for young people in wheelchairs to undertake their expedition in. However, other modes of travel may also be considered such as canoeing, rafted open canoes, on horseback or on adapted cycles.

These modes of travel may provide an ideal challenge and can also give participants the opportunity to learn new skills and link activities to their Physical section.

Success story

Vincent, a DofE Development Officer, embraced the underlying DofE principle 'achievable by all' when he was approached by a participant with a physical disability.

Elizabeth, who has long-term weakness on her left side, was aware that she would not be able to complete a walking expedition. However, as she was a keen horse-rider already, Vincent suggested that a horse riding expedition would suit her skills and provide a challenging DofE adventure.

By building on her existing skills and choosing horse riding, Elizabeth was able to complete her Bronze expedition with her friends.

During the expedition, the group explored the Galloway Hills and forest area to learn about the history and wildlife. Looking after horses proved to be a challenging task, but through working together, the group managed to complete an equally challenging and rewarding Bronze DofE expedition.

Condition 2: *All expeditions must be unaccompanied and self-sufficient.*

If a participant's medical conditions preclude the carrying of heavy loads, consider whether a different mode of travel such as canoeing or cycling might alleviate this, before using en-route equipment drop points by staff or pre-positioned kit at campsites.

Some groups of participants may require close adult support in order to complete their expedition. The DofE allows close supervision where it is necessary to ensure the safety and welfare of the young people involved.

Alternatively it may be possible for members of the team to be given training to provide support for the duration of the expedition, with or without additional adult assistance at the campsite(s).

Condition 3: *All expeditions must be supervised by an adult who is able to accept responsibility for the safety of the team.*

Teams are not usually accompanied by adults although they must always be supervised by an appropriately experienced individual. Very often Supervisors may observe teams from a distance to preserve the independence of the teams but they should visit teams as often as necessary to ensure their safety and well being.

For some teams at Gold level, it may be necessary for the Supervisor to stay on the same campsite as the participants. The Supervisor should give the team

The DofE Expedition Guide

as much independence as possible, staying as far away as possible on the same site, only coming closer to support with specific activities if required.

Advice from the experts...

Here are some useful points to consider, from The New Forest Open Centre and Sue Haysom, Additional Needs Co-ordinator, DofE South East Office:

- Talk with teachers, parents and carers – it is all about what the young people can achieve. Show videos and photos of previous expeditions to break down barriers where needed.
- Talk to the young person one to one and get a good understanding of what they want to get from their Expedition section and DofE programme.
- Use mixed ability/inclusive groups where possible, everybody benefits.
- Do be prepared to be flexible based on how the expedition is going. It is more important to have a great experience than to necessarily complete the plan for the day.
- After the expedition celebrate success and share the experiences as much as possible.

Condition 4: *The expedition must have an aim.*

Establishing the aim creates an opportunity for young people to take ownership of the expedition, shaping its purpose to their personal interests and strengths. The aim will usually provide many different ways for participants to be involved in the investigations and team responsibilities which best suit them.

Success story

At the Ysgol Penmaes DofE centre in Wales, four DofE participants, supported by their Leader Hannah, undertook an expedition in the Elan Valley. Using a wheelchair, walking and canoeing on the route, they completed a five day expedition and achieved their Gold Awards.

All four participants had complex needs including autism and cerebral palsy. Using mixed modes of travel meant the young people were not constrained by physical limitations, while maintaining a physical challenge and learning new skills.

Planning a mixed mode of travel route to include an electric wheelchair, needing overnight charging points, was not easy but they overcame these challenges. DofE Leader Hannah's most memorable experience from the expedition was seeing the young people being able to camp independently. They have developed great friendships through teamwork, increased their independence and their confidence has soared in a way not thought possible by staff and parents.

Success story

The DofE depends on inspirational Leaders, like Charlotte, to ensure that every section of the DofE is as accessible as possible.

The Expedition section, as Charlotte discovered, can sometimes be the most challenging but rewarding sections of the DofE for young people with additional needs.

Within Charlotte's Gold expedition group of four young cadets, three had cerebral palsy and the third hip dysplasia. As a result, all four had relative difficulty walking which meant that additional time and effort went in to planning the expedition, with two young people in a wheelchair.

The group were leant two 'jungle chairs', from a company called RGK, which meant that the rough terrain on the North York Moors was made more accessible for these participants. Their expedition project was entitled Disabled access in the North York Moors and was designed to explore how accessible their route was to other disabled explorers and what could be put in place to improve this.

Condition 5: *All participants must be properly equipped.*

Any specialist equipment required to support a participant must be checked with the same care as all other expedition equipment to ensure that it is in sound condition, is suitable for purpose and sufficiently robust to stand up to the task involved.

Equipment can be pre-positioned, based on the needs of the individual or team but not simply because of the difficulties of the expedition environment. If using some pre-positioned equipment, teams must still carry personal emergency equipment and agree this selection with their Licensed Organisation and Assessor.

When pre-positioning equipment, if possible, allow the team to set it up when they arrive so that they still feel in control of their expedition.

Condition 6: *Participants must have completed the required training and practice expeditions. All participants must complete the appropriate level of the Expedition Training Framework and mode of travel training.*

Identifying each participant's strengths is essential to ensure they have a full and valued role in the expedition. Each participant will learn at a different pace, so training plans need to be flexible.

Depending on the individual needs, the repetition of certain skills and creating routines in learning skills, may help participants to feel safe and comfortable while on expedition.

Confidence-building is essential preparation for all participants undertaking their Expedition section. Slowly build expedition experience during smaller camping trips or on trips to youth hostels, by using frame or large dome tents or even camping in the back garden at home. For some participants, preparing their own meal and using a sleeping bag may be challenges more easily tested and achieved for the first time at home or at the DofE centre.

Where expeditions have a shared emphasis on exploring and journeying, give sufficient training to the methods of investigation, observation and recording associated with the expedition aim.

Condition 7: *At least one practice expedition must be undertaken at each level of the programme, in the same mode of travel in a similar environment to the qualifying expedition.*

Some participants will need to undertake their practice and qualifying journeys in the same area to allow them to gain familiarity with the location and to feel more comfortable.

More than one practice expedition may be needed to help some teams take control of their qualifying expedition, so plan in time for this at the start of the section.

Success story

Valerie, a DofE Leader at St. Nicholas School in Chippenham, supported five participants who all had complex additional needs including autism and Down's syndrome to complete their expedition together. In preparation, the participants learnt key navigational skills including recognising the four main points of a compass.

The group focused on what equipment they would need and what they would need to pack in their rucksack. By visiting camping shops and taking pictures of the items they would need, the group could pack their rucksacks independently.

As most of the participants had never slept in a tent before, the group camped in the grounds of a house. This helped them feel comfortable with camping and was great preparation for their qualifying expedition. The group could camp in expedition conditions along a towpath. The wide range of abilities helped the participants develop their teamwork and communication skills and all went on to achieve their Bronze Awards.

Condition 8: *The team must plan and organise the expedition.*

Teams should plan their own routes and submit a route plan in an appropriate format for the participant's use. Navigation can be undertaken by various methods such as picture route cards, depicting landmarks and signs on laminated cards or smiley faces instead of OS maps. These can also be used alongside OS maps. Allow all members of the team to have access to the navigation tool.

The route must take into account the needs of all the participants, for example having accessible paths in case of emergency medical needs.

Condition 9: *Assessment must be by an approved Accredited Assessor.*

The Assessor must be notified if the team includes participants who have additional needs and must be aware of any approved variations before the expedition takes place.

Conditions 10-13: *Who, the level of assessment and how many in a team.*

All DofE teams must comprise between four and seven young people (eight for some tandem modes of travel). The DofE understands that forming teams specifically for young people with additional needs can be difficult and sometimes levels and abilities need to

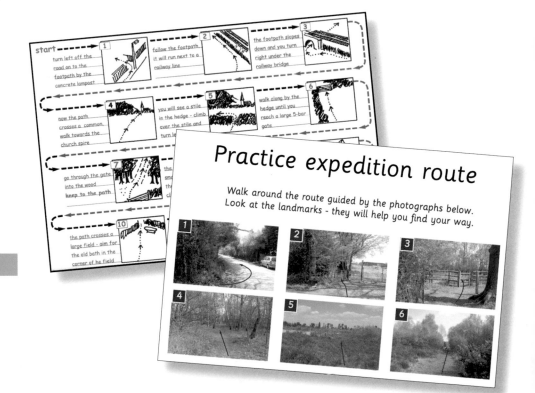

be mixed. This may also be the case for inclusive expeditions. Advice and support on this should be sought from the DofE Regional/Country Office.

Condition 14: *Accommodation should be by camping.*

Where camping is not possible and after discussion and agreement with the Licensed Organisation, other basic accommodation such as barns, bothies, mountain huts, or narrowboats may be used.

Take into account individual needs when considering which type of accommodation to use. For example camp beds sit higher off the ground so might be useful for young people who use wheelchairs.

Frame tents or large dome tents may provide a suitable introduction to camping and, for some, may be essential during the qualifying expedition.

Teams may also be allowed to use the same campsite for more than one night if necessary, either for their aim or because of the additional needs of the participants. Teams still need to travel to and from the campsite as part of their journeying, preferably using a clover leaf pattern of different routes.

Condition 15: *The expedition must be of the correct duration.*

All participants must complete an expedition of the required minimum duration.

Condition 16: *The expedition should normally take place between the end of March and the end of October.*

Plan the expedition for a time of year which will best suit the team and give them the best chance of success and enjoyment. This can be particularly important for participants with medical conditions which can be exacerbated by the weather.

Condition 17: *The expedition should take place in the recommended environment.*

All participants should follow the guidance on expedition recommended environments, set out in Chapters 2 & 5.1.

Environments at all levels have numerous tracks, bridleways, towpaths and disused railway lines that can be used, many are gradient free. At Gold level, all participants should aim for their expedition to take place in wild country. If this is not possible then open country is acceptable, agree this in advance with the Licensed Organisation and DofE Regional/Country Office.

Most areas of wild country have accessible tracts of level terrain on valley floors, moorlands or plateaus that can be used.

Some large country parks or private estates may also be used with the land owner's permission, providing an enclosed and remote area to explore safely.

Condition 18: *The expedition must meet the minimum hours of planned activity.*

TOP TIP...

Have patience and understanding as tasks can take much longer than anticipated. Try not to hurry or help participants too much, they can do it for themselves and the benefits are far greater.

Deborah Pierce,
Additional Needs Co-ordinator,
DofE Head Office

TOP TIP...

Use cooking as the expedition aim. Participants who cannot journey far could spend time preparing a multi course meal at their lunch stop, as part of their planned activity time. The team can prepare recipe cards with instructions to help. The Assessor to be the taster. This can keep everyone active, without simply having long rests.

Annabel Davies, DofE Supervisor,
Clapton Girls Academy,
Hackney.

Condition 19: *A substantial meal should be cooked and eaten by the participants each day.*

Participants need to cook and eat an appropriate meal each day (except the last expedition day). For some participants this may require close supervision. Young people's dietary needs, meal time routines and medication must be taken into account.

Condition 20: *A presentation must be prepared and delivered after the expedition.*

Give early attention to the aim and preparation of the presentation. There is a rich variety of presentation styles and techniques, ranging from poetry to film, painting to dance, written to oral, which are available to participants thus enabling them all to give an interesting and creative account of their expedition. See Chapter 11 for more advice, guidance and suggestions on presentations.

Blind determination

"Like all kids with a love for sport and adventure, I was devastated at around 16, when, through failing sight, all that had to pretty well stop!

Some 30 years on I was introduced to my first guide dog and oh how life suddenly changed, once again. My love for running took me into the history books in 2008, by becoming the first and only blind person in the world to run seven marathons in seven days, over seven continents.

Talking to people who dream of adventure they seem to look at the negative. But I always feel, regardless of being blind, disabled or able bodied, simply think of the adventure.

The excitement of the start, plotting and organising, what adventures and excitement awaits me, that is what spurs me on, the quiet confident belief in yourself and the fact that you believe you can do it.

For me it is a combination of body and mind working together. But I always say the hardest thing of all is stepping through your front door and going for it, it's so easy to say you'll do it tomorrow and sit down again.

What keeps me going and focused is the thought of finishing! But we all need something special in our armoury and for me it's the family.

With the 7 marathons, I had a photo of the family hanging on my chain; with the TOP2TOE event I had a photo of the family as the lens of my watch, it was so easy to pull strength from them, I know they wanted success for me and that thought alone worked for me."

Dave Heeley

Dave is the first blind person in the world to have completed the ultimate endurance challenge: seven marathons in seven days on seven continents.

What *The Handbook for DofE Leaders* says...

The DofE encourages participants at all levels to be adventurous and consider modes of travel of their expedition other than going on foot. Changing modes of travel as they progress from level to level can add interest and broaden horizons while being part of the challenge of progression.

Other modes of travel for DofE groups are cycling, canoe or kayak, rowing, horseback and sailing including dinghies, yachts or multihull and sail training vessels. However groups have also completed expeditions on other modes including camels, dog sled and skis.

Expeditions must be completed by the participants' own physical efforts with minimal external intervention and without motorised assistance.

Chapter 13.1
Cycling expeditions

What *The Handbook for DofE Leaders* says...

Cycle expeditions must meet all the DofE requirements and sectional conditions of DofE land based expeditions.

This includes the recommended areas and the need for isolation.

Cycle expeditions are a great and accessible alternative mode of travel for teams at all levels of the DofE. They offer a new perspective to DofE teams, travelling considerable distances and seeing much more of the countryside.

Depending on the team's expedition aim and their resources, expeditions can be carried out on road touring bikes using surfaced roads, hand powered bikes on appropriate surfaces or mountain bikes on bridleways or tracks,

Planning the expedition

As with all DofE expeditions the planning begins with the aim. Once cycling is chosen as the mode of travel all the normal requirements for the investigation and recommended environments apply. See Chapters 2 and 5.1.

Cycle expeditions may make more use of long distance cycle routes than expeditions on foot, but this use must still form only part of the expedition route, which participants create for themselves. Many teams who complete Bronze level on cycle will go on to complete all their DofE expeditions on cycle.

For a group based in the south of the UK their cycle expeditions through the levels may be:

- **Bronze:** The New Forest.
- **Silver:** Salisbury Plain or The Ridgeway.
- **Gold:** Dartmoor or Mid Wales

Linked into the above could be training and practices undertaken in the North and South Downs and a Gold practice on Exmoor.

For a group based further north it may be:

- **Bronze:** Some areas around low levels of the coast to coast route.
- **Silver:** Dalby Forest, North Yorkshire or the Tissington Trail in the Peaks.
- **Gold:** Cheviot Hills, Pennines or Isle of Man.

Linked into the above could be training and practices undertaken in the Yorkshire Wolds and Kielder Forest.

Other suggested areas may be Coed y Brenin, Afan Forest Park, Galloway Hills, Glentrool, 7 Stanes in Southern Scotland and trails in France and Holland. Some busy areas like the Lake District and Peak District may have too high a footfall for effective DofE cycle expeditions. Talk to experienced cyclists to find other interesting cycle areas.

Expedition routes should involve minor roads, lanes, tracks and bridleways. Teams need to avoid more major roads and towns. Many routes will pass though villages and hamlets but teams should plan their rests in more isolated areas.

Hours of planned activity and distance advice

Working out the speed of travel is key to successful expeditions and this should come from teams undertaking training and practice expeditions together.

When teams start to plan their route they should begin by assuming that they will travel for all of the required hours of planned activity, then deduct time for lunch, rests and project work.

It may be that additional activity time will be needed above the minimum DofE requirement in order to achieve the aim. For each team, the combination of this project and journeying will create a unique expedition.

The distance covered by a team will vary greatly depending on the factors influencing their speed. Their age, fitness, equipment, wind strength, project and location; whether the route

is on or off road, or mixed terrain and the condition or steepness of the trail will all have an effect.

A more complex route may require more stops for map reading. Equally, some aims will require frequent stops, while others may require fewer but longer stops.

The speed of teams will vary considerably, but an average team might travel:
- between 12-15km per hour or 7-9 mph on surfaced roads or
- between 6.5-8km per hour or 4-5 mph on tracks and trails.

As a rule of thumb 1 km/mile travelled on an unsurfaced bridleway or track is roughly the equivalent effort to 2 km/miles on surfaced roads. It is acceptable for cycle teams to climb more than 500m in a single day to achieve their aim.

Every team is different and the nature of their aim and personal situation means that it is hard to give estimates of common distances. However, to help Supervisors it is estimated that a team with an appropriate project and adequate breaks will normally achieve total distances of around:

	Hard surface	Off road
Bronze:	105 km/65 miles	53 km/33 miles
Silver:	177 km/110 miles	89 km/55 miles
Gold:	240 km/150 miles	120 km/75 miles

Some teams may travel much further, while others may put more time into their project. Whatever they do, it must be an appropriate challenge for them.

Cycle computers and sports trackers can be a good way to monitor average speeds on practices, to help with the planning for the final expedition. Many can create a mapping file which can be used as evidence for the section.

Cycle expeditions over large distances require careful planning and route cards should be practical and succinct. Teams may need to use either or both 1:25 000 and 1:50 000 maps depending on the expedition aim, although 1:50 000 is often sufficient.

Training

All the major cycling organisations/ bodies aim to support cyclists to have a good standard of competence and enjoy their activity, avoiding injuries or confrontations with others.

Several offer qualifications to Supervisors and participants for both on and off road cycling. Information can be found online.

Participants need to complete three areas of training:

1. The appropriate compulsory Expedition Training Framework for all DofE expeditions.
2. The three levels of The National Standard for Cycle Training, or an equivalent level of competence, to gain basic skills and cycle maintenance experience.
3. Additional skills specific to the expedition area, especially if outside the UK.

TOP TIP...

Tulip route cards, with a bit of thought, can be an effective way of navigating on bikes. Search online for examples and templates.

Aled Davies,
Mid Wales DofE Assessor
Network Co-ordinator

Cycle teams are governed by the Highway Code and must be aware of the Countryside Code and Mountain Bike Code.

Teams must follow all access laws and requirements. It is the responsibility of the team and Supervisor to be aware of relevant access issues which should be investigated at the planning stage.

Assessor Network Co-ordinators can provide up to date local information for wild country areas in the UK. Expedition Training Framework documents and cycle codes are available at **www.DofE.org/expedition**.

Training sessions and day rides give the Supervisor the opportunity to support participants to continue to develop their skills, improve fitness, solve mechanical problems and really enjoy the experience.

Licensed Organisations usually require Supervisors and trainers to have recognised outdoor and cycle qualifications to deliver the training standards and give enthusiasm and expertise to their team.

Fitness

Cycling expeditions can be demanding, using muscles not usually used in this way for prolonged periods. A planned fitness programme which becomes progressively more demanding is essential.

It cannot be stressed enough that the best training for long distance cycling is long distance cycling, and it should always be a mix of what the expedition will require; on and off road, hill climbing and load carrying. Participants should choose a selection of 10-25 mile training sessions (or rides), to complete with company or on their own and can complement these with gym fitness sessions.

Equipment

Personal and expedition equipment is the same for all expeditions and only some specific additional equipment, which can often be borrowed, is needed for cycle expeditions.

The bicycle

The cycle needs to be the right size and shape for the rider. Cost is usually what dictates which cycle is used, but use the best one that can be bought, hired or borrowed, either new or second hand. Shop around, ask for a discount as a DofE participant and look for adverts from people giving up the activity.

A good quality frame is expensive but it can be worth it as it responds to both the rider and the road.

Participants should research cycle parts to help them understand their equipment and value it. Invest in, and get used to using, a good quality saddle, available for males and females and which are designed to minimise the numbness of prolonged riding.

Tyre liners, which sit between the inner tube and tyre, provide an extra level of protection against sharp objects. Tyres should have puncture guards that deform around penetrating objects and push them out.

Getting the cycle to the expedition area may need some careful planning, particularly at Gold level or if travelling outside of the UK. It is usually easy to borrow cycle carriers for vehicles, if the team does not already have one. If travelling by train, check the booking space and company policy in advance. Remember that cycling to the start of the expedition cannot be included as part of the expedition.

Clothing

To find the right clothing do some research, talk to other cyclists and clubs and visit a cycle shop to see, feel and try the different options. However, participants don't always need the best kit, particularly at Bronze level. Encourage participants to borrow or use kit and clothes they already have. Outlined below is some advice on clothing:

- **Helmets:** DofE policy is that participants must always wear helmets whilst cycling. Ensure that these are comfortable (so they get used), secure, the right size and conform to safety standards.
- **Hats:** Specialist under helmet hats are available to help with comfort and warmth.
- **Waterproofs:** Jackets and trousers need to be close fitting and the jacket needs to be a bright colour/high visibility. Trousers should have a high back and be cut for cycling.
- **Windproof jackets, jerseys and base layers:** Warmth, flexibility and dryness at body layer are essential.
- **Shorts and trousers:** Choose items that are very comfortable over long distances and are cut and padded for cycling.
- **Gloves:** These essential items need to be both wind and waterproof with cushioning or padding.
- **A change of clothes:** at the campsite will be needed. If possible use this time to dry and air the cycling kit.

Footwear

Trail/touring shoes with stiffer soles for power and a recessed cleat for more comfortable walking when required, are ideal for DofE expeditions, particularly on harder surfaces and at Gold level expeditions.

Cleats allow the rider to pull on the pedals as well as push, greatly increasing cycle efficiency.

Multi-sports shoes (or even trainers) are fine for most shorter cycle expeditions. Many have dual density mid-soles for cycling efficiency and the need to do any walking or pushing up steep hills. These can be used with toe clips, but are not recommended for the more challenging, off-road expeditions.

Panniers (waterproofed) and cycle trailers

Food and equipment must be carried in panniers, not on participants' backs. A small day sack may be used for light items on training day rides.

The capacity of panniers may well be less than the average rucksack, so teams will need to think about bulk, size and weight of all food and equipment. Panniers on racks over the rear wheel with a joint capacity of 40 litres should be sufficient for DofE expeditions; others can be added to the handlebars and front wheel.

Panniers need to be securely and correctly fitted to the bike. Check frames and panniers are compatible before spending money.

Ensure that any straps and hooks are in good condition and any equipment attached to the top of the rack, such as tents or sleeping bags, are secure, stable and make a safe load. Ensure that all kit can be kept dry.

Similar to expeditions on foot, the weight of equipment is a handicap and must be reduced as much as possible. Cycles may need to be lifted over obstacles, pushed up steep hills or through deep mud.

Some teams like to use cycle trailers to increase their load bearing capacity. The same good practice advice for panniers generally applies to cycle trailers, and groups must get used to cycling with them.

TOP TIP...

Bar bags on handlebars are really useful to attach the map to, so you can see it without getting off.

Carol Tavemer,
DofE Award Facilitator,
Isle of Wight

General equipment

Make sure the cycle is in a suitable condition and fitted out ready for the expedition. It is disruptive and frustrating to keep stopping for repairs and it can undermine the enjoyment of the expedition. Participants will need the skills and repair kit/parts to be able

to maintain their cycles throughout their expedition and remain self sufficient.

Cycle clubs and shops can help with training sessions, but participants may need to be inventive to solve some problems.

A repair kit to carry out running repairs should include:
- Puncture outfit, spare valve, spare inner tube, tyre levers and pump.
- Spare brake blocks and brake cables.
- Spare gear cables.
- A chain tool.
- Two or three spare spokes and a spoke key.
- Spanners, allen keys, pliers and screwdrivers necessary for the above.
- Some rag and a very small plastic container of a liquid detergent.
- A bag of odd nuts, bolts, washers, screws, cable/zip ties, tape and some thin wire.
- It is helpful for Supervisors to carry spare wheels.
- Some items will be team based, e.g. spanner set, whereas others will need to be taken by each participant, e.g. inner tubes.

TOP TIP...

Cycles and their parts are mobile and easy to steal so a locking system is essential. Ask at campsites or farms if there is a safe storage area that can be used for cycles. Use a heavy duty plastic bag as a cover for the saddle if unable to keep the cycle undercover at night.

Alan Surtees,
DofE Expedition Advisory Panel

Safety

Through training and practice expeditions every team member must be fully competent in cycling with a fully loaded cycle. The balance of the panniers must be even and the centre of gravity kept low. The rack must be securely fitted and any items securely strapped on so nothing can fall off.

Maintenance

Participants will need to be trained through hands on experience to maintain their cycle.

All team members need to be able to:
- Keep the bike clean and oiled.
- Mend a puncture including removing and replacing the rear wheel.
- Adjust and replace brake blocks and a worn brake cable.
- Adjust the chain tension and repair a broken chain.
- Adjust derailleur gears.
- Undertake pannier and rack repairs.
- Remove and replace a broken spoke.

Complete a check of the cycle and its parts before departure to identify any areas of wear.

Participants must take care on all roads and tracks for vehicles and other users, particularly on narrow country roads and lanes with blind corners and bends.

Riding in a group is very different to cycling alone. Teams should ride in single file and keep at least two bike lengths apart, extending to 30 metres when descending hills or in difficult terrain.

The experience and thrill of off-road cycling must be set against respecting the surfaces used which can often be unstable with odd cambers, potholes, tyre grooves, mud and gravel. Riders should be aware of, and avoid, the deep grooves left in tracks by 4x4 and agricultural vehicles. Training in dealing with, and cleaning out cuts and grazes is essential.

Be aware of roaming animals, for example sheep, ponies, cattle and deer, as accidents involving them can have serious consequences. Remember that walkers often have dogs with them.

The weather in the UK is very changeable and teams must be prepared for poor visibility by wearing brightly coloured tops and having reflector strips on their panniers. Additionally, every bike must have adequate lighting with spares carried.

TOP TIP...

Train' different team members of the expedition team to high levels for different areas of maintenance – brakes, gears and so on.

Chris Floyd,
DofE Expedition
Advisory Panel

Responsible cycling and code of behaviour

Cycling, particularly off-road cycling, can conflict with other countryside users and all DofE participants have a responsibility to maintain the good reputation of the DofE, always being courteous and considerate by:

- Approaching other users carefully and letting them know riders are approaching. Slow down and give audible warning while still some distance away. If necessary, stop and dismount.
- Riding slowly on crowded trails.
- Passing others with care and courtesy.
- Sharing the track with others; bikers should give way to walkers and horses.

- Changing the route if the trail is closed or heavily muddy.
- Staying on the route and trying not to create extra width.
- Never having a confrontation with other users or doing any stunts and tricks while cycling. All of these are strictly against DofE safety conditions.

Supervision and assessment

Cycle expeditions are supervised and assessed in the same way as all other expeditions. See Chapters 8 and 10.

Due to the long distances involved, both the Assessor and Supervisor need to carefully plan their roles and routes during the expedition.

The Supervisor must be an experienced and appropriately qualified cyclist, approved by the Licensed Organisation and/or Approved Activity Provider.

The Supervisor must bring not only technical competence but also equipment skills, team management and consideration for the environment, giving confidence to the team and fostering success and enjoyment.

Whilst the Assessor does not have to have cycling experience, it can add positively to the expedition experience for the participants if they do.

Many local Assessor groups and DofE Assessor Networks will have cycling enthusiasts with excellent local knowledge who can help participants get the most out of their expedition.

Cycling – the multi-skill sport

Cycling is the best form of transport by far, it gives you the freedom to explore in the open fresh air.

With the ability to cover much greater distances than by foot from a very young age, cycling is often our first experience of true independence.

It is also the only mode of land transport that enhances fitness, can be done from aged 8-80 and causes almost zero pollution.

It is quite simply a wonderful skill to learn and way to get around and explore. And remember that practice and time is all it takes to perfect a skill like cycling.

If you decide you want to cycle for your expedition, write up a training schedule with details like distances and different terrains covered; it will help you track your progress and see how far you have come when you've achieved your Award.

It can be easy to forget how hard you have worked and it's something you can look back on and feel proud that you have stuck with and achieved your goal.

Chris Boardman MBE

Chris is an Olympic cycling champion winning Gold in the 400m pursuit in Barcelona, 1992, and is now Director of Coaching for the world leading British Cycling's Olympic programmes and Head of Research and Development for the British Olympic Cycling Team

Chapter 13.2
Horseback expeditions

What *The Handbook for DofE Leaders* says...

Horseback expeditions must meet all the DofE requirements and sectional conditions of DofE land based expeditions. This includes the recommended areas and the need for isolation.

There are additional guidance and approaches set out in this guide that DofE teams need to follow.

Possibly the most rewarding mode of travel, horseback expeditions are a unique challenge for DofE participants and can provide a sense of adventure unlike any other. It is a mode of travel which requires careful planning to ensure success and to overcome some of the barriers that participants will come across.

Riding expeditions should only be undertaken by participants who regularly ride in rural areas, and who are competent in the skills set out in the Training framework for horseback expeditions approved by the British Horse Society.

Horses and horse care

Horses are creatures of habit with their own personalities. They do not always like new surroundings, are as affected by weather conditions as much as their riders and, as such, can express their discomfort in forceful ways.

Any horse should be accustomed to the other horses in the group or else there can be problems when being stabled or turned out at the end of the day.

Turning horses out to graze in corrals created with electric fencing to separate them is a suitable and safe alternative to stabling, reducing the risk of injury from kicks or bites.

It is often difficult and expensive to hire suitable horses. Many stables are not suitably insured or are reluctant for their horses to be stabled away from their home base and will require participants to provide insurance.

Horses and ponies need to be prepared and conditioned for the demands, fitness and duration of DofE expeditions as thoroughly as their riders. At Bronze level a participant's own horse or pony may need little preparation other than practice in load-carrying.

At Silver level, and especially at Gold level, where expeditions are several days long and take place in open or wild country, horses must be very fit, suitable for, and used to, meeting the demands made by the terrain involved in the long journey.

A fitness and feeding plan will usually be needed to help prepare the horses. Horses should be shod within two weeks before the start of the expedition.

Teams should aim to use the same horse throughout the expedition as this is a partnership between horse and rider. However, with the agreement of the Supervisor and Assessor, substitute horses may be permitted if the original mount sustains an unforeseeable injury/ ailment. The replacement will need to have completed appropriate fitness training and preparation.

A person knowledgeable in working with horses should ensure that the horses are fit before the team sets out and after the expedition has ended. At the beginning and end of each day participants should ensure that their horses are sound and fit enough to continue with the expedition and a daily check by a knowledgeable adult is recommended.

Some equipment may be pre-positioned, see page 242 for details.

Planning the expedition

As with all expeditions, the planning begins with the aim. Once horseback is chosen as the mode of travel, all the normal requirements for the investigation and recommended environments apply. See Chapters 2 and 5.1.

As vehicles pose the greatest danger on horseback expeditions, teams should avoid the use of surfaced roads as much as possible and only use open country, bridleways and tracks.

Hours of planned activity and distance advice

When teams start to plan their route they should begin by assuming that they will travel for all the required hours of planned activity, then deduct time for lunch, rests and project work. It may be that additional activity time will be needed above the minimum DofE requirement in order to achieve the aim.

For each team, the combination of this project and journeying will create a unique expedition. Time spent travelling to the team's expedition start point cannot count towards hours of planned activity.

It takes time to prepare horses for travel, feeding, tacking up and so on. More time is also needed at the end of the day's journey compared with other modes of travel. At Bronze level up to an hour of the minimum planned activity time can be allocated to do this and up to two hours at Silver and Gold levels. The minimum hours of journeying at each level must still be achieved (three at Bronze, three and a half at Silver and four at Gold).

Teams undertaking horseback expeditions should choose an aim which is achievable without using too much planned activity time during the day, as this will largely be taken up with journeying and caring for the horses.

The speed of teams will vary considerably due to the rider, horse, weather, route, aim and project. As a rough guide for planning, an average team might travel at 4km an hour.

Teams should also plan 15-minute breaks every two hours, plus 30 minutes to one hour for lunch. Bronze teams may often only average 3kmph. Speed varies greatly from team to team so they should use their practice journeys as a guide to their speed over ground.

Fit horses carrying saddlebags and riders with day-sacks will travel at 4–5kmph on good tracks but will probably only average 3kmph across rough ground and moorland. Most of the route will be completed at walk with occasional trotting. Cantering is discouraged whilst carrying loads.

An average team at each level might travel:

■ **Bronze:** 24-32km (15-20 miles)
■ **Silver:** 60-75 km (37-46 miles)
■ **Gold:** 80km-100km (50-62 miles)

Reconnoitring

Whilst at Silver and Gold levels the expedition environment must be unfamiliar to the participants, a limited amount of reconnoitring may take place to ensure that tracks and bridleways can be negotiated on horseback.

If routes are obstructed this can result in lengthy route changes and may force teams onto roads. The local BHS bridleways representative or the local council rights of way officer can often look at the route and warn of any known obstructions.

Participants should assess the chosen route before setting out, including risk assessing any small lanes and road or rail crossings.

> **TOP TIP...**
> For horseback expeditions it is essential to start early in the day to ensure teams have plenty of spare daylight in case things don't go according to plan. There is still a great deal to do once teams get into camp.
> Mary Harper,
> DofE Manager,
> Dorset

Campsites

Careful route planning is needed to identify campsites and landowners who can provide for both the needs of horses (water, secure pasture or stabling) and participants. Ask if establishments require the horses to be in possession of a current vaccination certificate.

Teams still need to ensure campsites are sufficiently separated to allow for appropriate hours of journeying. Bivouacking in a hay loft or barn is permitted, but extreme care must be taken while cooking.

> **TOP TIP...**
> If in doubt, or for more local information, contact the relevant Expedition Assessor Network Co-ordinator for the wild country area.
> Paul Smith,
> DofE Assessor,
> Yorkshire Dales & Pennines
> and North York Moors.

Training

Participants should regularly ride in rural areas and must complete the following three areas of training. This should be delivered by an appropriately qualified or experienced person approved by the Licensed Organisation or AAP:

1: The appropriate level of the DofE Expedition Training Framework.

2: The skills set out in the DofE Training framework for horseback expeditions, approved by the British Horse Society, including training in riding and road safety to a standard the supervisor is satisfied with. The DofE recommends participants complete the BHS Riding and Road Safety Test or the Pony Club Road Rider test or are trained to these standards.

3: Additional skills specific to the expedition area and country.

Horseback teams are governed by the Highway Code and must be aware of the Countryside Code.

Teams must follow all access laws and requirements. It is the responsibility of the team and Supervisor to be aware of relevant access issues which should be investigated at the planning stage. Assessor Network Co-ordinators can provide up to date local information for wild country areas in the UK.

Expedition Training Framework documents and the complete DofE training framework for horseback expeditions are all available at **www.DofE.org/expedition**.

All participants must be competent in ensuring the well-being of the horse for the full duration of the expedition without direct staff supervision or intervention.

All participants must be able to recognise difficult and dangerous going and know the action to be taken in the event of an accident to horse or rider. First aid training must include treatment of an unconscious casualty and head injuries.

Practice expeditions

Both rider and animal must be prepared for the challenge of the qualifying expedition. It is likely that groups will complete more than one practice expedition, for example one on foot and one on horseback. This helps to ensure that they are competent and confident in the skills needed for the DofE level and the demands of the expedition area, particularly if in wild country.

The need for these practices will depend on the experience of both the participants and the horses. These practices may be in the same area each time.

Equipment

Pre-positioned equipment

Some teams set out to be entirely self-sufficient, using very lightweight and minimal equipment and such efforts should always be commended. However, horses can only carry so much weight, both rider and equipment. Horseback teams may pre-position some of their equipment which is over the load-bearing capacity of the animal on expedition.

For expeditions in remote areas, or at Gold level, participants should be encouraged to carry as much as they can safely manage. This is an expedition, not a series of day rides with overnight stops.

Pre-positioned equipment must be of the same lightweight type that would have been used if travelling on foot. Participant camping equipment and food may be pre-positioned at campsites, but emergency equipment, food for the day and sleeping bags must always be carried.

Participants' emergency equipment, listed on the DofE website and items associated with the essential well-being of the horse must be carried each day.

These include:
- Numnah, head collar and rope.
- Hoof pick.
- First aid equipment for the horse which should include antiseptic cream or powder, cotton wool and a leg bandage.
- Fly repellent.
- Bailer twine to tie up gates, repair bridle etc.
- A penknife or pocket tool.

If within the horses' load-bearing capacity, teams should take a sleeping bag and a lightweight tent as additional emergency equipment.

This equipment should be carried in saddlebags and/or a small, lightweight day-sack. Day sacks can rub and cause sweating and, if used, they must be small so as not to bump on the back of the saddle or impede the rider. Day sacks must be secured with a waistband and not have a frame. A small hip bag is useful for bits and pieces needed during the day.

Arrangements for watering, especially in hot weather, should be made with the Supervisor as suitable drinking troughs/streams may not always be available. A large water container and bucket is easily carried in the back of a car.

Equipment which may be pre-positioned at rest stops and campsites include:
- Fodder and haynets.
- Grooming tools, sponges/towels, sweatsheets, rugs, spare numnahs and girths.
- Water and feeding buckets.
- Camping equipment. Lightweight equipment to allow teams to cook and camp in the usual two or three person units.
- Food for the rest of the expedition.
- Corralling equipment and mucking out tools may also be needed.

Any pre-positioning of equipment will require the involvement of the Supervisor, staff or parent but this must not extend beyond the delivery of the equipment and the usual duties of remote supervision.

Clothing and footwear

Every participant must wear a hard hat with a safety strap at all times when riding, approved to the current BSI safety standard. Normal expedition and riding clothing can be used, as long as it is appropriate for the expedition area and conforms to current good practice.

All participants should carry or wear riding gloves. Footwear must be appropriate to ride in. Footwear, the hard hat and clothes should be checked by the team's Supervisor.

Many participants find a sheepskin 'seat-saver' to go over the saddle increases their comfort level.

The usual outdoor good practice of using layers of clothing, which may be removed or added to as weather conditions and body warmth dictate, should be followed.

Waterproof outer clothing such as a cagoule may be worn, but should not impede the vision, hearing or control of the horse, and should not flap in the wind, as this could startle the horse.

Safety note

- Participants should undo the waistbands and chest harnesses on day sacks when passing under low trees or crossing water.
- Nothing solid, such as a Trangia stove or a compressed sleeping bag in a stuff sack, should be carried in the day sack as falling onto it from a height could cause serious injury.
- Saddlebags may need to be removed to pass safely through narrow gates.

- A mobile phone should be carried within the team, as in the event of a fall of horse or rider serious injuries may be sustained.

Map reading

Using a map while in the saddle can be difficult, especially if the map needs to be spread out. Horses may be startled if they see maps flapping about in their peripheral vision.

As well as the usual route card, horseback teams should create an itinerary allowing them to follow the route without having to dismount to read the full map, which every team must still carry. Software like eDofE Mapping allows A4 route sections to be printed, which can then be laminated.

TOP TIP...

Remember to laminate the group's route cards to ensure they last the expedition – safety info and phone numbers can also be added.

Kellie Ross,
DofE Development Worker,
Leicestershire.

Supervision and assessment

Horseback expeditions are supervised and assessed in the same way as all other land based expeditions. See Chapters 8 and 10. The Supervisor must be an appropriately qualified and experienced person approved by the Licensed Organisation or AAP. The Supervisor must bring not only technical competence but also equipment skills, team management and consideration for the environment. They should give confidence to the team and foster success and enjoyment.

Either the Supervisor, or the Supervisor working with another appropriately qualified and experienced person, must be able to take responsibility for the safety, care and welfare of the horses for the duration of the expedition. They will also advise on the pre-positioning of equipment if required and assess the horses before and after the expedition.

Supervisors should use normal remote supervision methods, meeting the team at checkpoints en-route.

As part of effective remote supervision, the teams may be more closely supervised for parts of the journey where there are specific hazards such as water crossings or fast or 'blind' road crossings. This close supervision must be kept to a minimum.

When horses are involved, the DofE recommends that adult assistance is on hand at night. B&Bs attached to farms work well, allowing the Supervisor and staff to be out of the way but easily contactable if needed.

A horse box or trailer, placed in a strategic location, may help in recovering a horse if it should go lame, lose a shoe or require veterinary care. Participants should know the location and telephone number of the local vet or blacksmith, as it may be possible for a blacksmith to re-shoe a horse or a vet to treat a minor injury at the campsite.

Whilst the Assessor does not have to have riding experience, it can add positively to the expedition experience for the participants if they do. Many local assessor groups and DofE Assessor Networks will have riders with excellent local knowledge, who can help participants get the most out of their expedition. The Assessor role has no responsibility for the care of the horses.

The positive outcomes and sense of achievement for all involved on successful completion are immensely rewarding.

The DofE Expedition Guide

A magnificent way to travel

For the past few years I have been on an amazing expedition on horseback, travelling from Beijing to London in between the Olympic Games.

I have found travelling by horse gives you such fantastic benefits; like the opportunity to explore your surroundings up close but at the same time, to cover distances impossible by foot.

You don't have to go as far as China either! Everyone has a chance to be a modern day explorer, and a DofE expedition is a great way to begin.

If going on horseback though, it is incredibly important to look after the horses on the expedition and make sure they are well fed and rested, especially when they are carrying all of the equipment as well as the rider.

Make sure both the rider and the horse are well trained and prepared. Participants should aim to have the same respect for the horses as they would the rest of their team and they will provide them with the most magnificent way to travel and explore.

Meghan Lewis

Meghan is the first person on record to ride on horseback the entire distance from one end of the Great Wall of China to the other. Over four years she rode 8,000 miles from Beijing to London, The Long Ride, in between the Olympic Games, spanning nine countries and raising money for charity.

Chapter 13.3
Water expeditions - overview
and general considerations

What *The Handbook for DofE Leaders* says...

To facilitate and encourage these other modes of travel, the DofE provides specific advice to support their delivery.

Water based expeditions can give an entirely different perspective on journeying, immersing participants into a new environment and experience. The DofE encourages participants to take up a new mode of travel and the extra challenge of developing new skills is recognised by the DofE as part of the core outcomes of the section, rather than in addition to them.

Participants who have experience in watercraft can be ambitious in their aim and planning, developing these as they progress through the DofE levels. As with all expeditions, teams should create a challenge appropriate to their skills and experience.

It is more in keeping with the outcomes of the Expedition section for teams to travel unaccompanied and be self-sufficient on less demanding water with Supervisor visits. However, the DofE does also recognise the teamwork outcomes of expeditions on larger sail training vessels, where the presence of a Supervisor is mandatory.

Water expeditions provide an opportunity for those with mobility problems or who are less physically able or confident, to participate in a full and demanding expedition.

Water expeditions have the added advantage of causing no pollution or erosion of the river banks – and water does not wear out.

Successful water expeditions

The keys to success in water expeditions are a well-chosen aim, appropriate water, suitable craft and the right team members. Local access to suitable water and craft is the decisive factor, but there are also many open expeditions available all around the UK and beyond.

Select water within the team's capability

It is in the team's own interests to select water and craft which give an excellent chance of bringing the expedition to a successful conclusion. Select water which is suitable for the craft involved and well within the team's level of skill, so there is less chance of adverse weather or environmental conditions affecting the journey.

Participants must be able to train and carry out practice expeditions on water of a similar degree of difficulty, to gain experience of successfully dealing with any problems.

Alternative campsites and flexible start and finish times should be included in the expedition plan.

A paddle or rowing expedition on a Grade 1 or 2 river is less likely to be affected by the weather than a sailing expedition on an estuary but rivers are subjected to occasional flood conditions, even during the summer months.

Levels of wind may make journeying difficult or impossible for sailing. On exposed water, strong winds create the additional problem of rough water.

More time to plan and prepare

Teams and participants who have little or no experience in the chosen mode of travel and are having to learn new skills from scratch, will require more time to plan, train and prepare than for a normal expedition on foot.

It can help by planning to have the expedition at the end of the participant's DofE programme.

Participants undertaking a new mode of travel from that at their previous DofE level(s) may need to complete extra practice journeys.

Incorporate greater flexibility into planning and execution

Weather affects all expeditions on land or water, but the effect on water expeditions is greater and more immediate. The distance travelled by a team will vary depending on a headwind, no wind or a strong current, so it is essential to plan with this in mind.

Build alternative back-up dates into the planning

Weather or water conditions can bring a premature end to even the most carefully planned and flexible of water based expeditions. This is a reality that has to be accepted by all who engage in outdoor pursuits and particularly by DofE participants nearing their 25th birthday.

At least one back-up date should be arranged for all qualifying expeditions on inland water and multiple dates should be considered for estuaries, coastal waters and the open sea.

Involve experienced, adaptable Supervisors and Assessors

Use Supervisors and Assessors who can accommodate flexibility in distances and back-up dates. Local Supervisor pre-expedition checks are essential at all levels, especially where craft are then being trailored to distant locations.

Safety afloat

Water is a very exciting and challenging environment, but also a very demanding one. Water conditions and situations can change with frightening rapidity. Safety must always come first and be the vital consideration for everyone involved.

All participants undertaking water based expeditions must complete the Expedition Training Framework to at least the Silver level.

Particular attention should be paid to basic first aid concerned with:

- Resuscitation - participants should be able to administer resuscitation on and in the water, as well as adjacent to it;
- The ability to recognise and treat hypothermia/hyperthermia. Cold water and wet clothing drain heat from the body quickly and many craft are unsheltered which can lead to sun exposure.

The participants should be water confident and a buoyancy aid or lifejacket, suitable clothing and footwear must be worn

Supervisors need to be confident in the ability of participants to be able to get to safety in an emergency and follow agreed emergency procedures.

It is the responsibility of the Supervisor and Licensed Organisation/AAP to ensure these procedures and agreed levels of participant training, water confidence and competence are in place.

All participants must wear a buoyancy aid or life-jacket when on or close to the water as the unexpected can happen at any time. Specific exceptions for rowing are set out in the Training framework for boatwork at **www.DofE.org/expedition**.

Do not trust anyone else to check this equipment: test buoyancy aids and life-jackets to ensure they are sound. Buoyancy aids and lifejackets provide high visibility in the event of an emergency; brightly coloured headwear or upper body clothing can add to this visibility.

Suitable dress for a particular activity should be determined by current good practice. Clothing must give protection during the activity and when immersed in water, but not restrict movement. Wet suits are rarely needed as they only work when wet and can lead to participants overheating in normal conditions. Clothes made from modern synthetic materials can give very good insulation without absorbing as much water as the more traditional materials.

It is vital that participants protect their extremities against heat loss:

- **Head:** A thermal hat provides cheap and effective protection for the head, especially if used with a waterproof hood.
- **Hands:** Gloves or paddle mitts protect against blisters and the cold.
- **Feet:** Feet should always be protected; deck shoes, plastic sandals or old trainers are a necessity for all water expeditions to avoid cuts from broken glass, abrasions and the possibility of infection. Wet suit bootees are not satisfactory for river

expeditions, unless an over-shoe is also worn.
- **Sun protection:** Cover skin and use strong sun block, a sun hat and sunglasses as craft often have little shade. Light is reflected from the water and it is usually difficult to change posture or position, exposing the same area of skin for long periods.

A craft with adequate buoyancy

All craft should have sufficient built-in buoyancy to stay afloat and support all the occupants. If the buoyancy is not built into the craft, then it must be firmly secured. The buoyancy of all borrowed or hired craft should always be tested by the users. In the event of a capsize, the golden rule is 'always stay with the boat', it is much more visible than a head bobbing up and down in the water.

A practiced and predictable response to sudden immersion

Sudden immersion in cold water is very possible, so all training must take place with this in mind to prepare participants and help them overcome any fear of this. As well as individuals being prepared for

the shock of sudden immersion in cold water, the team must also be trained to give a practiced response in rescuing the participants and all of the kit, in the least possible time.

Suitable clothing may go a considerable way to reducing this shock.

Proficiency in capsize and recovery drills

Complete an intensive period of capsize and recovery drill, including outdoor swimming with and without a buoyancy aid. Participants are often reluctant to get into, the usually cold, UK water so drills are best learned at the end of the training session, so participants don't stay wet and cold.

Capsize should always bring about a predictable, automatic, reflex response to sudden immersion through drill practice, ensuring that participants are not overcome by panic. Capsize must be followed by recovery. Rescue and recovery techniques vary and participants must have the appropriate training and experience, including a 'man overboard' drill for vessels in open water.

Have the relevant water based qualifications or equivalent competence or experience

The Royal Yachting Association has qualifications and syllabuses for sailing and the British Canoe Union has qualifications and syllabuses for canoeing that might be undertaken by participants. Qualifications for canoeing are not necessary but all participants must have completed the Training framework core paddling skills.

For rowing expeditions, where there is no appropriate national qualification, participants must complete the Training framework for boatwork. All DofE Expedition Training Framework documents are available online at **www.DofE.org/expedition** The Sea Cadets, The Scout Association, Girlguiding UK and some Licensed Organisations have their own courses of instruction.

Training must be supported by experience. It is important that regular practice is spread over a period of time. It is all too easy for participants to give the appearance of competence and respond in the correct manner, yet still lack the depth of experience and confidence to cope with an emergency.

Being able to assist each other when in difficulty

The Expedition section is all about a team working together. Participants will have to depend on each other to succeed and develop the skills needed to be able to help other team members. As part of wider training, participants need to have the ability to use a throwline accurately, right an upturned boat and administer resuscitation. The skills related to the activity and to survival are vital, but they need to be supported by having a confidence in each other, developed through shared training and practices as a team.

Train for an expedition – not just the technical skills

Training should focus on the completion of a journey on water, not just mastering technical skills for handling a particular craft. Developing an awareness of the environment, surroundings, potential threats and unexpected hazards is essential.

Participants need to be aware of dangers including Weil's disease (leptospirosis), blue-green algae and water pollution. As good practice, all participants should ensure that any open cuts are protected by adhesive waterproof dressings, and wash their hands before eating. Participants who have been properly trained by knowledgeable and experienced instructors are in no greater danger than those engaged in land expeditions.

Participants canoeing, sailing and rowing on rivers and canals should use the standard approach to navigation set out in EX[2]. Only when tidal waters, estuaries and coastal waters are being used is it necessary to use charts and change to marine navigation.

Mobile phones

Mobile phones can provide 'ship to shore' communication between participants and supervisors. Equipment should be tested in the area of the expedition prior to the qualifying expedition and be protected from immersion in the water. For more detailed information on mobile phones, refer to Chapter 9.

The DofE Expedition Guide

"Sailing and rowing expeditions rock!"

I was 14 when I started my DofE programme at school and I haven't looked back since. Completing my expedition spurred me on to take my passion for adventuring and turn it into a career. For the last ten years my job title has been 'Professional Adventurer' and has driven me to row solo across the Atlantic, sail around Antarctica, canoe the Yukon, dragonboat the English Channel, surf kayak in the Indian Ocean and many other challenges. The Atlantic row, in particular, caused me to face some of the toughest moments of my life, in some of the most horrendous conditions, but because I was doing what I loved and following my passion, it helped get me through the lows.

I had no rowing experience before I set out to row the Atlantic and had not sailed before taking on the might of the Southern Ocean! As with all expeditions, with the right training and preparation anything is possible. So if you want to avoid carrying a heavy rucksack and walking in wet boots then rowing or sailing might be for you! They let you travel greater distances and see your surroundings completely differently.

I can't promise it will always be easy, but it will be worth it. When we push ourselves outside our comfort zones those life-changing moments tend to happen. Battling waves as big as houses during my ocean crossings has taught me how to handle incredibly tough situations. Conversely, on the calm days, the peace and tranquillity of travelling by boat and harnessing the power of nature to propel you is truly awe-inspiring. Just remember to 'choose your attitude' no matter what the expedition throws at you, because that is the one thing you will always have a choice about. But make sure it's a positive one because negative attitudes are banned from the boat!

Debra Searle MBE

DofE Trustee and Gold Award holder Debra completed a solo row across the Atlantic (3,300 miles) when she spent three and a half months alone at sea. Since then, amongst other things, she has completed the longest canoe race in the world and sailed around Antarctica, as well as presenting a number of TV programmes.

What *The Handbook for DofE Leaders* says...

Paddle and rowing expeditions must meet all the DofE requirements and sectional conditions of DofE expeditions.

There are additional approaches and guidance advice which must be followed in addition to the usual requirements.

Paddle and rowing expeditions are an increasingly popular alternative to walking. They offer a wide range of varying environments and craft where participants can develop their skills, both personally and as a member of a team.

The expedition could be as wide-ranging as a journey along the local canal network, or down one of the rivers such as the Severn, Wye or Thames, to a remote expedition on a Scottish loch or abroad.

A paddle or rowing expedition gives an entirely new perspective on journeying. The subsequent development of new skills and experiences frequently leads young people into an activity which may last a lifetime. One of the elements that may attract participants to undertake a paddle expedition is that they do not have to carry a rucksack on their back.

Participants can gain the levels of paddle or rowing skills and experience needed as they undertake the rest of their DofE programme, undertaking their expedition as one of the last activities. Paddle or rowing expeditions lend themselves well to exploring and provide an opportunity to engage in fresh areas of study in stimulating surroundings. They also offer an exciting form of travel, which can lead to new interests and awareness of oneself and the environment.

The craft
Open canoe

The open canoe, with its origins in the Canadian canoes of the North American Indians and the Voyageurs, is an ideal craft for expeditions. It is an excellent vehicle for carrying equipment. It allows for companionship, usually carrying two or three people, and is safe insofar as if young poeple fall into the water, they fall clear of the vessel. Rafted open canoes or similar craft that can accommodate the whole team can be used as they provide a very stable platform.

Sea kayaks and touring kayaks

The sea kayak is an excellent craft in which to undertake a camping expedition. With their length and keel they are easy to paddle in a straight line

and there is ample room for camping equipment. Though designed for the sea, they are suitable for use on the type of river involved in DofE expeditions, and paddlers who camp and travel long distances prefer them.

Purpose-built touring kayaks are ideal for DofE expeditions as they are able to carry sufficient camping gear and food to enable self-sufficiency.

The low volume white water kayak, though being very common and great for sport, is not a very suitable craft in which to carry out a journey and should only be used for training or the Physical section. Their small size does not enable self-sufficiency and many young people find them difficult and tiresome to paddle in a straight line for hours at a stretch.

Rowing

A rowing expedition in a gig or whaler epitomises the concept of teamwork where a team has to work in harmony to ensure their success.

There are many thousands of rowing boats of all shapes and sizes, ranging from those capable of carrying pairs of participants and their gear, to gigs, whalers and ex-ship lifeboats which can carry a group of seven on rivers, canals and sheltered estuaries.

Rowing expeditions must take place in a boat which has been designed for rowing. The broad beam of sailing dinghies, their design and lightness makes them extremely frustrating and tiresome to row over an extended period of time.

It should be remembered that rowing boats cannot be carried for any distance and it is essential that there are locks at all weirs and sluices in addition to slipways for launching and recovery.

Using a lock may take up to 20-30 minutes and, if there is a lock keeper, use may be restricted to the working day, frequently with a break for lunch; all this detail needs to be determined beforehand and built into the planning.

Team composition

As with all expeditions, the minimum number of participants in any expedition team must be four. For tandem canoes/kayaks or craft designed for multiple occupancy, the maximum team size is eight otherwise seven as for other modes of travel.

The number of craft in the team must be agreed with the Licensed Organisation/Approved Activity Provider after an appropriate risk assessment has been completed.

Water

Access to canals is easy in the UK. Many young people will start their DofE canoeing experience in this type of environment. Even in large urban areas canals can offer good opportunities for training. Access to rivers in the United Kingdom is often difficult, except for where they have been turned into navigations or there is a tradition of access.

Navigations usually involve the lower reaches of rivers, which in many cases are still used for commerce and recreational boating. They include many local canals and rivers, such as the Wye, the Severn, the Yorkshire Ouse, the Great Ouse, the Thames and the Trent.

Paddlers and rowers require licences for all English and Scottish canals and some canalised rivers. The British Canoe Union has negotiated a special arrangement with the Canals and Rivers Trust/Thames Licence whereby their waters are included in the BCU Licence, which is included as part of BCU membership.

Separate licences are required for many of the larger rivers, such as the Great Ouse. The relevant details may be obtained from the local BCU Access Officers. It is the responsibility of the team and the Supervisor to ensure the correct permissions and licences are in place.

On the continent there are thousands of miles of suitable rivers used by tens of thousands of touring paddlers on a scale difficult to imagine in Britain. Most have their source in the Alps or the Massif Central. Their upper reaches have a limited place in the Expedition section and their lower reaches are frequently polluted and highly commercialised. However, the middle sections, often extending for hundreds of miles, are ideal for DofE paddlers and rowers.

The Dordogne, the Ardèche, the Rhine, the Rhône and the Danube are typical examples and provide wonderful, stimulating environments for paddle expeditions. Some rivers have been canalised with locks, and licences may be required.

Planning the expedition

Where to do the expedition

Participants should choose water which is suitable for the aim of the expedition, the type of craft and, above all else, that is well within their competence and experience. A principal condition of the Expedition section is that all expeditions must be unaccompanied and self-sufficient, providing a sense of isolation and remoteness.

The choice of where an expedition is carried out will depend to a large extent on its aim, but referring to guides or asking those with experience will help inform the choice.

Guides provide detailed advice on rivers as well as details of access and rights of passage.

The BCU will also be able to give advice on many of the overseas waterways, or advise where the information is available.

Recommended environments for paddle and rowing expeditions:

Bronze
- Canals, rivers or other inland waterways and lakes.
- The water and area may be familiar to participants.

Silver
- Canals, rivers or other inland waterways and lakes in rural areas.
- The water must be unfamiliar to the participants and present an appropriate challenge. There is an expectation that the conditions will be related to the age and experience of the participants and represent a progression between Bronze and Gold.

Gold
- Rivers or other inland waterways and lakes in rural areas, sheltered coastal waters or estuaries.
- The water must be unfamiliar to the participants and must present an appropriate challenge. At Gold level routes should be in or pass through wild country. Moving water, either by current or tide, or large bodies or water, should be sought where possible.
- It should be remembered that the challenge is the journey and not individual, or sets of, rapids.

The water used for Silver and Gold levels must be unfamiliar to the participants but teams may reconnoitre parts of the route beforehand from the bank. It is essential that access to the water, launching and recovery points, mooring sites and campsites are identified before the expedition.

Like all expeditions, the weight and bulk of camping gear and food should be kept to a minimum when paddling or rowing.

Do not be tempted to take additional or non-essential equipment. Portages are not only at the beginning and end of the day but frequently during the journey itself around weirs, locks and some rapids. The Canal & River Trust (formerly British Waterways), unlike the Environment Agency, Thames Region, does not allow certain craft to use locks.

Supervisors and participants will need to check with the relevant agency/authorities with regard to whether locks can be accessed, or whether they have to be portaged.

Portage can be a strenuous activity, especially for younger participants, and frequently involves several trips between the place of disembarkation and re-embarkation.

It is important for health and safety reasons, to train all participants in effective lifting procedures.

Hours of planned activity and distance advice

Every team is different and the nature of their aim and personal situation means that it is hard to give estimates of common distances covered during the hours of planned activity. This is particularly hard for paddle and rowing expeditions as they are so highly affected by factors such as the number of locks, the amount of head winds and the strength of the current.

To help Supervisors, it is estimated that an average team, with appropriate breaks and project investigations, will normally achieve total distances of around those stated in the table below:

Hours of planned activity and distance advice

Bronze	A team could realistically cover around 16-20km (10-12.5 miles) on each day, resulting in a journey of around 32-40km (20-25 miles) over the two days.	Some teams may travel much further, while others may put more time into their project. Whatever they do, it must be an appropriate challenge for them.
Silver	A team could realistically cover around 22km (13.5 miles) a day, resulting in a journey of around 65 kilometres (40 miles) over the three days.	
Gold	A team could realistically cover around 32 kilometres (20 miles) a day according to the wind, current or tide, resulting in a journey of around 128 kilometres (80 miles) over the four days.	

Training

There are training requirements which are split into four sections:

- The Expedition Training Framework, which is compulsory for all expeditions.
- Training framework core paddling skills, which are compulsory for all paddling expeditions or the Training framework for boatwork, which is compulsory for all rowing expeditions.
- Learning of skills that are specific to the environment.
- Any additional Licensed Organisation/AAP requirements.

All training documents are available at **www.DofE.org/expedition**.

Many Licensed Organisations/AAPs will require appropriately qualified coaches, such as those holding BCU qualifications, to deliver this training.

The DofE has developed a set of guidelines to assist coaches/trainers of paddle or rowing expeditions in developing their own training programmes to meet the aim of the expedition and the needs of the participants. A number of these key elements have been taken directly from the BCU awards that are appropriate to the expedition being undertaken.

The training requirements programme has been developed to identify the additional training required to ensure that participants can expedition safely with remote supervision in their chosen environment. Trainers will need to select the appropriate training elements specific to the environment in which the expedition will take place and that they feel will fulfil the 20 conditions.

There is no substitute for experience and teams should spend enough time on the water so that the craft becomes an extension of the user, or until they are at home in the environment.

When the basic skills have been acquired, it is essential that experience be built up using the same kind of water that is to be used for the qualifying expedition.

Minimum training requirements

The nature of paddling and rowing expeditions is such that the minimum training requirements for all these expeditions is the Silver level Expedition Training Framework and mode of travel requirements. Some areas will require all elements of the Gold level framework.

Expedition Training Framework documents and paddle/rowing training programmes are available at **www.DofE.org/expedition**.

All participants undertaking a paddle or rowing expedition must:

- Observe the Countryside Code when using inland waters.
- Know the Water Sports Safety Code, the basic rules of the water – priorities, the sound signals used on water and distress signals.
- Know the rules of conduct for the water on which they are journeying, including the courtesies, customs and etiquette associated with boating and sailing.

- Be adequately trained to:
  - Ensure they meet the 20 conditions of the Expedition section.
  - Satisfy the Supervisor that they have completed the required training and reached the necessary level of competence for the conditions and environment of their expedition. If the Assessor is not satisfied with the level of competence or evidence then they may withdraw their services. See Chapter 10.
  - Satisfy the Supervisor that their craft, equipment and clothing is suitable for the expedition.
  - Demonstrate that their equipment is waterproofed and watertight.

Equipment

All craft must be sound, suitable, fitted out for the conditions in which they are to be used and approved by the Supervisor for use.

They must have integrated buoyancy, or buoyancy which is securely attached

to the boat. Boats must have bow and stern toggles, loops or buoyant painters fore and aft, which are properly secured.

Personal and expedition equipment

Personal, emergency and expedition equipment is the same for all expeditions and can be found at **www.DofE.org/expedition**.

The list below is intended as a starting point when considering additional equipment for paddling and rowing expeditions:

- Buoyancy aid or life-jacket as appropriate, with whistle attached.
- Repair kit.
- Waterproof or water-resistant watch.
- Knife.
- Maps/charts in or with water resistant protection.
- Matches in a waterproof container.
- Throw line/towline and a spare.
- Water-resistant torch with a spare bulb and batteries.
- Spare paddle (per boat).
- A bailer and large sponge.
- Flares (if relevant to the environment).
- Helmets should be considered where relevant to the environment.
- For rowing expeditions, crutches must be tied to the boat, a spare oar and crutch should be carried

and the repair kit should also include canoe tape and very thick flexible plastic sheeting.

Clothing

The list of personal equipment given at **www.DofE.org/expedition** will provide a basis for the kit list for paddling expeditions. This equipment can be supplemented with appropriate specialised clothing.

Considerations must be made for the environment that the participants will be working in. Shade is often unavailable and therefore protection for the head, hands and feet is particularly important. Feet must be protected at all times, old trainers may be used. The ability to carry and keep a complete change of dry clothing is essential.

Personal and team camping equipment: This equipment list is the same for land and water expeditions, although paddlers are often able to carry more equipment for some extra comfort. Craft, paddling and portaging (if required) must be considered when equipment is selected.

> TOP TIP...
>
> For canoeing expeditions carry a group tarp if the weather is bad, so you will be able to make a shelter to eat under as a group.
>
> Darryl Grout,
> Supervisor and Assessor,
> Central England

Food and drink

Paddle expeditions offer the opportunity for a wide and varied menu. This can include fresh produce and tinned food, which could not be carried on a foot expedition. Teams are also able to take water filtration units for wilderness expeditions.

Expeditions on salt water will need to ensure they carry sufficient drinking water and have access to fresh drinking water at campsites.

Waterproofing equipment

All clothing, plus most of the camping gear and food, will need to be protected in effective waterproof containers or dry bags. Large plastic drums with an efficient seal are popular with open canoeists.

Waterproof bags inside rucksacks are an alternative, being particularly useful at portages and adjusting the trim of the craft. Spare clothing and sleeping bags should be given the additional protection of being individually sealed by whatever waterproofing method is chosen.

In all craft the storage of equipment affects the trim and stability. Equipment should be stored to ensure that the craft is appropriately trimmed for the prevailing conditions, and that heavy items are stored as low as possible to increase stability.

Supervision

The Supervisor is the person responsible for the safety and welfare of the participant whilst on their expedition and must be approved by the Licensed Organisation or Approved Activity Provider. They must be familiar with their role and responsibilities.

Supervisors must have considerable experience of water similar to that being used by the expedition team and must also be competent in assessing water and weather conditions. For all paddle expeditions the Supervisor must be in the area of the expedition.

TOP TIP...

Heavy rain and water penetrates even the most expensive rucksack. Invest in a dry bag to make sure your kit (and especially your sleeping bag) stays dry.

Tony Cluxton,
DofE Manager,
Birmingham City Council

The BCU offers appropriate qualifications for paddlesport coaches to operate in the environment of the expedition, but these should be supported by experience which should also be seen as a valuable asset.

Rivers and canals

The sense of isolation and solitude experienced during an expedition is one of the essential experiences to meet the outcomes for the section. Accordingly, it should not usually be necessary for Supervisors to shadow teams on the water.

If the Supervisor feels that this is necessary then it may be that the team is not sufficiently well trained for the chosen environment. However, as highlighted in condition 2b of the 20 conditions, Supervisors can shadow the team on the water where specific, hazardous areas are unavoidable. In this environment it is usual to supervise teams by meeting them at checkpoints during the day, in a similar way to expeditions on land.

Sheltered coastal waters and estuaries

For teams in sheltered estuaries or sheltered coastal waters, Supervisors must provide safety cover afloat. Contact should not be made with the team during the expedition except for the usual needs of supervision.

The safety cover must be sufficiently remote from the participants to avoid destroying the team's sense of remoteness and self-sufficiency and yet be able to render assistance in an emergency within a reasonable amount of time.

The safety cover may consist of the Supervisor and the Assessor shadowing the team at an appropriate distance.

Success story

A DofE group from Daffryn Taff School in Wales show how you don't have to have prior skills or knowledge to be able to complete a fantastic water expedition.

Eight novice paddlers completely embraced the DofE spirit of adventure when they decided they wanted a different challenge for their Gold expedition.

After undertaking six months of preparation including intensive training, fitness, sea navigation and learning to read weather charts they set out on an adventure of a life-time within the Pembrokeshire coast national park, travelling by sea kayak.

After four days of exhausting paddling, they emerged triumphant having faced some great challenges like the unpredictable weather and even capsizing, but they are sure they would do it all again!

By learning a new skill, embracing adventure and all the while discovering the landscape by water and exploring its wildlife, this group had a chance to do something completely different which they will never forget.

Where a safety boat is used it must be sufficiently seaworthy and fitted out to cope with any water conditions which may arise in the sea area being used.

It is desirable that all craft used on open water should be highly visible.

What if the DofE centre does not have any paddle or rowing qualified Supervisors?

When a Licensed Organisation or DofE centre does not have the necessary coaches to be able to deliver the training required for an expedition they can use the help of BCU-approved coaches, clubs or centres. However, the practice or qualifying

expedition must be delivered by DofE Leaders or staff who are registered with the Licensed Organisation, or by an Approved Activity Provider (AAP).

Assessors

Paddle and rowing expeditions are assessed in the same way as all other expeditions. See Chapter 10.

Whilst the Assessor does not have to have paddle or rowing experience, it can add positively to the expedition experience for the participants if they do.

If they need to assess on water then the Licensed Organisation or AAP must approve their competence and experience to do so.

It may be difficult to find an Accredited Assessor with competence and experience on water in the mode of travel. In these cases it may be appropriate to use an Assessor who works alongside another adult with the specific mode of travel skills, this might be the Supervisor.

Many of the DofE's Assessor Networks have expert paddlers amongst their members who are qualified and willing to assess paddle expeditions.

Holding a BCU coaching qualification does not give the automatic right to assess DofE expeditions.

Getting a unique perspective

The DofE offers a wonderful way for a young person to grow and learn and explore all sorts of things. I think it was through my DofE programmes that I really got a taste for expeditions.

I did all my expeditions in the hills but would have loved the opportunity to get out on the water, rowing.

I find being on the water gives you a unique perspective as well as unique challenges. The water gives me something deeper too - sort of spiritual and I love the wildlife that I meet out there!

Sarah Outen MBE
Sarah is a record breaking explorer who became the first woman to row solo across the Indian Ocean in 2009 and is now completing a London2London round-the-world expedition by bike and boat.

Chapter 13.5
Sailing expeditions

What *The Handbook for DofE Leaders* says...

Sailing expeditions can provide participants at all levels the opportunity to develop themselves and learn a range of new skills.

Sailing expeditions need to follow normal DofE requirements and Expedition section conditions, however, there are a wide variety of vessels participants can use and numerous flexibilities allowed for these modes of travel.

Sailing expeditions provide an outstanding way to undertake a DofE expedition. From sailing dinghies and keelboats to yachts and sail training vessels, these expeditions can be the beginning of a new interest or the culmination of many years experience.

There is a vast range of environments where these can take place and DofE participants often sail around lakes and estuaries all over the UK as well as longer expeditions around the world, including Norway, the Mediterranean and the West Indies.

Choosing sailing as a new mode of travel

A sailing expedition gives an entirely new perspective on journeying and the DofE encourages participants to undertake a challenge in this mode of travel.

One of the elements that may attract participants to undertake a sailing expedition is that they do not have to carry a rucksack on their back. Participants can gain the levels of sailing skills and experience needed as part of

other sections of their DofE programme, and then undertake their expedition as one of the last activities.

For young people, learning the skills to undertake this as a new mode of travel is part of the challenge of the Expedition section. While their expedition will challenge them, it might not cover the same distances or be as technically demanding as those who have more sailing experience.

The boat

It is essential participants choose their mode of travel at the start of their Expedition section when they develop their aim as this will determine their choice of boat, appropriate water and all their preparations and training. There are several very different kinds of boats participants can choose to use for their sailing expedition.

Dinghies and open keelboats

Sailing dinghies, such as a Wayfarer and an open 'day-sailing' keelboat, enable participants to journey in the boat and then set up camp each evening. Some participants, using open keelboats, might choose to put up a tarpaulin bivouac and sleep on bottom boards.

Dinghies and open keelboats are readily available all over the UK in outdoor centres and clubs allowing regular access to build up experience. These boats are cheap and easy to maintain and can be easily transported by trailer to suitable water. They are excellent boats for expeditions on rivers, sheltered estuaries, lochs and lakes.

There would usually be a minimum of two boats per expedition to provide

TOP TIP...

Due to the flexibility of distance covered, the Assessor might struggle to find the team at the campsite/ anchorage. The use of a text message before disappearing from reception, or the ability to communicate with one another by VHF radio can assist both participants and Assessor in fulfilling their aims.

Chris Floyd,

DofE Expedition Advisory Panel

mutual support and, where appropriate, these boats should be swamp tested.

Yacht and multihull vessels

Yachts are excellent for expeditions in estuaries, coastal waters or for passage out into open sea. To be able to handle a yacht competently is a very satisfying and rewarding experience and, for many sailors, represents the fulfilment of their aspirations.

Yachts have built-in sleeping accommodation so participants live and sleep aboard the vessel for the duration of the expedition, operating, navigating and crewing the yacht as a team. It is these aspects which makes such adventures unique and enjoyable.

Sail training vessels

Sail training vessels are an excellent way for participants to undertake a sailing expedition in coastal waters and the open sea. They also provide good access and support for participants who are new to sailing or who have additional needs. Such vessels also allow for excellent expeditions with a project focus as they can carry much more investigation equipment, allowing teams to extend the scale and scope of expedition aims and projects.

There are a number of vessels and organisations around the UK which support DofE expeditions in sail training vessels.

Sail training vessels may require more than seven people to sail them safely. In these cases up to 12 young people can be organised into 'watches' (nautical term for a working shift).

Each watch operates independently from each other except in the case of an emergency or an exceptional task on board that requires more hands than one watch can provide. This system maintains the spirit of the Expedition section, but allows these vessels to be used. Watch patterns normally allow for two four hour watches a day meaning that participants at any DofE level complete eight hours of planned activity.

The size of sail training vessels can mean that participants might specialise their skills through a structured training programme. This allows team members to play to their strengths while also developing other specific areas where they are less confident.

Planning the expedition
Where to carry out the expedition

Participants should choose water which is suitable for the aim of the expedition, the type of craft and, above all else, that is well within their competence and experience.

The choice of where an expedition is carried out will depend to a large extent on its aim, but referring to guides, clubs or asking those with experience will help inform participant's choice. Information on water access is set out on page 258.

It is the responsibility of the team and the Supervisor to ensure the correct permissions and licences are in place. Select water which is suitable for the craft involved and well within the team's level of skill so there is less chance of adverse weather or environmental conditions affecting the journey.

Recommended environments for sailing expeditions

For sailing expeditions the conditions teams choose to go out in can be more important than the area of water.

Often the same area of water can be completely altered during different weather conditions. It can therefore be used for both practice and qualifying expeditions if required.

Suitably experienced and competent Bronze teams might use a Silver or Gold environment in very calm good weather if it is local to their sailing centre or vessel. The water used for Silver and Gold levels must be unfamiliar to the participants but teams may reconnoitre parts of the route beforehand from the bank as appropriate.

It is essential that access to the water, launching and recovery points, mooring sites and campsites are identified before the expedition.

Condensed programmes for expeditions in coastal areas and the open sea

Some programmes, considered by the DofE on a case by case basis, will undertake the qualifying expedition immediately after the

---

Recommended environments for sailing expeditions

Bronze	Inland waters or sheltered estuaries well within the participants' competencies. The water and area may be familiar to participants.	All expedition routes and expedition areas must present an appropriate challenge for the DofE team.
Silver	Inland waters, estuaries or sheltered coastal waters. The water must be unfamiliar to the participants and present an appropriate challenge. There is an expectation that the conditions will be related to the age and experience of the participants and represent a progression between Bronze and Gold.	Ideally, practice and qualifying expeditions should take place in different areas. Where this is not practical, different routes over the same area can be used.
Gold	Inland waters, estuaries or sheltered coastal waters. Yachts and sail training vessels may be used in open sea areas. The water must be unfamiliar to the participants and must present an appropriate challenge. At Gold level routes should be in or pass through wild country or use remote and quieter coastal waters and open sea areas.	

---

practice expedition. This ensures knowledge is retained by participants and removes the need for an additional acclimatisation day.

In these cases the DofE recommends that time is made, usually at least one night in port, to distinguish between the practice and qualifying expeditions and to enable the expedition team to reflect on what they have learnt.

If this approach is being considered, Supervisors must be prepared to add in additional days to the practice expedition, if required, to ensure participants are ready to take appropriate control of the vessel for their qualifying expedition.

Planning flexible routes and hours of planned activity

As highlighted in the general advice on water based expeditions, Chapter 13.3, teams need to build a greater amount of flexibility into expedition planning and execution.

The distance travelled by teams may vary greatly depending on the weather, so alternative campsites and flexible start and finish times should be included in the expedition plan.

Sailing expeditions on the open sea can be particularly affected by the weather, so teams should focus on the number of hours of planned activity each day rather than set routes and distances.

Some general considerations:
- Teams still need to submit route plans and notifications in the

normal way, following appropriate Licensed Organisation procedures and DofE processes set out at **www.DofE.org/expedition**.
- An acclimatisation day at Gold level is still required and is recommended for all expeditions using coastal waters and open seas so participants can get used to the motion of the vessel.
- All sailing must be planned for completion during daylight hours, as far more training is required for night sailing.
- It is common for groups sailing in open water to complete the DofE expedition as part of a longer passage or period of sailing from one port to another.

Weather or water conditions can bring a premature end to even the most carefully planned and flexible of water-based expeditions.

This is a reality that has to be accepted by all who engage in outdoor pursuits and particularly by DofE participants nearing their 25th birthday.

At least one back-up date should be arranged for all qualifying expeditions on inland water and multiple dates should be considered for estuaries, coastal waters and the open sea.

Use Supervisors and Assessors who can accommodate flexibility in distances and back-up dates.

Local Supervisor pre-expedition checks are essential at all levels, especially where craft are then being trailered to distant locations.

Flexibilities to the 20 conditions for sailing expeditions

Sailing expeditions need to follow normal DofE requirements and Expedition section conditions. However, there is a wide variety of vessels participants can use and numerous flexibilities allowed for these modes of travel. These flexibilities are set out below, and the full 20 conditions of the Expedition section can be found on pages 12-13.

Condition	Dinghy variations	Yacht/multihull variations	Sail training vessel variations
1	No outboard motors to be used.	Motors may be used when appropriate including in harbours, berths and when good seamanship and safety dictates. Motors may also be used when there is a lack of wind in order to maintain the spirit of adventure and personal development of the expedition.	
2	Staff may not be aboard the participant's vessels. The team may be accompanied by a safety boat.	Staff may be aboard the vessel. The Supervisor and Assessor should not be involved in the skippering, crewing, navigation, control or management of the boat, except in an emergency for reasons of safety. Regular contact with coastguards should be maintained.	
3	The Supervisor must have appropriate qualifications, relevant to environment and the mode of travel. If the Supervisor is an Accredited Assessor then they may be both the Assessor and Supervisor. Thus minimising adult intervention.		

Condition	Dinghy variations	Yacht/multihull variations	Sail training vessel variations
6	Participants should be appropriately trained, using the RYA training framework as a reference and have completed the Expedition Training Framework for the appropriate DofE level and environment.	Participants must be competent at the mode of travel to complete their expedition and reference could be made to the RYA cruising syllabus. Week-long experiences that include training and a final expedition may be considered by the DofE on a case by case basis. Acclimatisation is essential at all levels in anticipation of seasickness. Ideally, practice and qualifying expeditions should take place in different areas, where this is not practical, different routes over the same area can be used.	
	Participants must have completed the Expedition Training Framework for the appropriate DofE level and mode of travel. Ideally, practice and qualifying expeditions should take place in different areas, where this is not practical, different routes over the same area can be used.		
8	Participants must be able to demonstrate the ability to passage plan their expedition. However, dynamic planning will always be a feature of all sailing expeditions.		
9	Where expeditions take place in inland waters, lakes, lochs and sheltered estuaries, the Supervisor should, where safe and practical, accompany the expedition in another vessel. For expeditions on sheltered coastal waters and open sea areas the Assessor should be aboard the vessel and hold relevant qualifications. Where Accredited Assessors hold the relevant qualifications and are approved by the Licensed Organisation, then the Assessor may also be the Supervisor. Ideally the Assessor should still meet the appropriate level of independence from the team, particularly at Gold level.		
10	None.	None.	Groups of up to 12 are acceptable where watch teams of up to six are used to ensure that team dynamics remain within the spirit of the Expedition section.
16	It should be noted that towards the end of the season, particularly in higher latitudes, daylight hours are reduced so consideration should be given to ensuring that groups are not benighted.		

Training

There are training requirements which are split into four sections:
- The Expedition Training Framework, which is compulsory for all expeditions.
- Training framework for sailing expeditions, which sets out DofE requirements and recommendations.
- Learning of skills that are specific to the environment.
- Any additional Licensed Organisation/ AAP requirements.

All training documents are available at **www.DofE.org/expedition**.

Many Licensed Organisations/AAPs will require appropriately qualified instructors, such as those holding RYA Yachtmaster/ Senior Dinghy Instructor certificates of competence, to deliver this training.

The DofE sets out core training requirements that participants must know. Additionally Licensed Organisations and AAPs will usually recommend the appropriate levels of competence required with reference to the RYA training framework. Trainers will need to select the appropriate training elements specific to the environment in which the expedition will take place and that they feel will fulfil the 20 conditions.

There is no substitute for experience and teams should spend enough time on the water so that the craft becomes an extension of the user, or until they are at home in the environment.

When the basic skills have been acquired, it is essential that experience be built up using the same kind of areas of water that are to be used for the qualifying expedition.

Minimum training requirements

The nature of sailing expeditions is such that the minimum level for sheltered water is the Silver level framework and the DofE Training framework for sailing expeditions. All other expedition areas require training to the Gold level framework.

All participants undertaking a sailing expedition must:
- Observe the Countryside Code when using inland waters.
- Know the Water Sports Safety Code (see **www.DofE.org/expedition**), the basic rules of the water – priorities, the sound signals used on water and distress signals.
- Know the rules of conduct for the water on which they are journeying, including the courtesies, customs and etiquette associated with boating and sailing.
- Be adequately trained to:
  - Ensure they meet the 20 conditions of the Expedition section.
  - Satisfy the Supervisor that they have completed the required training and reached the necessary level of competence for the conditions and environment of their expedition. If the Assessor is not satisfied with the level of competence or evidence then they may withdraw their services. See Chapter 6.10.
  - Satisfy the Supervisor that their craft, equipment and clothing are suitable for the expedition.
  - Demonstrate that their equipment is waterproofed/watertight.

Safety

The participants should be water confident and a buoyancy aid or lifejacket, suitable clothing and footwear must be worn. All expeditions must follow their Licensed Organisation or AAP safety policies. For more information please refer to the safety section in Chapter 13.3.

An example Gold itinerary for DofE expeditions aboard sail training vessels

Months 1-3
It can be beneficial for participants to gain some local sailing experience in small vessels to build confidence, skills and physical fitness.

Month 4
A two day, one night taster and training session. This is especially important for sail training vessel expeditions to ensure participants are capable and competent to operate a vessel safely. This also allows inexperienced young people to try out this mode of travel without committing themselves to the full programme and gives them time to improve skills and fitness as necessary. It may also be possible for participants to complete the RYA Start Yachting Certificate in these two days. Participants may complete the RYA Essential Navigation and Seamanship Course

Month 5
Complete the practice expedition. This is likely to be to be a minimum of two days and two nights at all DofE levels and may be longer depending on the competence of the team.

Month 6
Complete the qualifying expedition, with acclimatisation day. Participants must have the competence, skills and physical fitness to undertake their qualifying expedition.

This could also be completed immediately after the practice expedition as a condensed programme with out the need for an additional acclimatisation day.

See guidance on condensed programmes: on page 272.

Equipment

All boats and equipment must be approved for use by the Supervisor and follow any Licensed Organisation requirements, particularly concerning wearing appropriate personal flotation devices.

As with all expeditions, participants need to be self-sufficient, so Supervisors cannot carry additional equipment, other than drinking water, in a safety boat to give to teams.

Boats

Regardless of the type of sailing boat used, it must be sound, suitable and fitted out for the conditions in which it will be used. Sailing dinghies and keelboats must be fitted with adequate buoyancy, securely attached to the boat.

The buoyancy must be tested. It is expected that sailing dinghies and keelboats will be stowed, moored or securely anchored overnight. Yachts and sail training vessels must be in a sound condition and equipped to modern good standards of custom and practice, with suitable life-saving and emergency equipment. They should also comply with the appropriate and current RYA recommendations for the type of vessel.

Crew equipment

The crew of each boat should carry a range of general equipment for their vessel. The list below is only intended as a starting point when considering additional equipment for DofE sailing expeditions:

- Anchor and warp.
- Throwing/tow line.
- Painters and/or spare line.
- Bucket, bailer/bilge pump and sponge.
- Charts/maps in water resistant protection.
- Compass(es).*
- Repair kit.
- Buoyant knife.
- Powerful water-resistant torch. *
- Flares, air horn.*
- Emergency water supply.*

These may not be necessary for all inland/ river sailing locations.

Clothing

In addition to the standard clothing needed for all DofE expeditions, each participant should ensure they have suitable clothing for their sailing expedition, including:

- Protection for their head, hands and feet.
- A complete change of clothing in a waterproof container.
- Appropriate footwear, such as dinghy or wetsuit boots or deck shoes.

Personal equipment

Every participant must have the necessary personal and emergency equipment for the expedition mode of travel.

TOP TIP...

Shipping forecasts are important, but make sure you listen to the inshore forecast for sea based expeditions too for more accurate weather reporting – these are broadcast by the Coastguard at 4 hourly intervals.

Barry Fisher,
DofE Director,
Scotland

The list below is intended only as a starting point of some important items for sailing expeditions:

- Life-jacket or buoyancy aid with attached whistle. It is essential to have a suitable personal flotation device (buoyancy aid or lifejacket) which must conform to current standards and be appropriate for the area that the expedition is conducted in.
- Bivvy bag (poly-bag).
- Waterproof or water-resistant watch.
- Sailor's knife with blade, tin-opener and spike.
- Matches in a waterproof container.
- Personal first aid kit.
- Emergency rations.
- Small water-resistant pocket torch with spare bulb and alkaline batteries.
- Waterproof notebook and pencil.
- Mobile phone (in a sealed waterproof bag).
- Coins/phonecard for a landline.
- VHF radio.

Camping equipment

If participants are camping at the end of each day, they will need the same personal and team equipment as expeditions on land. However, all items should be stored in waterproof containers rather than in a rucksack.

Like all expeditions, the weight and bulk of camping gear and food should be kept to a minimum when sailing. Do not be tempted to take additional or non-essential equipment.

Yachts and sail training vessels will allow participants to live and sleep aboard the vessel for the duration of the expedition. The style of catering and menu choices should be adapted accordingly.

> **TOP TIP...**
> Always remember to reef down early – better to sail slightly slower but with no sudden dramatic panics than being caught out with full sail in a strong breeze – a DofE expedition is not a race!
>
> Barry Fisher.
> DofE Director.
> Scotland

Supervising and assessing sailing expeditions

Sailing expedition Supervisors must have considerable experience of the water that is being used and be competent in assessing water safety in all weather conditions. All Supervisors and Assessors must be approved by the Licensed Organisation/AAP.

Assessors and Supervisors should follow the guidance set out in chapters 8 and 10 as for all other expeditions.

The requirements for the location of the Supervisor and Assessor during sailing expeditions are set out in point three and nine in the Flexibilities to the 20 conditions for sailing expeditions chart on pages 274 and 275.

The Supervisor and Assessor should remain as remote as possible, interacting with the teams only as needed for effective remote supervision and to support the team in an emergency situation.

Supervisors may control larger vessels to safely see them in and out of port. However, passage planning should be completed in such a way to ensure that participants can be in control of the vessel as much as possible to reduce adult intervention. For example, through use of anchoring in quiet bays.

Whilst the Assessor does not have to have sailing experience, it can add positively to the expedition experience for the participants if they do. If they need to assess on water then the Licensed Organisation or AAP must approve their competence and experience to do so.

It may be difficult to find an Accredited Assessor with competence and experience on water in the mode of travel. In these cases it may be appropriate to use an Assessor who works alongside another adult with the specific mode of travel skills, this might be the Supervisor.

Alternatively, to help reduce the level of adult intervention and enhance self-reliance, an appropriately experienced individual may act as both the Assessor and the Supervisor or an expedition support staff member.

Holding an RYA Yachtmaster certificate of competence does not give the automatic right to assess DofE expeditions.

Advice from the experts...

- It's important that everyone is clear about their role and responsibility before starting a task so always allow time for a proper briefing first.
- Always tell the coastguard about your passage plan each day, including your destination and ETA.
- Don't forget to visit the heads (toilets) before putting your waterproofs and lifejacket on. It takes a while to get them off again.
- If you're worried about sea-sickness, check with your doctor and get some pills. Read the instructions and make sure you take the pills before setting sail. If you feel queasy, wrap up warm and stay in the fresh air where you can see

the horizon. Drink plenty of fluids and eat some ginger biscuits. Keep busy, helming is great for this. If feeling ill lie flat on your back in your bunk with the lee cloth up and a bucket. Avoid being sick over the windward side of the boat or you'll give everyone a nasty surprise!

Nick Fleming, DofE Supervisor and RYA Yachtmaster Instructor Examiner.

Essential decision-making skills

I sailed the Atlantic Ocean many times as a teenager but an accident which broke my neck when I was 18 put an end to that period of my life. As I relearned life skills as a disabled person, I realised the sea was where my future lay. I had experienced first-hand the enjoyment and pleasure it gave me, so I set about helping other disabled people share that experience and worked to help establish the RYA Sailability charity.

I set myself small sailing goals at sea to begin with. At first, my biggest hurdle was to sail solo, on my own, for the first time since being disabled. It was great making my own decisions without others telling me what to do. The next step was racing, improving my skills until I was winning races, beating able-bodied racers, not through strength, but through skill.

Then came my first long distance challenge, my personal Everest. Inevitably, the next challenge was always going to be the Atlantic Ocean. Aided only by a nurse to help with my medical needs, after a four week, 3,000 mile crossing I sailed the Atlantic Ocean in January 2010.

To succeed you need to believe in yourself. In these adventures, I have learnt you have to trust your judgment, take advice of course, but ultimately your safety and your success lies in your hands. Remember, your achievements in life may well inspire others too.

Geoff Holt MBE

Paralysed in an accident at 18, Geoff went on to become the first disabled person to sail single-handed around Great Britain and the first quadriplegic sailor to sail unassisted across the Atlantic Ocean in 2010, among numerous other achievements.

Additional information and references

There is an enormous amount of support, books and websites which can help sailing expeditions. Participants might consider visiting the following:

- **www.asto.org** – Association of Sail Training Organisations, list of members.
- **www.rya.org.uk** – Royal Yachting Association.
- **www.rnli.org.uk** – Royal National Lifeboat Institute.
- **www.dft.gov.uk/mca** – Maritime and Coastguard Agency.
- **www.wayfarer.org.uk**

Chapter 14
Something else...

What *The Handbook for DofE Leaders* says...

The Expedition section aims to inspire young people to develop initiative and a spirit of adventure and discovery.

The DofE encourages and will always consider innovative and creative expedition proposals from participants even if they do not meet all of the 20 conditions.

While the Expedition section, as part of their wider DofE programme, is carefully designed to foster specific outcomes and benefits for young people, it is also an innovative and creative section.

The DofE will always look to encourage and support young people, at any DofE level, who want to do 'something else' which is very unusual, but of equal or greater challenge than a more traditional expedition.

These will be one-off expeditions and a written proposal must be submitted to the DofE Head Office in Windsor for consideration, at least 12 weeks prior to the date of departure. Participants should seek the guidance of their DofE Manager at least six months prior to the expedition and before they have committed any expenditure. This is also the best time to talk to the DofE Head Office.

Even for potential one-off expeditions, several of the 20 conditions (see pages 12-13) are not flexible as they are essential to the definition of the section. These are conditions: 1, 4, 5, 7, 8, & 20.

Additionally, the conditions below must still be met to some degree:

Condition	Details
2	Participants should be unaccompanied.
3	There must be a Supervisor or support team involved in some way with experience of the appropriate kind of expedition.
6	Appropriate training and practices must be completed to adequately prepare participants for the expedition.
11	Participants can undertake an expedition in this category at any DofE level, **but they must be aged over 16.**
15, 17 & 18	Teams should still aim to meet the minimum requirements of the section.

TOP TIP...

Don't be afraid to ask others for advice when planning an expedition. First hand knowledge of an area can pin-point amazing places to visit!

Shelli Randall,
DofE Supervisor,
Embassy Open Award Centre,
Bournemouth

In this way, the expedition must still meet many of the outcomes of the section; planning, training for and completing an adventurous and remote journey, and travelling by the participant's own physical effort and without motorised assistance.

It is important that these undertakings come from and are planned by the participant(s), who have a passion for them and are seeking a different challenge. They may not simply be part of someone else's event, doing it just to be different or to undertake something chosen by staff to fulfil their own interests. Be aware that often what the young people are planning may well be a better fit for their Residential section.

Participants must discuss their plans with their Licensed Organisation and agree with them what role, if any, their Licensed Organisation will play in the expedition.

It is the participant's responsibility to ensure that it is clear to everyone where insurance and responsibility for health and safety rests, either with themselves, their parents/guardians, their Licensed Organisation or an Approved Activity Provider.

Note: In giving approval for such expeditions, The Duke of Edinburgh's Award only confirms that the expedition complies with the aim, principles and purpose of the Expedition section. We do not accept any responsibility concerning the suitability of the expedition for the participants' health and safety, the adequacy of training, emergency procedures or public liability insurance.

TOP TIP...

Be ambitious and plan, plan, plan, well ahead; the more you prepare the better the expedition will turn out and the bigger the challenge you can take on!

Robert Campbell Mayers,
DofE Leader & Mourne
Expedition Assessor,
Northern Ireland

Advice on setting up a unique challenge

Such expeditions should not be undertaken lightly and very careful planning, probably over a significant amount of time, must be put in place.

Participants should still start with the aim, principles and benefits of the Expedition section. They should think about how these can be used with boldness, imagination and enterprise to build for themselves their unique expedition.

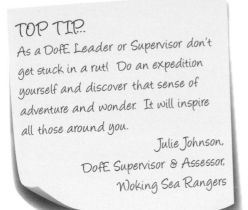

TOP TIP...

As a DofE Leader or Supervisor don't get stuck in a rut! Do an expedition yourself and discover that sense of adventure and wonder. It will inspire all those around you.

Julie Johnson,
DofE Supervisor & Assessor,
Woking Sea Rangers

Participants should create a project plan carefully at the earliest opportunity. This helps them understand the time scales, costs, potential barriers, paperwork, training, practices and equipment that will be needed to make the expedition a success.

Participants should also try to contact people who have undertaken a similar kind of expedition to that which they are considering, in order to get advice and guidance.

Appropriate training for the mode of travel and completing as many practice expeditions as necessary remains an essential part of the preparation process.

Participants need to complete three areas of training:
- At least one UK practice expedition will be needed in an appropriate area.
- Participants must have completed the Gold level Expedition Training Framework.
- The participant(s) must be sufficiently trained and skilled so that their safety does not depend on adult intervention.

For such expeditions, outside of the UK, it is likely that some extended time may be spent in the destination country or countries. Training in the customs, culture and lifestyle of the destination is usually required and enhances the whole experience. Training must also include knowledge of essential local language(s) for greetings, logistics and emergencies, emergency contact procedures and an understanding of local laws and restrictions. See Chapter 5.2 on expeditions outside of the UK.

Cost can be one of the biggest barriers to bold and unique expeditions. Fundraising will probably be an essential part of the planning and build-up process but cannot count towards the Volunteering section. Individual sponsorship, fundraising events and even corporate sponsorship may be needed. It must be made very clear to everyone, exactly what any monies are being used for.

The Duke of Edinburgh's Award is a registered Charity and its name and charity number must not be used to raise money to fund an individual going on an expedition. Participants can state that they are raising money to pay for themselves to go on an expedition as part of their DofE programme.

Making a stand for unusual expeditions

I first got into adventuring and exploring with a gap year at the age of 19. I have completed some amazing adventures like paddle-boarding the length of the Mississippi and skating the length of the British Isles. With great achievement always comes great challenges and I have definitely had some ups and downs on my journeys!

The most important thing to remember is the expedition gives you a chance to go on an adventure of your making. The more exciting and challenging you make it, the more likely you are to complete it and get the most out of it. Every time we experience new things we develop ourselves and our understanding of our place in the big wide world.

And just remember that comfort kills ambition. Do something new every day, if you become bored then you're not using your time wisely. We live once, so make the most of your time, go get 'em! So make sure you take full advantage of this opportunity you have through the DofE and who knows where you will end up!

Dave Cornthwaite

Dave has broken five world records, crossed Australia on a skateboard, kayaked Australia's largest river and descended the Mississippi by stand-up paddleboard. Dave aims to complete 25 separate journeys of 1,000 miles or more, each using a different form of non-motorised transport.

Chapter 15
Glossary of roles and D*of*E Expedition section terminology

20 conditions

The 20 conditions of the Expedition section set out the criteria all DofE participants must fulfil in order to complete their Expedition section. The first 19 conditions are assessed by the DofE Expedition Assessor on the qualifying expedition and the 20th condition is completed after the expedition.

Achievement Pack

A book containing pictorial evidence and records of a young person's activities undertaken as part of their DofE programme, compiled through eDofE.

Acclimatisation day

A day spent in the expedition environment to allow participants to adjust to the expedition area, prepare themselves and their equipment and meet their DofE Expedition Assessor.

Aim

The expedition must have an aim which is related to the interests and abilities of those taking part and the area they will be travelling through. This is the key to any expedition's success. From thinking about the aim come all the other decisions such as location and mode of travel.

Alternative poor weather routes

To allow teams to manage the risk and impact of poor weather on expedition, participants plan alternative, low level (lower risk) routes that can be used to enable the team to reach its intended destination, meeting the 20 conditions and avoid the full impact of weather-related hazards.

Approved Activity Provider (AAP)

Organisations licensed by The DofE to provide expedition and residential opportunities that have been proven to meet DofE requirements and conditions and so can count towards the achievement of an Award.

Assessor Network

A group of accredited DofE Expedition Assessors, co-ordinated by an Assessor Network Co-ordinator for a specific area of UK wild country.

Assessor Network Co-ordinator

A DofE Expedition Assessor who co-ordinates the Assessor Network, all expeditions and a number of volunteer Network Assessors for a given area of UK wild country.

Assessor's report

An Assessor's report is completed by the Assessor for a particular section of a participant's programme. In the Expedition section it constitutes a review of the expedition that the young person has undertaken and evidences the qualifying expedition as complete. The report can be recorded online via **www.DofE.org/assessor**, a voice recording, or using the *Keeping Track* booklet.

Award holder

A young person who has achieved a Duke of Edinburgh's Award by completing their DofE programme.

Campcraft

Expedition campcraft is the ability to provide food and shelter under all conditions likely to be encountered in the outdoors. The skills and confidence of participants to do this are developed by practice and experience.

Directly Licensed Centre (DLC)

A Directly Licensed Centre is a type of Licensed Organisation which holds a licence to deliver DofE programmes to young people on its own premises.

Directly Licensed Centres can include schools, youth clubs and young offender institutions, which do not run their DofE provision under a licence provided by an Operating Authority.

DofE centre

A location where the DofE is run, for example, a school, youth centre or young offender institution. There may be one or more groups at a centre.

DofE Co-ordinator

The person who sets up and manages the DofE in a centre. They support the Leaders and oversee the groups.

DofE Expedition Assessor

An adult who checks on a young person's progress and agrees the completion of the Expedition section of their programme. They will provide an Assessor's report to confirm this (see Assessor's Report). In the Expedition section, qualifying expeditions must be assessed by a competent adult who is approved by the Licensed Organisation or AAP and accredited by The Duke of Edinburgh's Award Charity. DofE Expedition Assessors are also known as Accredited Assessors. Some Assessors are members of volunteer networks which are managed directly by the DofE. Each network is based in a wild country area and members provide a service for Licensed Organisations, assessing expedition teams. For details see **www.DofE.org/go/expeditionareas**

DofE Expedition Assessor's debrief

The meeting between the DofE Expedition Assessor and the DofE team they have been assessing which comes immediately at the end of the expedition. This meeting is the opportunity for the Assessor to share in the team's success and congratulate them. The Assessor will help the young people review their expedition and express their feelings and reactions.

DofE Expedition Assessor's pre-expedition check

The meeting between the DofE Expedition Assessor, DofE Expedition Supervisor and the DofE team they are supporting, at which they agree their contract before the start of the expedition.

DofE Expedition Supervisor

A Supervisor is essential for the Expedition section as they are responsible for supervising and supporting a team of participants to ensure their safety and well-being whilst they are undertaking their expedition.

DofE Expedition Supervisor's pre-expedition check

The Supervisor's pre-expedition check is intended to prevent participants travelling to an expedition area only to find that their equipment or training is inadequate. It should take place at the team's home base, normally between seven and ten days before departure for the expedition, to enable teams to bring all their equipment together but still have time to make any necessary changes.

DofE group

A group of young people who are working together on their DofE programmes, with one or more DofE Leaders.

DofE Leader

The adult responsible for a DofE group. They lead, guide and encourage young people, agree their programme choices and sign off *Keeping Track* booklets and their *eDofE* evidence.

DofE Manager

The named person in a Licensed Organisation who is responsible for the day-to-day delivery of the DofE. There will often be other assistants, administrators and staff involved.

DofE expedition team

This is to describe participants who are working as an expedition team. Expedition teams will have four to seven participants (eight for modes of travel which have tandem).

eDofE

The online system for managing and recording young people's progress through their DofE programmes.

eDofE Mapping

eDofE Mapping is a free expedition route submission tool designed to create standard DofE route cards and route summaries. It can be used by anyone using eDofE and helps speed up the route approval process.

Emergency escape routes

Easy to follow, non-hazardous emergency escape routes to agreed locations where participants can get help while on expedition. These routes must be in place for all DofE teams and recorded on their route card.

EX²

The DofE interactive expedition training tool which contains practical advice, detail and training support advice for expedition Supervisors, instructors and DofE Leaders. EX² is available from the DofE shop, **www.DofEshop.org**.

Expedition environment

The area in which practice and qualifying expeditions take place. Each level of the DofE has recommended environments where expeditions may be undertaken by participants. These environments become increasingly isolated and challenging as participants progress through the DofE levels.

Expedition presentation

All participants must deliver a presentation, related to the expedition's aim, in order to complete the section. It is entirely up to the team how their presentation is delivered – it could be in any format. The presentation should also include an account of the journey to encourage participants to reflect on their experiences.

Expedition season

The UK expedition season is between the end of March and the end of October, covering the British summer.

Expedition support staff

Staff or volunteers for a Licensed Organisation or AAP who help the Supervisor deliver an expedition safely.

Expedition Training Framework

The Expedition Training Framework consists of a number of areas in which young people must prove their competence before they can undertake their DofE expedition. This skills training helps to ensure their safety.

Instructor

Staff or volunteers for a Licensed Organisation or AAP who deliver training to DofE participants. The training is then signed off by the Supervisor.

Licensed Organisation (LO)

Licensed Organisation is the umbrella term used for the four different types of organisation that can hold licences to deliver DofE programmes. The four different types of organisation are:
- Directly Licensed Centre (DLC)
- National Operating Authority (NOA)
- Operating Authority (OA)
- DofE Business Partner

Mode of travel

Mode of travel means the method of journeying selected by participants for their expedition which uses their own physical effort. Modes of travel include expeditions on foot, cycle, horseback, paddle, rowing, sailing and by wheelchair. Other rarer modes include cross-country skiing and dog-sled.

Modular Training Framework

The DofE maintains a number of training modules to help all adults involved in the DofE to develop the skills that they need to carry out their role effectively. Collectively, these modules are referred to as the Modular Training Framework.

National Operating Authority (NOA)

A National Operating Authority is a type of Licensed Organisation which holds a licence to deliver DofE programmes to the young people with whom they work in one or more of the UK nations.

Network Assessor

An accredited DofE Expedition Assessor who is a member of an Assessor Network for a UK wild country area and has volunteered to assess expeditions on behalf of the DofE in that area.

Open expedition

Open expeditions are DofE expeditions made available to all DofE participants, to join as an individual, and can run at all levels and in all modes of travel. Open expeditions enable independent participants, those who missed their own group's expedition or those unable to form a viable team, to complete practice and qualifying expeditions.

Operating Authority (OA)

An Operating Authority is a type of Licensed Organisation which holds the licence to deliver DofE programmes in a specified geographic area. Operating Authority licences are often held by local authorities.

Participant

Any young person who is doing a DofE programme. Some participants enter directly at Silver or Gold level.

Practice expeditions

Good practice expeditions prepare participants for the challenges of their qualifying expedition, allowing them to avoid problems like poor time-keeping, overweight packs, lack of fitness and blistered feet while under assessment. Practice expeditions must replicate as closely as possible the conditions of the qualifying expedition. This must include sufficient experience of being unaccompanied and remotely supervised.

Qualifying expedition

To achieve their Expedition section all participants must complete a qualifying expedition which is assessed by a DofE Expedition Assessor and meets the 20 conditions of the Expedition section.

Remote supervision

A style of safe expedition supervision where the Supervisor remains out of the sight and hearing of the team and allows the team to get on with the expedition without intervention, intervening if absolutely necessary or if requested. The Supervisors will have a good idea of roughly where the team is and how the participants are progressing, periodically observing the team without intervening.

Route card

All DofE teams complete a route card form detailing their intended expedition route and then submit their route card for approval. The route card is a key tool in enabling participants to identify and manage risk in their expedition route. A route card template is available from **www.DofE.org/expedition.**

Something else

A very unusual and one off expedition, of equal or greater challenge to a more traditional expedition, which does not meet all of the 20 conditions and is submitted to the DofE Head Office for consideration.

Variations

Where participants have individual needs that mean one or more of the 20 conditions cannot be met, they may apply for a variation to enable them to complete their DofE expedition.

Wild country

Wild country is defined as an area remote from habitation. The expectation at Gold level is that all expeditions take place in wild country. In the UK, expedition assessment in areas of wild country are co-ordinated by an Assessor Network Co-ordinator.

Index

A

B

C

D

E

Quotes:

Quotes: